Immigration
and
Ethnicity

AMERICAN GOVERNMENT AND HISTORY INFORMATION GUIDE SERIES

Series Editor: Harold Shill, Chief Circulation Librarian, Adjunct Assistant Professor of Political Science, West Virginia University, Morgantown

Other books in this series:

HISTORICAL SOURCES ON U.S. RELIGION AND CHURCH HISTORY— *Edited by Garth Rosell**

HISTORICAL SOURCES ON U.S. CULTURAL HISTORY—*Edited by Philip I. Mitterling**

U.S. CONSTITUTION—*Edited by Earlean McCarrick**

U.S. FOREIGN RELATIONS—*Edited by Elmer Plischke**

U.S. POLITICS AND ELECTIONS—*Edited by David J. Maurer**

SOCIAL HISTORY OF THE UNITED STATES—*Edited by Donald F. Tingley**

U.S. WARS AND MILITARY HISTORY—*Edited by Jack Lane**

PROGRESSIVISM—*Edited by John D. Buenker and Nicholas C. Burckel**

*in preparation

The above series is part of the
GALE INFORMATION GUIDE LIBRARY

The Library consists of a number of separate series of guides covering major areas in the social sciences, humanities, and current affairs.

General Editor: Paul Wasserman, Professor and former Dean, School of Library and Information Services, University of Maryland

Managing Editor: Denise Allard Adzigian, Gale Research Company

Immigration
and
Ethnicity

A GUIDE TO INFORMATION SOURCES

*Volume 1 in the American Government
and History Information Guide Series*

John D. Buenker

*Professor of History
University of Wisconsin-Parkside*

Nicholas C. Burckel

*Director, Archives and Area Research Center
University of Wisconsin-Parkside*

Preface by Rudolph J. Vecoli

*Professor of History
Director, Immigration History Research Center
University of Minnesota*

Gale Research Company
Book Tower, Detroit, Michigan 48226

Library of Congress Cataloging in Publication Data

Buenker, John D
　　Immigration and ethnicity.

　　(American Government and history ; v. 1) (Gale
information guide library)
　　Includes index.
　　1. United States--Emigration and immigration--
Bibliography. 2. United States--Foreign population
--Bibliography. 3. Ethnicity--Bibliography.
I. Burckel, Nicholas C., joint author. II. Title.
III. Series.
Z7165.U5B83　[JV6465]　　　016.32573　　　74-11515
ISBN 0-8103-1202-6

For Lee and Lenore

VITAE

JOHN D. BUENKER is professor of history at the University of Wisconsin-Park-side. He holds his Ph.D. from Georgetown University and has previously taught at Prince Georges College and Eastern Illinois University. He is the author of URBAN LIBERALISM AND PROGRESSIVE REFORM and of the forthcoming THE INCOME TAX AND THE PROGRESSIVE ERA, and coauthor of ESSAYS IN ILLI-NOIS HISTORY, THE STUDY OF AMERICAN HISTORY, and PROGRESSIVISM. He has written articles and reviews for the JOURNAL OF AMERICAN HISTORY, the AMERICAN HISTORICAL REVIEW, the NEW ENGLAND QUARTERLY, the HISTORIAN, MID-AMERICA, ENCYCLOPEDIA AMERICANA, the DICTIONARY OF AMERICAN BIOGRAPHY, ROCKY MOUNTAIN REVIEW, and the state historical journals of Illinois, Indiana, Ohio, Pennsylvania, New York, Connecticut, New Jersey, and Rhode Island. He is the recipient of the William Adee Whitehead Award of the New Jersey Historical Society and the Harry E. Pratt Award of the Illinois Historical Society, and was a John Simon Guggenheim Memorial Fellow.

NICHOLAS C. BURCKEL has served as assistant archivist at the University of Wisconsin-Madison, and then as director of University Archives and Area Research Center at the University of Wisconsin-Parkside. Since 1975 he has also served as executive assistant to the chancellor. He received his B.A. from Georgetown University and his M.A. and Ph.D. in history from the University of Wisconsin. He has published reviews and articles on history and archives in COLLEGE AND RESEARCH LIBRARIES, AMERICAN HISTORICAL REVIEW, AMERICAN ARCHIVIST, MIDWESTERN ARCHIVIST, MID-AMERICA, HISTORY TEACHER, HISTORY: REVIEWS OF NEW BOOKS, WISCONSIN MAGAZINE OF HISTORY, and the FILSON CLUB HISTORY QUARTERLY. In 1977 he edited RACINE: GROWTH AND CHANGE IN A WISCONSIN COUNTY. He is an active member of the Organization of American Historians, American Historical Association, American Association for State and Local History, and the Society of American Archivists, as well as a variety of local and state archival and historical organizations.

CONTENTS

Contents

PREFACE

In recent years American immigration studies have experienced a rebirth in response to the rediscovery of ethnicity. Scholarship concerned with immigrants had originated in the controversies swirling about the question of immigration restriction. Much of the early writing was of a polemical nature, arguing the positive or negative influence of the foreign influx upon American morals, institutions, and stock. During this initial stage, sociologists, social workers, economists, or biologists, but few historians, participated actively in the debate. With the enactment of the immigration laws of the 1920s, immigrants receded from the center of public and scholarly attention. Now that immigration had become a thing of the past, it became fit game for the historian. From the 1920s on, a small number of scholars began to write the history of American immigration. Although they produced important works of lasting value, immigration history remained the province of a few, on the periphery of the central concerns of American historiography. And so things stood until the 1960s.

In the sixties Americans suffered a series of traumas which undermined their faith in the American civil religion. Vietnam, Watergate, and domestic violence challenged beliefs in the omnipotence, righteousness, and stability of the Republic. The "Black Revolution" shattered the complacent assimilationist ideology. From this ferment emerged a new emphasis on the particularities which provide the basis for distinct group identity and solidarity. A search for roots expressed itself in a resurgence of ethnic consciousness and activities. Social scientists were startled by the surfacing of white ethnic groups long thought to have been assimilated. Immigration and its impact upon American society became once more a lively issue in scholarly inquiry and discussion. Not since the 1920s was so much attention focused upon questions of group characteristics, assimilation, and ethnic maintenance. As historians searched the past from a pluralistic perspective, social scientists sought to analyze the contemporary workings of ethnicity. The result has been a veritable flood of books, articles, and dissertations dealing with the role of immigration and ethnicity in the American past and present.

This bibliography is an attempt to bring some measure of order and control to the "knowledge explosion" in the field. Anyone who has attempted to survey even a portion of the literature on immigration and ethnicity must admire the courage of John D. Buenker and Nicholas C. Burckel in assuming the task of compiling a comprehensive guide to published materials. Scholars themselves, of course, do not agree on the precise parameters of the subject: were African slaves immigrants? are American Jews ethnics? Beyond that thorny problem, there are the complexities inherent in the wide diversity which has characterized American immigration; scholarship has reflected that diversity in specialized literatures on each national, racial, or religious group. Then too, these topics have been studied in one aspect or another by practically every humanistic and social science discipline.

Buenker and Burckel have struggled with these problems, and have produced a comprehensive guide to information sources which will be of great value to students, librarians, teachers, and anyone else interested in immigration and ethnicity. Containing more than 1,500 annotated entries, this is certainly the most inclusive, as well as up-to-date, bibliography available on the subject. Yet by necessity this represents a selection of the total literature, and it follows that the inclusion or omission of any particular item was a matter of judgment on the part of the compilers. Certain editorial decisions are obvious: Afro-Americans and native Americans are not included; foreign language materials, which at least equal in volume those in English, are seldom cited; and only a sampling of the more than 1,000 doctoral dissertations devoted to immigration topics appears in this guide. Clearly to have included those categories of materials would have made this a multivolume work. Although older studies of established value are included, the compilers chose to emphasize the publications of the last two decades. This also reflects the fact that more has appeared in this field in the last twenty years than in the previous fifty.

Of course, to attempt a bibliography of the immigration and ethnicity literature at this time is like taking a snapshot of an avalanche. It inevitably will be dated the moment it appears. Yet it will serve and serve well the needs of today. As a research tool it will facilitate greatly the work of all of us engaged in this field of study. On behalf of my colleagues as well as myself, I extend our thanks and our compliments to John D. Buenker and Nicholas C. Burckel on a job well done.

Rudolph J. Vecoli
University of Minnesota

INTRODUCTION

Because of its interdisciplinary nature, this guide should be of value to teachers and students of a wide variety of disciplines, including history, sociology, anthropology, political science, cultural geography, linguistics, and social studies, at the college, university, and senior high school levels. In addition to containing the most important sources of information on all the major immigrant groups from colonial times to the present, it draws together in the most comprehensive form yet published the most significant literature on the vast subjects of immigration and ethnicity. The volume also contains items dealing with the contemporary debate over immigration restriction in the 1920s and devotes nearly an entire chapter to government documents, committee hearings, and other official publications. It also lists numerous ethnic societies and archival and manuscript depositories, as well as their major holdings and the journals that they sponsor. The guide ought also to be of use to many of the rapidly proliferating ethnic organizations seeking to inform their members about their history and cultural heritage. School systems planning bilingual and multicultural programs will find it extremely helpful in planning course outlines and reading lists. Finally, the renewed interest in ethnic studies that has arisen in the past decade makes this guide a valuable addition for public libraries in any city with an ethnically diverse population.

In compiling this list of sources, we first consulted a variety of standard secondary sources with extensive bibliographic information. These sources included John J. Appel, ed., THE NEW IMMIGRATION; Frank Freidel, HARVARD GUIDE TO AMERICAN HISTORY; Roy L. Garis, IMMIGRATION RESTRICTION; Maldwyn Jones, AMERICAN IMMIGRATION; Franklin D. Scott, THE PEOPLING OF AMERICA: PERSPECTIVES ON IMMIGRATION; and numerous special subject bibliographies. In addition we culled all issues of the JOURNAL OF AMERICAN HISTORY, AMERICAN HISTORICAL REVIEW, topical journals whose subject area is immigration and ethnicity, and AMERICA; HISTORY AND LIFE. For repositories and societies we consulted the NATIONAL UNION CATALOG OF MANUSCRIPT COLLECTIONS, GUIDE TO MANUSCRIPT COLLECTIONS IN THE UNITED STATES, DIRECTORY OF HISTORICAL SOCIETIES AND AGENCIES, and ENCYCLOPEDIA OF ASSOCIATIONS, plus more specialized regional and subject listings. From these major sources and others we compiled approximately 3,500 potential entries, and read and annotated more than 1,800 books, articles, dissertations, and government documents. The number and variety of fictional and autobiographical works as well as film and phonograph recordings relating to the immigrant experience is so great that we felt it was impractical to include them in this volume. Almost no foreign language sources are cited. The bibliography also does not include the Afro-American or Indian-American experience in the United States. There is enough source material on these two groups that, rather than being treated inadequately within the space limitation of this bibliography, they merit separate consideration.

Even this method of surveying the field of immigration and ethnicity does not guarantee that all sources have been consulted, but the selections which follow include the major works in the field and an extensive number of sources reflecting the available scholarship. If, therefore, certain immigrant groups or time periods loom larger than others in number of entries, this merely reflects the general availability of material, not necessarily the importance which the authors ascribe to certain immigrant groups.

As to format, we have tried to combine a chronological and topical arrangement where possible. In some cases that has forced us to be arbitrary. Jews, for instance, were immigrants throughout American history, but because the bulk of them came during the "new immigration" of the 1880s and after, all Jewish immigrants have been included in chapter 3. We have sought to solve some of these anomalies through cross-referencing in the index. The index is to individual entry number, rather than to page, and this provides a more specific guide for users.

For the initial encouragement to undertake this project we owe a special thanks to Arthur D. Larson. In the preparation of the volume we are indebted to a number of students and staff who laboriously checked bibliographic details, typed drafts of the manuscript, and secured copies of articles and books through interlibrary loan: Lenore Burckel, Karen Gombar, Judith Hamilton, Patricia Knorn, Bridget Peterson, Christine Piwoni, Margaret Principe, and Patricia Regner. We also appreciate the expeditious handling of the manuscript by the series editor Harold B. Shill and Gale Research Company. We particularly appreciate the support of Chancellor Alan E. Guskin who supported the final typing of the manuscript prior to publication.

J.D.B.
N.C.B.

Chapter 1

GENERAL ACCOUNTS AND MISCELLANEOUS

GENERAL ACCOUNTS

001 Adamic, Louis. FROM MANY LANDS. New York: Harper & Brothers, 1940. 349 p. Notes.

Focuses upon the experiences of representative immigrant families and individuals from all over Europe as well as Japan and Mexico. Concludes with the creation of a survey project to uncover more information on the ethnic origins of Americans.

002 _____. NATIONS OF NATIONS. New York: Harper & Brothers, 1945. 350 p. Notes, index.

Chronicles experiences and achievements of immigrants from Italy, Mexico, France, Holland, Sweden, Russia, Germany, Africa, Yugoslavia, Norway, Greece, Poland, and Ireland. Focuses largely on representative individuals.

003 Ander, O[scar]. Fritiof, ed. IN THE TREK OF THE IMMIGRANTS: ESSAYS PRESENTED TO CARL WITTKE. Rock Island, Ill.: Augustana College Library, 1964. 325 p. Notes, index.

A festschrift by colleagues in immigration history including essays by Harvey Wish, Oscar Fritiof Ander, Carlton Qualey, Clarence Cramer, Edward Hutchinson, Charlotte Erickson, Francis Weisenburger, John Flanagan, Oscar Winther, Kenneth Bjork, William Hoglund, Walter Forster, Wilbur Shepperson, Theodore Saloutos, James Rodabaugh, and Iverne Dowie. The essays span all aspects of immigrant history and the annotation of each essay may be found under the immigrant group with which it deals.

004 Anderson, Charles H. WHITE PROTESTANT AMERICANS: FROM NATIONAL ORIGINS TO RELIGIOUS GROUP. Ethnic Groups in American Life Series, edited by Milton Gordon. Englewood Cliffs, N.J.: Prentice Hall, 1970. 188 p. Appendices, footnotes, index.

1

Defining white Protestants as English, Welsh, Scottish, Scotch-Irish, Swedes, Norwegians, Danes, Finns, Germans, and Dutch, the author first studies the assimilation of these groups into a core society. In the second half of the book he evaluates the current status of white Protestants from several aspects.

005 Blegen, Theodore C. GRASS ROOTS HISTORY. Minneapolis: University of Minnesota Press, 1947. 266 p. Index.

Drawn from American immigration and regional history, this book contains a series of papers by Blegen. Although his examples are mainly from Norwegian immigration and settlement in the upper Midwest, his emphasis on the unlettered and the average indicates the general importance of such studies for social historians.

006 Brandenburg, B. IMPORTED AMERICANS. 1904. Reprint. New York: F.A. Stokes Co., 1940. 303 p.

First person account by an American who poses as an Italian immigrant in order to experience difficulties of steerage and Ellis Island. Recommends protection and regulation of immigration.

007 Brown, Francis J., and Roucek, Joseph S., eds. ON AMERICA: HISTORY CONTRIBUTIONS AND PRESENT PROBLEMS OF OUR RACIAL AND NATIONAL MINORITIES. 3d ed. Englewood Cliffs, N.J.: Prentice Hall, 1952. 631 p. Appendices, selected bibliography, index.

Anthology by numerous scholars dealing with the whole range of ethnic, racial, and religious minorities, their institutions, political involvement, educational, and religious practices. Concludes with several essays on "trends toward cultural democracy in America."

008 _____. OUR RACIAL AND NATIONAL MINORITIES: THEIR HISTORY, CONTRIBUTIONS AND PRESENT PROBLEMS. Englewood Cliffs, N.J.: Prentice Hall, 1952. 877 p. Maps, illustrations.

A general textbook dealing with the immigration, culture, assimilation, and contributions of America's minority groups. Also examines the problems of majority-minority relations and intergroup conflict.

009 Brunner, Edmund de S. IMMIGRANT FARMERS AND THEIR CHILDREN: WITH FOUR STUDIES OF IMMIGRANT COMMUNITIES. Garden City, N.Y.: Doubleday, Doran & Co., 1929. 277 p. Appendices, index.

The first section deals generally with the question of foreign-born farmers, their number, distribution, characteristics, intelligence levels, intermarriage, social life, and religion. The second section focuses on the Danes in Minnesota, Czechs in Virginia, Poles in New England, and a mixed group of immigrant farmers in North Carolina.

010 Carpenter, Niles. IMMIGRANTS AND THEIR CHILDREN, 1920: A STUDY BASED ON CENSUS STATISTICS RELATIVE TO FOREIGN BORN AND THE NATIVE WHITE OF FOREIGN OR MIXED PARENTAGE. Washington, D.C.: Government Printing Office, 1927. 431 p.

Statistical analysis of first and second generation immigrants with respect to territorial distribution, length of residence, nationality, race, sex, language, age, fecundity, vitality, marital condition, intermarriage, illegitimacy, citizenship, and occupation.

011 Chickering, Jesse. IMMIGRATION INTO THE UNITED STATES. Boston: Little and Brown, 1848. 66 p. Appendix.

Documents the substantial increase in immigration after 1830 and urges favorable and considerate treatment toward immigrants to facilitate assimilation.

012 Coleman, Terry. PASSAGE TO AMERICA. London: Hutchinson & Co., 1972. Reprint. New York: Anchor Press, 1973. 317 p. Illustrations, appendices, footnotes, sources, bibliography, index.

A journalist's account of the people who emigrated from Great Britain and Ireland from 1846 to 1855, the greatest period of emigration up to that time. Argues that it was technological change brought by the steamship, rather than the reforms of any government, that made the Atlantic crossing tolerable for the immigrants.

013 Commager, Henry S., ed. IMMIGRATION AND AMERICAN HISTORY: ESSAYS IN HONOR OF THEODORE C. BLEGEN. Minneapolis: University of Minnesota Press, 1961. 154 p. Bibliography, index.

Collection of reinterpretative and exploratory essays on various phases of immigration studies, especially fiction, demography, ideas, and the respective images of Yankees and Europeans.

014 Commons, John R. RACES AND IMMIGRANTS IN AMERICA. 1907. Reprint. New York: Augustus M. Kelley, 1967. 242 p. Illustrations, footnotes, index.

After a historical survey of immigration including a chapter on blacks, the economist turns to the immigrant's role in labor, industry, politics, and urban life.

015 Corsi, Edward. IN THE SHADOW OF LIBERTY: THE CHRONICLE OF

ELLIS ISLAND. 1935. Reprint. New York: Arno Press, 1969. 315 p. Illustrations, index.

Written by commissioner of Ellis Island from 1931-34. First part: autobiography from Italian emigration in 1907 to appointment as commissioner. Second half: vignettes and anecdotes of famous incidents on Ellis Island.

016 Cullen, Joseph P. "To America Via Hell." AMERICAN HISTORY ILLUSTRATED 1 (1966): 14-23.

Describes the difficult and perilous journey of immigrants to America, the problems involved in getting to a ship, the overcrowded conditions, fetid water, spoiled food, inadequate air, and often brutal treatment on the voyage and their frequent defrauding at the point of entry.

017 Dinnerstein, Leonard, and Reimers, David M. ETHNIC AMERICANS: A HISTORY OF IMMIGRATION AND ASSIMILATION. New York: Dodd, Mead & Co., 1975. 204 p. Appendix, bibliography, index.

A historical overview of non-English American immigration and assimilation, which focuses on the communication problems faced by all new ethnic Americans, their struggles and conflicts, and their patterns of mobility and assimilation. An attempt to delineate the broad themes which characterize the immigrant experience.

018 Eaton, Allan H. IMMIGRANT GIFTS TO AMERICAN LIFE: SOME EXPERIMENTS IN APPRECIATION OF THE CONTRIBUTIONS OF OUR FOREIGN-BORN CITIZENS TO AMERICAN CULTURE. New York: Russell Sage Foundation, 1932. 185 p. Illustrations, appendix, bibliography.

A catalog of ethnic exhibitions which are held in an attempt to preserve the mores and traditions of immigrant groups through various ethnic festivals and displays. The displays described in the book emphasize the material contributions of immigrants to American life.

019 Fleming, Donald, and Bailyn, Bernard, eds. DISLOCATION AND EMIGRATION: THE SOCIAL BACKGROUND OF AMERICAN IMMIGRATION. Perspectives in American History Series, vol. 7. Cambridge, Mass.: Charles Warren Center for Studies in American History, 1974. 635 p. Footnotes.

A series of eight previously unpublished articles each of which is separately annotated under the individual author's name: Maldwyn A. Jones, Malcolm Gray, Alan Conway, Johann Chmelar, Theodore Saloutos, Leo Schelbert, Wolfgang Kollmann, and Arthur F. Corwin.

020 Greenleaf, Barbara. AMERICA FEVER. New York: Four Winds Press, 1974. 201 p. Illustrations, selected bibliography, index.

A brief, popular survey of immigration patterns written by a journalist. Stresses continuity of experiences of all immigrants.

021 Handlin, Oscar. THE AMERICAN PEOPLE IN THE TWENTIETH CENTURY. 2d ed., rev. Cambridge, Mass.: Harvard University Press, 1966. 248 p. Notes, index.

Examines the interaction between the forces of unity and nationalism and those of cultural diversity in the twentieth-century United States and speculates on their future relationship.

022 _____. A PICTORIAL HISTORY OF IMMIGRATION. New York: Crown, 1972. 328 p. Maps, illustrations, charts, tables, bibliography, index.

Narrative arranged in chronological order from the arrival of the Amerindians to the present. Contains hundreds of photographs.

023 _____. THE UPROOTED: THE EPIC STORY OF THE GREAT MIGRA-TIONS THAT MADE THE AMERICAN PEOPLE. Boston: Little and Brown, 1951. 307 p.

Pulitzer Prize-winning saga of the traumatic impact of urban-industrial life in America upon the culture and institutions of predominantly peasant immigrants.

024 _____, ed. CHILDREN OF THE UPROOTED. New York: George Brazil-ler, 1966. 551 p.

Handlin wrote the introduction to this collection of thirty-four essays (written by prominent children of immigrants) on the difficulties of being second generation Americans.

025 _____. IMMIGRATION AS A FACTOR IN AMERICAN HISTORY. Englewood Cliffs, N.J.: Prentice Hall, 1959. 206 p.

Collection of documents, letters, autobiographies, and essays on various aspects of immigrant life and institutions with a commentary by the editor.

026 Hansen, Marcus Lee. THE ATLANTIC MIGRATION, 1607-1860, A HISTORY OF THE CONTINUING SETTLEMENT OF THE UNITED STATES. Edited with a foreword by Arthur M. Schlesinger. Cambridge, Mass.: Harvard University Press, 1940. 306 p. Illustrations, notes, bibliography.

This account of immigration from the founding of Jamestown to the Civil War stresses European causes for migration and American socioeconomic mobility.

027 _____. THE IMMIGRANT IN AMERICAN HISTORY. Edited with a fore-
word by Arthur M. Schlesinger. Cambridge, Mass.: Harvard University
Press, 1940. Reprint. New York: Harper Torchbooks, 1964. 217 p.
Index.

A series of topical essays by the father of immigration history
summing up his lifetime work. The last essay cogently delineates the outlines of "immigration as a field for historical
research."

028 _____. MINGLING OF THE CANADIAN AND AMERICAN PEOPLES.
New Haven, Conn.: Yale University Press, 1940. 264 p. Maps, index.

Details the causes and course of "perhaps the longest single
reciprocity in international migration"--the exchange of Canadian and American migrants from 1604 to 1938.

029 Higham, John. "Immigration." In THE COMPARATIVE APPROACH TO
AMERICAN HISTORY, edited by C. Vann Woodward, pp. 91-105. New
York: Basic Books, 1968.

Urges the use of comparative history to explore immigration
"as a source of distinctions, divisions and changes within the
United States," thus stressing it as an important differentiating
force.

030 Hoff, Rhoda. AMERICA'S IMMIGRANTS: ADVENTURES IN EYEWITNESS
HISTORY. New York: Henry Z. Walch, 1967. 162 p. Bibliography.

Collection of forty-two first person accounts by American observers and immigrants ranging from Benjamin Franklin in 1784
to Rene Dubos in 1966. Most deal with advice to perspective
immigrants or reports on their conditions in the United States.

031 Hutchinson, Edward P. IMMIGRANTS AND THEIR CHILDREN, 1850-1950.
New York: Wiley, 1956. 278 p. Appendices, index.

A survey and guide to the census data on immigration, its
changing composition, geographical and occupational distribution, contribution to the American economy, and the effect
of restriction on foreign stock peoples.

032 Huthmacher, J. Joseph. A NATION OF NEWCOMERS: ETHNIC MINOR-
ITIES IN AMERICAN HISTORY. New York: Delacorte Press, 1967.
132 p. Illustrations, bibliography.

Deals primarily with the Irish, Italians, Chinese, Japanese,
Puerto Ricans, and Negroes: the ethnic groups that have pro-
voked the most antagonism among members of the core culture.

033 Ifkovic, Edward. AMERICAN LETTERS: IMMIGRANT AND ETHNIC WRIT-
ING. Englewood Cliffs, N.J.: Prentice Hall, 1975. 386 p. Bibliography.

Collection of letters and writings by Americans of nearly every
ethnic heritage, organized around the general topics of American identity, remembrances of the Old Country, adjustment of
the foreign born to America, alienation or assimilation of their
children, and the future of the melting pot and cultural pluralism. Also contains a workshop section with suggestions for
projects to involve students in ethnic studies.

034 Janeway, William Ralph. BIBLIOGRAPHY OF IMMIGRATION IN THE
UNITED STATES, 1900-1930. 1934. Reprint. San Francisco: R and E
Research Associates, 1972. 132 p.

An exhaustive bibliography, topically arranged, of books, documents, and periodical literature. General topics include immigration backgrounds, cultural heritage, social adjustments,
race relations, assimilation, and immigration restriction. Of
particular importance for popular periodicals.

035 Jones, Maldwyn Allen. AMERICAN IMMIGRATION. The Chicago History of American Civilization Series. Chicago: University of Chicago
Press, 1960. 319 p. Illustrations, appendix, bibliography, index.

A chronological account of immigration from earliest foundations to the present written by an English scholar. Frequently
used as a textbook in college level courses on immigration.

036 Kaplan, Louis. A BIBLIOGRAPHY OF AMERICAN AUTOBIOGRAPHIES.
Madison: University of Wisconsin Press, 1962. 325 p. Subject index.

Contains bibliographical and biographical information on 6,377
autobiographies. Includes those of many prominent immigrants
such as Louis Adamic, Mary Antin, Andrew Carnegie, Samuel
Gompers, and Carl Schurz. Useful reference tool.

037 Kennedy, John F. A NATION OF IMMIGRANTS. Rev. and enl. New
York: Harper & Row, 1964. 122 p. Illustrations, appendices.

Brief survey of immigration patterns and contributions and an
argument for liberalizing the quota legislation in the early
1960s. Introduction by Robert Kennedy written after his broth-
er's assassination.

038 Kohler, Max J. IMMIGRATION AND ALIENS IN THE UNITED STATES:
STUDIES OF AMERICAN IMMIGRATION LAWS AND THE LEGAL STATUS
OF ALIENS IN THE UNITED STATES. New York: Bloch Publishing Co.,
1936. 459 p. Notes, index.

Discusses administration of immigration laws, the right of asylum, racial discrimination, the special problems of Jews and
Chinese, the legal status and registration of aliens, naturalization, and deportation.

039   Kolm, Richard. BIBLIOGRAPHY OF ETHNICITY AND ETHNIC GROUPS.
      Washington, D.C.: National Institute of Mental Health, 1973. 250 p.
      Index.

      Contains 451 annotated books and articles on ethnicity and
      ethnic groups and an additional 1,244 items without annotation.

040   Kraus, Michael. IMMIGRATION, THE AMERICAN MOSAIC: FROM
      PILGRIMS TO MODERN REFUGEES. Princeton, N.J.: Van Nostrand,
      1966. 202 p. Appendix, bibliography, index.

      A brief survey of immigration from colonial times to 1965, ac-
      companied by a series of readings by and about a wide variety
      of immigrants.

041   Maisel, Albert Q. THEY ALL CHOSE AMERICA. New York: Thomas
      Nelson and Sons, 1957. 280 p.

      A chapter devoted to each of the following immigrant groups:
      Dutch, English, French, Germans, Greeks, Irish, Italians,
      Japanese, Jews, Mexicans, Poles, Scots, Swedes, Swiss, and
      blacks.

042   Mann, Arthur. IMMIGRANTS IN AMERICAN LIFE: SELECTED READ-
      INGS. Boston: Houghton Mifflin Co., 1974. 262 p. Appendix, bib-
      liography, index.

      Features selections by numerous scholars and political figures
      dealing with the various streams of migration, immigrants' jobs,
      housing, community life, politics, and assessments of success.
      Also discusses nativism, concepts of assimilation and Americani-
      zation, changes in immigration policy, and the revival of eth-
      nicity.

043   Mayo-Smith, Richmond. EMIGRATION AND IMMIGRATION: A STUDY
      IN SOCIAL SCIENCE. New York: C. Scribner's Sons, 1890. 302 p.
      Bibliography, index.

      Attempts to study emigration and immigration with the tools of
      the new social sciences. Focuses on demography, political
      effects, economic impact (especially on native American labor),
      social disorganization, efforts to protect immigrants by law,
      and the growth of restriction.

044   National Industrial Conference Board. THE IMMIGRATION PROBLEM IN
      THE UNITED STATES. New York: 1923. 133 p. Charts, tables, ap-
      pendix, footnotes.

      A survey of the history and causes of immigration, the relation
      of immigration to the American economy and culture, the de-
      velopment of federal immigration legislation, and an in-depth
      study of the 1921 immigration law with accompanying sugges-

tions for revision. Recommends a modified quota system.

045 Neidle, Cecyle S. GREAT IMMIGRANTS. The Immigrant Heritage of America Series. New York: Twayne, 1973. 295 p. References, bibliography, index.

Selects a dozen immigrants from the eighteenth to twentieth century and writes a biographical chapter on each: Albert Gallatin, Johann Roebling, John Peter Altgeld, Abraham Jacobi, E.L. Godkin, Johann Most, Nikola Tesla, Anton Carlson, O.E. Rolvaag, Selman Abraham Waksman, David Dubinsky, and Herman Badillo.

046 _____. THE NEW AMERICANS. New York: Twayne, 1967. 342 p. Notes, bibliography.

A lengthy general introduction provides the background to a series of nearly seventy-five selections of writings by immigrants and foreign observers on their own experience in America from colonial times to the present. The arrangement is chronological and each selection has a biographical introduction.

047 Novotny, Ann. STRANGERS AT THE DOOR: A HISTORY OF AMERICAN IMMIGRATION BETWEEN 1855-1934. Riverside, Conn.: Chatham Press, 1971. 150 p. Illustrations, appendix, bibliography, index.

Contains a selection of photographs, drawings, and essays which provide a pictorial narrative of the evolution and decline of Castle Garden and Ellis Island as immigrant reception centers.

048 Panunzio, Constantine. IMMIGRATION CROSSROADS. New York: Macmillan Co., 1927. 307 p. Footnotes, index.

A broad survey by a social economist of the contributions of immigrants, the changing attitudes of Americans toward the immigrants, and suggestions for immigration policy.

049 Pitkin, Thomas M. KEEPERS OF THE GATE: A HISTORY OF ELLIS ISLAND. New York: New York University Press, 1975. 226 p. Illustrations, notes, bibliography, index.

Chronological account of the Ellis Island immigrant reception center from 1892 to its closing in 1954. Focuses upon legislative changes, political squabbles, and the use of the island as a detainment center in war years.

050 Rischin, Moses, ed. IMMIGRATION AND THE AMERICAN TRADITION. The American Heritage Series. Indianapolis, Ind.: Bobbs-Merrill Co., 1976. 456 p. Index.

A collection of articles by historical figures and modern day scholars organized around the general topics of assimilation, labor, the yellow peril, World Wars I and II, self-determination, world revolution, restriction, acculturation, the presidential campaigns of Al Smith and John Kennedy, and the nation's post-1965 immigration policy.

051 Schmid, Hans. "Die Verschiedenen Einwandererwellen in die Vereiningten Staaten von Nord-Amerika von den Anfangen Bis Zur Quotengesetz-gebung." HISTORISCHES JAHRBUCH (West Germany) 85 (1965): 323-61.

Surveys the various migrations to the United States, beginning with the Indians and Eskimos of prehistoric times to the New Immigrants of 1890-1920. Discusses the reasons for this migration, the various forms and areas of settlement, and the common problems of assimilation.

052 Scott, Franklin D. THE PEOPLING OF AMERICA: PERSPECTIVES ON IMMIGRATION. AHA Pamphlet no. 241. Washington, D.C.: American Historical Association, 1972. 75 p. Footnotes.

This is a revision of EMIGRATION AND IMMIGRATION, published in 1963 and 1966 as part of a series of historiographical pamphlets by the Service Center for Teachers of History.

053 Shalloo, J.P. "United States Immigration Policy, 1882-1948." In ESSAYS IN HONOR OF GEORGE H. BLAKESLEE, edited by Dwight E. Lee and G.E. McReynolds, pp. 126-52. Worcester, Mass.: Clark University Publication, 1949.

Discusses the provisions of the major immigration laws passed between the Oriental Exclusion Act and the Displaced Persons Act and analyzes their impact upon the magnitude and ethnic composition of immigration during that period.

054 Smith, Darrell H., and Herring, H.G. BUREAU OF IMMIGRATION: ITS HISTORY, ACTIVITIES AND ORGANIZATION. Institute for Government Research, Service Monograph of the United States Government, no. 30. Baltimore, Md.: Johns Hopkins Press, 1924. 247 p. Appendices, bibliography, index.

One of a series of monographs that was designed to assist legislators and administrators who needed information about the topic in order to implement effective legislation. It is descriptive and it presents the activities, plans, organization, personnel, and laws of the bureau as of 1924.

055 Steiner, E.A. THE IMMIGRANT TIDE, ITS EBB AND FLOW. New York: F.H. Revell Co., 1909. 370 p.

Summarizes the author's twenty-five-year acquaintance with

New Immigrants from all parts of Europe. Gives a sympathetic picture of their adjustment to American life.

056 _____. ON THE TRAIL OF THE IMMIGRANT. New York: F.H. Revell Co., 1906. 364 p. Illustrations, appendix, index.

Highly personalized account focusing on southern and eastern European immigrants, their journey to America, and the flavor of their various ethnic enclaves.

057 Stephenson, George M. A HISTORY OF AMERICAN IMMIGRATION, 1820-1924. Boston: Ginn, 1926. 282 p. Select bibliography, index.

Discusses in general terms the European background of various national groups, their adjustment to American life, especially in politics, and the changing attitudes of the American people and government toward immigration.

058 Taylor, Philip A.M. THE DISTANT MAGNET: EUROPEAN EMIGRATION TO THE U.S.A. New York: Harper & Row, 1971. 326 p. Maps, illustrations, charts, tables, notes, bibliography, index.

A British scholar synthesizes existing published accounts of the immigrant experience in Europe, during the Atlantic crossing and finally in America. It does not propound any new theses but presents the story of the immigrants in an interesting fashion for the general reader.

059 U.S. Library of Congress, Division of Bibliography. IMMIGRATION IN THE UNITED STATES: A SELECTED LIST OF RECENT REFERENCES. 1943. 94 p.

Contains entries under the following headings: general, history, crime and the immigrant, deportation, restriction, statistics, nationalities, refugees, citizenship, and naturalization. Includes an author and a subject index.

060 Vecoli, Rudolph J. "European Americans: From Immigrants to Ethnics." In THE REINTERPRETATION OF AMERICAN HISTORY AND CULTURE, edited by William H. Cartwright and Richard L. Watson, Jr., pp. 81-112. Washington, D.C.: National Council for the Social Studies, 1973.

A historiographical essay on European immigration and the role of the immigrant in American life. Regards the melting pot theory as inadequate and focuses upon works dealing with the persistence of ethnic identity.

061 Wittke, Carl F. WE WHO BUILT AMERICA: THE SAGA OF THE IMMIGRANT. Englewood Cliffs, N.J.: Prentice Hall, 1939. 538 p. Index.

Survey of immigration from colonial times to the restriction of the 1920s. Emphasizes continuity of the immigrant experience and the sources of nativism.

062 Ziegler, Benjamin Munn. IMMIGRATION, AN AMERICAN DILEMMA. Boston: D.C. Heath & Co., 1953. 166 p. Bibliographical essay.

Selections by ten authors on the historical evolution of American immigration and its cultural, social, economic, political, and international implications. Contains some tables and government documents.

IMMIGRATION TO A SPECIFIC LOCALITY

063 Appel, Livia, and Blegen, Theodore C. "Official Encouragement of Immigration to Minnesota during the Territorial Period." MINNESOTA HISTORY BULLETIN 5 (1923): 167-203.

A brief historical introduction is followed by a dozen representative primary sources dealing with immigration to Minnesota. Sources include reports of officially appointed immigration agents, the first immigration law of 1855, a newspaper editorial, correspondence, and broadsides.

064 Belissary, C.G. "Tennessee and Immigration, 1865-1880." TENNESSEE HISTORICAL QUARTERLY 8 (1949): 229-48.

Investigates the efforts of many Tennessee politicians, professionals, and businessmen to attract immigrants to their state in the post-Civil War era. Despite their efforts, the author argues that high land prices, racial problems, and Southern xenophobia combined to discourage large scale immigration.

065 Blegen, Theodore C. "The Competition of the Northwestern States for Immigrants." WISCONSIN MAGAZINE OF HISTORY 3 (1919): 3-29.

Indicates that the large number of Germans, Norwegians, and Swedes who came to Wisconsin, Minnesota, and Iowa in the 1870s and 1880s did so at the express invitation of states which needed an influx of population for development.

066 Bodnar, John E., ed. THE ETHNIC EXPERIENCE IN PENNSYLVANIA. Lewisburg, Pa.: Bucknell University Press, 1973. 330 p.

A collection of essays on different immigrant groups settling the state, including essays by Caroline Golab on the Polish experience, Richard Juliani on Italians in Philadelphia, and other studies on Croatians, Serbs, and Ukrainians.

067 Brandfon, Robert L. "The End of Immigration to the Cotton Fields." MISSISSIPPI VALLEY HISTORICAL REVIEW 50 (1964): 591-611.

Discusses the efforts of Delta planters to attract Italian immigrants to work on their cotton plantations. Only a few came,
however, and they were frustrated by their inability to rise
above the tenant level and by their relegation to the same
social status as the Negro. After 1910 almost all Italian immigrants left the cotton fields.

068   Brown, Arthur J. "The Promotion of Emigration to Washington 1854-1909."
PACIFIC NORTHWEST QUARTERLY 36 (1945): 3-17.

Deals largely with efforts to attract settlers to Washington from
the Midwest and East with little or no discussion of how many
of those who came to Washington were foreign born.

069   Bushee, Frederick A. ETHNIC FACTORS IN THE POPULATION OF BOS-
TON. 1903. Reprint. New York: Arno Press and New York Times,
1970. 171 p. Tables, index.

Analyzes the causes of immigration, characteristics, living
standards, vitality, occupations, poverty, crime, naturalization,
and intermarriage of a wide variety of Boston ethnic groups.
Definite undertones of nativism.

070   Crockett, Norman L. "A Study in Confusion: Missouri's Immigration Program, 1865-1916." MISSOURI HISTORICAL REVIEW 58 (1963): 248-60.

Chronicles Missouri's program of encouraging immigration through
promotional literature, state and local immigration boards, immigration agents, and the railroads. The program was ham-
pered by poor organization and timing as well as "a rural and
racial attitude reflecting a contradiction of ideas."

071   Davis, Allen F., and Haller, Mark H. THE PEOPLES OF PHILADELPHIA:
A HISTORY OF ETHNIC GROUPS AND LOWER CLASS LIFE, 1790-1940.
Philadelphia: Temple University Press, 1973. 290 p. Index.

Collection of thirteen essays by various scholars analyzing the
life of lower class Philadelphians from the late eighteenth to
early twentieth century. About one-half deals with specific
ethnic groups and the remainder with such common problems
as poverty, housing, crime, violence, and residential mobility.

072   Esslinger, Dean R. "The Urbanization of South Bend's Immigrants, 1850-
1880." Ph.D. dissertation, University of Notre Dame, 1972. 227 p.

Uses South Bend as representative of a small midwestern town
experiencing the transition from commerce to industry, accompanied by a significant population increase, especially among
the immigrants. Geographical and occupational mobility are
studied as well as the rise of immigrants to positions of community leadership.

073 Fleming, Walter L. "Immigration to the Southern States." POLITICAL
     SCIENCE QUARTERLY 20 (1905): 276-97.

     Argues that the South is becoming more receptive to immigrants
     as a labor force to replace Negroes and outlines new patterns
     of settlement and efforts to encourage immigration.

074 Frakes, George E., and Solberg, Curtis B., eds. MINORITIES IN CALI-
     FORNIA HISTORY. New York: Random House, 1971. 280 p.

     Book of readings divided into two sections. Part 1 covers the
     role of minorities in the historical development of the state
     until the end of World War I. Part 2 concentrates on the
     current minorities in California, which are blacks, Indians,
     Mexican Americans, and Orientals. Contributors range from
     Huey Newton to Ronald Reagan.

075 Freeman, Felton D. "Immigration to Arkansas." ARKANSAS HISTORICAL
     QUARTERLY 9 (1949): 210-19.

     A sociologist's review of the policies and promotional means
     used to induce immigration to Arkansas in the second half of
     the nineteenth century.

076 Galford, Justin B. "The Foreign Born and Urban Growth in the Great
     Lakes, 1850-1950: A Study of Chicago, Cleveland, Detroit and Milwau-
     kee." Ph.D. dissertation, New York University, 1957. 388 p.

     In each of these cities, Germans or Irish were the predomi-
     nant ethnic group between 1850 and 1870. However, since
     1910 the leading nationalities have been the Germans in Mil-
     waukee, Canadians in Detroit, Poles in Chicago, and Poles or
     Czechoslovaks in Cleveland. Aside from personal whim, in-
     fluences affecting immigration to certain cities included a fa-
     vorable employment situation, industrial recruitment, and social
     and cultural considerations.

077 Gates, Paul Wallace. THE ILLINOIS CENTRAL RAILROAD AND ITS
     COLONIZATION WORK. Cambridge, Mass.: Harvard University Press,
     1934. 374 p. Bibliography, index.

     Deals with efforts of the railroad and the state of Illinois to
     promote immigration between 1850 and 1880. Concerned largely
     with the relation of immigration to land usage and the role of
     the railroad in town promotion.

078 Green, Richard A. "Origins of the Foreign-born Population of New Mexico
     during the Territorial Period." NEW MEXICO HISTORICAL REVIEW 17
     (1942): 281-87.

     Based upon census data, this article demonstrates that New

Mexico's population was "surprisingly cosmopolitan as to origin if not as to culture." Although Mexicans were by far the largest segment of the foreign-born population, there were significant numbers from Italy and various northern and western European countries.

079 Hedges, James B. "The Colonization Work of the Northern Pacific Railroad." MISSISSIPPI VALLEY HISTORICAL REVIEW 13 (1926): 311-42.

In the twenty-five years following the chartering of the Northern Pacific in 1864, the railroad completed colonization as far west as the Missouri River and had begun settlement of the region further west. It handled the greatest number of immigrant settlers in the early 1880s.

080 _____. "Promotion of Immigration to the Pacific Northwest by the Railroads." MISSISSIPPI VALLEY HISTORICAL REVIEW 15 (1928): 183-203.

Tells the story of railroad magnate Henry Villard's efforts at organizing immigration settlement of the Pacific Northwest. This was done largely without state support and before completion of railroad links with the rest of the country.

081 Leonard, Stephen J. "Denver's Foreign-born Immigrants, 1859-1900." Ph.D. dissertation, Claremont Graduate School, 1971. 271 p.

Posits three periods of development. They are: (1) 1859-74, frontier period in which immigrants were recruited and welcomed; (2) 1875-92, period of rapid growth with somewhat fewer opportunities for immigrants, especially Italians and Chinese; (3) 1893-98, period of economic decline and rise of American Protective Association.

082 Menard, Russell R. "Immigration to the Chesapeake Colonies in the Seventeenth Century: A Review Essay." MARYLAND HISTORICAL MAGAZINE 68 (1973): 323-29.

A detailed review of Wesley Frank Craven's WHITE, RED, AND BLACK: THE SEVENTEENTH CENTURY VIRGINIAN, a set of three essays for the James L. Richard Lectures in History delivered at the University of Virginia in 1970.

083 Petersen, Harold F. "Some Colonization Projects of the Northern Pacific Railroad." MINNESOTA HISTORY 10 (1929): 127-44.

Traces the role of the Northern Pacific in establishing four colonies in the three counties of Becker, Clay, and Wadena in the 1870s and 1880s. Stresses the interdependence of the railroad and of northern Minnesota.

084 Petersen, William J. "Immigrants from Near and Far." PALIMPSEST 49

(1968): 295-302.

The story of immigration to Iowa in the 1850s with emphasis on popularizing immigration through pamphlets and newspaper editorials and advertisements.

085   Pozzetta, George E.   "Foreigners in Florida: A Study of Immigration Promotion, 1865-1910."   FLORIDA HISTORICAL QUARTERLY 53 (1974):   164-80.

Discusses Florida's efforts to displace black labor with cheap immigrant labor from Europe, in order to rebuild the South and make possible segregation and disfranchisement.   Contact with immigrants aroused nativist feelings and led to an anti-foreign, anti-Catholic upsurge in the state.

086   Rischin, Moses.   "Beyond the Great Divide: Immigration and the Last Frontier."   JOURNAL OF AMERICAN HISTORY 55 (1968):   42-53.

First surveys published studies of immigration west of the Rockies, then calls for a reexamination of the social and immigration history of the area rather than merely reapplying old theses to new situations.

087   Ristuben, Peter John.   "Minnesota and the Competition for Immigrants."   Ph.D. dissertation, University of Oklahoma, 1964.   305 p.

Between 1855 and 1927 Minnesota sought to attract new settlers by employing honorary and salaried agents, by advertising in American and foreign newspapers, by erecting displays at fairs, and by distributing over three million pieces of promotional literature.

088   Schell, Herbert.   "Official Immigration Activities of the Dakota Territory."   NORTH DAKOTA HISTORICAL QUARTERLY 7 (1932):   5-24.

Details the activities of the territory in recruiting primarily Scandinavian and Russo-German immigrants in the 1870s and 1880s.   The Dakota Immigration Bureau issued reams of promotional and informational publications, maintained recruiters in seaports, and built an "immigration house" to aid in settlement.

089   Shannon, James P.   CATHOLIC COLONIZATION ON THE WESTERN FRONTIER.   New Haven, Conn.:   Yale University Press, 1957.   302 p.   Illustrations, footnotes, sources, index.

Bishop John Ireland's colonization efforts in Minnesota where he established ten rural villages and farming communities in five western counties between 1876 and 1881.

090   Shepperson, Wilbur S.   RESTLESS STRANGERS: NEVADA'S IMMIGRANTS

AND THEIR INTERPRETERS. Reno: University of Nevada Press, 1970. 287 p. Illustrations, notes, bibliography, index.

Part 1 places the immigrant in the Nevada setting and describes the immigrant's response. The second part, which comprises most of the book, presents the immigrants as portrayed by journalists and novelists.

091 Taylor, Paul S. "Colonizing Georgia, 1732-1752: A Statistical Note." WILLIAM AND MARY QUARTERLY 22 (1965): 119-27.

Traces the shift from public to private promotion of colonization in colonial Georgia after the period of trusteeship. Concludes that most colonists were financed by private funds and that over 70 percent were servants transported because the head right system based the size of the land grant on the size of a person's household.

092 Tindall, George B. "Beyond the Mainstream: The Ethnic Southerners." JOURNAL OF SOUTHERN HISTORY 40 (1974): 3-18.

Presidential address at the annual meeting of the Southern Historical Association in 1973, surveying the current trend toward popularizing ethnicity and then analyzing that trend in the context of recent studies of the South.

093 Treat, Victor Hugo. "Migration into Louisiana, 1834-1880." Ph.D. dissertation, University of Texas, 1967. 764 p.

Examines census records to determine the sources, rates, and characteristics of migration. Analyzes both the metropolitan urban area of New Orleans and the rural areas of the state. Indicates that there was very little foreign-born immigration but a large amount of migration from other slave states.

094 Vecoli, Rudolph J. THE PEOPLE OF NEW JERSEY. Princeton, N.J.: Van Nostrand, 1965. 278 p. Appendices, bibliography, index.

Views the peopling of New Jersey in terms of successive waves of immigration and problems of adjustment over three centuries.

095 Weisenburger, Francis P. "A Brief History of Immigrant Groups in Ohio." In IN THE TREK OF THE IMMIGRANTS: ESSAYS PRESENTED TO CARL WITTKE, edited by O. Fritiof Ander, pp. 81-93. Rock Island, Ill.: Augustana College Library, 1964.

Traces the changing patterns of immigration to the Buckeye State from colonial times to the present, stressing the wide variety of national origins involved.

ECONOMICS OF IMMIGRATION

096   Eckler, A. Ross, and Zoltnick, J. "Immigration and the Labor Force."
ANNALS OF THE AMERICAN ACADEMY OF POLITICAL AND SOCIAL
SCIENCE 262 (1949): 92-101.

Demonstrates that, after the Civil War, the volume of immigration corresponded to the peaks and valleys of the business
cycle, underscoring the importance of immigration in swelling
the nation's labor force.

097   Erickson, Charlotte. AMERICAN INDUSTRY AND THE EUROPEAN IM-
MIGRANT, 1860-1885. Cambridge, Mass.: Harvard University Press,
1957. 269 p. Appendices, notes, index.

Deals mainly with the immigrants and the more general problem
of contract labor. Shows that those few immigrants who actually came to America under contract were skilled craftsmen.
But another less formal system of contract labor involved
mortgage-secured loans provided to immigrants needing fare
to America by steamship companies.

098   Gallaway, Lowell E.; Vedder, Richard K.; and Skukla, Vishwa. "The
Distribution of the Immigrant Population in the United States: An Economic Analysis." EXPLORATIONS IN ECONOMIC HISTORY 11 (1974):
213-26.

Takes issue with the argument that immigrants arrived in the
eastern industrial centers unaware of where economic opportunity could be found. The authors found that "the pattern of
distribution of immigrants to the United States at the beginning
of this century did reflect the changing nature of American
economic life and was consistent with an optimal allocation of
labor resources."

099   Handlin, Oscar. "International Migration and the Acquisition of New
Skills." In THE PROGRESS OF UNDERDEVELOPED AREAS, edited by
B.F. Hoselitz, pp. 54-59. Chicago: University of Chicago Press, 1952.

Discusses the migration of skilled laborers to the United States
and their impact upon the national economy. Also considers
the switch from skilled to unskilled labor and the need for
immigrants to adapt their skills to the changing needs of society.

100   Higgs, Robert. "Race, Skills and Earnings: American Immigrants in 1909."
JOURNAL OF ECONOMIC HISTORY 31 (1971): 420-28.

Argues that it is incorrect to blame the relatively lower pay
of the New Immigrants solely on ethnic discrimination. Believes that skill differentials provide an explanation for earning differentials in certain industries.

101 Hourwich, Isaac A. IMMIGRATION AND LABOR. New York: G.P.
Putnam's Sons, 1912. 554 p. Illustrations, diagrams.

Wealth of statistical data marshalled to challenge the Dillingham Commission's conclusions on the impact of immigration on
the labor market, the standard of living, home ownership,
wages, working conditions, pauperism, crime, and industrial
accidents.

102 Jerome, Harry V. MIGRATION AND BUSINESS CYCLES. New York:
National Bureau of Economic Research, 1926. 256 p. Charts, appendix,
footnotes, index.

An economist's study of immigration from the Civil War to 1920
which seeks to determine the relationship between employment
and migration. Devotes a chapter to economic conditions in
Europe leading to emigration.

103 Kuznets, Simon, and Rubin, Ernest. IMMIGRATION AND THE FOREIGN
BORN. Occasional Paper no. 46. New York: National Bureau of Economic Research, 1954. 103 p. Tables, graphs, appendices.

Analyzes the economic impact of immigration especially from
1870 to the 1920s. Concentrates on its effect on business cycles.

104 Neal, Larry. "A Neglected Source of American Economic Growth, 1790-
1912." OXFORD ECONOMIC PAPERS (Great Britain) 24 (1972): 68-88.

Concludes that immigration had an important positive impact
on the capital stock accumulation and economic growth of
the United States by the early part of the twentieth century.

105 Poulson, Barry W., and Holyfield, James, Jr. "A Note on European Migration to the United States: A Cross Spectral Analysis." EXPLORATIONS
IN ECONOMIC HISTORY 11 (1974): 299-310.

Concludes that "changes in relative income between the United
States and European countries of origin appear to be most re-
velant in explaining the surge in immigration and the long
swings in immigration to the United States from the United
Kingdom."

106 Spengler, Joseph J. "Some Economic Aspects of Immigration Into the United States." LAW AND CONTEMPORARY PROBLEMS 21 (1956): 236-55.

After surveying the historical background of the economic dimensions of American immigration, he provides an outline of
the implications of economic-demographic theory in terms of
the "capacity of the American economy to absorb immigrants."

107 Williamson, Jeffrey G. "Migration to the New World: Long Term In-
     fluences and Impact." EXPLORATIONS IN ECONOMIC HISTORY 11
     (1974): 357-89.

     Concludes that immigration fostered industrialization, suppressed
     real wage improvements, and did not have a very significant
     effect on aggregate growth. Argues that the latter seems a
     reasonable price, given the need to absorb refugees from Europe's
     social dislocation.

IMMIGRATION AS A FIELD OF STUDY

108 Addams, Jane. "Immigration: A Field Neglected by the Scholars."
     COMMONS 10 (1905): 9-19.

     A convocation address at the University of Chicago in which
     she calls for more research on immigration in the general frame-
     work of American culture. From this she hopes to disprove
     that further immigration will degrade American culture and
     values.

109 Ander, Oscar Fritiof. "Four Historians of Immigration." In his IN THE
     TREK OF THE IMMIGRANTS: ESSAYS PRESENTED TO CARL WITTKE,
     pp. 17-32. Rock Island, Ill.: Augustana College Library, 1964.

     Deals with the contributions of Carl F. Wittke, George M.
     Stephenson, Marcus Lee Hansen, and Theodore C. Blegen, all
     second generation Americans and all from the Midwest. Sees
     them as "grass roots" historians, concentrating on regional,
     state, and local history and using newspapers, letters, and
     European archives to tell the saga of immigration.

110 Appel, John J. "Immigrant Historical Societies in the United States,
     1880-1950." Ph.D. dissertation, University of Pennsylvania, 1960. 448 p.

     "This study of selected historical societies founded by Scotch-
     Irish, Irish, Jews, Germans and Scandinavians in the United
     States emphasizes connections between their origins, their
     founders' idealogies and the history produced or neglected by
     them." Disagrees with Marcus Hansen's contention that third
     generation immigrants founded historical societies as a return
     to ethnic consciousness by showing that most societies formed
     before 1910 were founded by an ethnic elite who promoted
     immigrant history "to challenge established historical theory
     and to influence issues closely related to ethnic group interests."

111 Cross, Robert D. "How Historians Have Looked at Immigrants to the Uni-
     ted States." INTERNATIONAL MIGRATION REVIEW 7 (1973): 4-11.

Briefly surveys the attitude of historians from early times to the present, stressing the evolution from restrictionist and filiopietistic views to more balanced, interdisciplinary analyses.

112 Curti, Merle, and Birr, Kendall. "The Immigrant and the American Image in Europe, 1860-1914." MISSISSIPPI VALLEY HISTORICAL REVIEW 37 (1950): 203-30.

Discusses various agencies, public and private, which recruited immigrants on the themes of standard of living, social mobility, and freedom from military service. Sees little difference in America's image over time or place.

113 Forster, Walter O. "The Immigrant and the American National Idea." In IN THE TREK OF THE IMMIGRANTS: ESSAYS PRESENTED TO CARL WITTKE, edited by O. Fritiof Ander, pp. 157-75. Rock Island, Ill.: Augustana College Library, 1964.

Discusses the obstacles to estimating the impact of immigrant groups upon U.S. society, especially upon America's self-image and definition. Tries to place the nativist outburst of the 1840s and 1850s and the anti-German hysteria of World War I into a wider historical context.

114 Handlin, Oscar, and Handlin, Mary. "New History and the Ethnic Factor in American Life." In PERSPECTIVES IN AMERICAN HISTORY, edited by Donald Fleming and Bernard Bailyn, pp. 5-24. Perspectives In American History Series, vol. 4. Cambridge, Mass.: Charles Warren Center for Studies in American History, 1970.

Focuses on the evolution of ethnic themes as a case study of the assumptions and methods of new social historians who emerged in the 1920s and speculates on the need for greater insights into America's cultural diversity.

115 Hutchinson, Edward P. "Notes on Immigration Statistics of the United States." JOURNAL OF THE AMERICAN STATISTICAL ASSOCIATION 53 (1958): 963-1025.

These notes provide in more detail than STATISTICAL ABSTRACT OF THE UNITED STATES the changes that have taken place in the methods of reporting immigration from 1820 to 1958.

116 Qualey, Carlton C. "Marcus Lee Hansen." MIDCONTINENT AMERICAN STUDIES JOURNAL 8 (1967): 18-32.

Faults Hansen for his limited and narrow research techniques, especially in demography, for his failure to make use of the monographic works of scholars in other fields, and for his oversimplified, neo-Turnerian views of population movement.

Praises him for his pioneering efforts to clarify and emphasize the need for organized study of a neglected field. Also contains a commentary by Victor Greene cautioning that Hansen was severely limited by the lack of published sources and the lack of communication among social scientists, but still faulting him for overgeneralization.

117 Saveth, Edward N. AMERICAN HISTORIANS AND EUROPEAN IMMIGRANTS, 1875-1925. New York: Russell and Russell, 1948. 244 p. Footnotes, references, index.

Includes the attitude toward immigrants of John Fisk, John W. Burgess, Henry Cabot Lodge, Henry Adams, Francis Parkman, Theodore Roosevelt, Frederick Jackson Turner, Woodrow Wilson, Herman Eduard Von Holst, James Schouler, James Ford Rhodes, John B. McMaster, Ellis P. Oberholtzer, Edward Channing, and H.L. Osgood. Provides an introductory chapter on the context of late nineteenth-century historiography.

118 Smith, Timothy L. "New Approaches to the History of Immigration in Twentieth-Century America." AMERICAN HISTORICAL REVIEW 71 (1966): 1265-79.

Urges researchers to emphasize cultural and structural assimilation instead of ethnic exclusiveness. Suggests the importance of the behavioral sciences and quantitative and comparative methodologies.

119 Wish, Harvey. "Carl Wittke, Historian." In IN THE TREK OF THE IMMIGRANT: ESSAYS PRESENTED TO CARL WITTKE, edited by O. Fritiof Ander, pp. 3-16. Rock Island, Ill.: Augustana College Library, 1964.

Discusses the works of Carl Wittke, himself the son of German immigrant parents, rating him one of the first historians to take immigration history out of the ranks of filiopietism and to apply systematic analysis. Also sees him as one of the first to study the development of immigrant groups, instead of viewing them as static.

INTERNATIONAL MIGRATION

120 Davie, Maurice R. WORLD IMMIGRATION: WITH SPECIAL REFERENCE TO THE UNITED STATES. New York: Macmillan Co., 1949. 585 p. Index.

A general chronological and topical treatment, including chapters on characteristics of immigrants, development and administration of immigration policies and laws, Americanization, assimilation, and naturalization.

121 Davie, Maurice R., et al. REFUGEES IN AMERICA. New York:
     Harper & Brothers, 1947. 453 p.

     Capsulizes the report of the Committee for the Study of Recent
     Immigration from Europe on refugee migration to the United
     States since 1933. The report is based upon case histories,
     life stories, special census data, alien registration material,
     and 50,000 questionnaires. Details the causes of migration,
     socioeconomic and psychological characteristics of the migrants,
     and their occupational, social, and residential adaptations.

122 Dollot, Louis. RACE AND HUMAN MIGRATIONS. Translated by Sylvia
     and George Leeson. New York: Walker, 1964. 153 p. Bibliography,
     index.

     A survey of international migration patterns with limited refer-
     ence to the United States.

123 Jackson, J.A., ed. MIGRATION. London: Cambridge University Press,
     1969. 304 p. Footnotes, index.

     A collection of ten articles by sociologists dealing with migra-
     tion throughout the world. Essays with information on U.S.
     immigration include articles by G. Beijer on "Modern Patterns
     of International Migratory Movements"; Charles Price on "The
     Study of Assimilation"; and A.H. Richmond on "Sociology of
     Migration in Industrial and Post-industrial Societies."

124 Saloutos, Theodore. "Exodus U.S.A." In IN THE TREK OF THE IMMI-
     GRANTS: ESSAYS PRESENTED TO CARL WITTKE, edited by O. Fritiof
     Ander, pp. 197-215. Rock Island, Ill.: Augustana College Library,
     1964.

     Investigates the topic of immigrants, especially from southern
     and eastern Europe, who returned to their native land after
     spending time in the United States. Analyzes the reasons for
     their return and the attitudes of those here and abroad toward
     them.

125 Tabori, Paul. THE ANATOMY OF EXILE: A SEMANTIC AND HISTORI-
     CAL STUDY. London: Harrap, 1972. 432 p. References, bibliography,
     index.

     A "history of exile from pre-Christian antiquity to the end of
     the nineteenth century...and the general attitude of the host
     countries to the exiles and expatriates." The United States is
     discussed in the larger pattern of world migration.

126 Taft, Donald R. HUMAN MIGRATION: A STUDY OF INTERNATIONAL
     MOVEMENTS. New York: Ronald Press, 1936. 590 p. Tables, foot-
     notes, references, index.

Emphasis is on early twentieth-century immigration to the United States accompanied by a discussion of other national movements and world migration "where they give perspective for an understanding of the American problem."

127 Taft, Donald R., and Robbins, Richard. INTERNATIONAL MIGRATIONS, THE IMMIGRANT IN THE MODERN WORLD. New York: Ronald Press, 1955. 670 p. Footnotes, index.

A four-part study including a description of important factors in migration, an analysis of world migration from World War I to 1955, the processes of immigration in the United States as a case study, and the relation between war and migration. Also makes suggestions for future migration policy.

128 Thomas, Brinley, ed. ECONOMICS OF INTERNATIONAL MIGRATIONS. London: Macmillan Co., 1958. 502 p. Tables, index.

The published proceedings of the seventh conference of the International Economic Association. Each chapter was written by a different economist. The most useful sections provide a comparative study of different countries' governmental policies in response to population migration.

129 Wenk, Michael. "The Refugee: A Search for Clarification." INTERNATIONAL MIGRATION REVIEW 2 (1968): 62-69.

Makes a distinction between "refugees" as those removed from their native country and "victims of armed conflict" who are those driven from their home, but who remain in their native country.

130 Willcox, Walter F., ed. INTERNATIONAL MIGRATIONS. Vol. 1: STATISTICS. 1,112 p. Tables, bibliography, index. Vol. 2: INTERPRETATIONS. 685 p. Appendices, index. 1929-31. Reprint. New York: Gordon & Breach Science Publishers, 1969.

Volume 1 deals with proletarian mass migrations in the nineteenth and twentieth centuries and includes a much larger section on the statistics of migration with tables for each country. Volume 2 deals with the countries of immigration including the United States, Canada, Argentina, Brazil, Australia, and New Zealand; and countries of emigration, notably European and Asian countries. A chapter is devoted to each country and written by a different author. One of the appendices is a critique of U.S. Immigration Service statistics.

Chapter 2

OLD IMMIGRATION

BRITISH (CORNISH, ENGLISH, SCOTCH, SCOTCH-IRISH, WELSH)

131 Berthoff, Rowland T. BRITISH IMMIGRANTS IN INDUSTRIAL AMERICA, 1790-1950. Cambridge, Mass.: Harvard University Press, 1953. 296 p. Notes, index.

Includes Scotch and Welsh along with English when discussing British immigration. "The Economic Adjustment," which forms the first part of the book, deals with the importance of the large number of skilled British workers and their role in the trade unions. In "The Cultural Adjustment" the author stresses that while the British were more at home in America than other immigrant groups, they nevertheless maintained their own cultural identity.

132 Black, George Fraser. SCOTLAND'S MARK ON AMERICA. 1921. Reprint. New York: R and E Research Associates, 1972. 126 p. Index.

Primarily a listing of prominent Scots involved in major events of U.S. history and in major occupations. Also contains a treatment of Scottish societies in the United States.

133 Burchell, Robert A. "British Immigrants in Southern California, 1850-1870." SOUTHERN CALIFORNIA QUARTERLY 53 (1971): 283-301.

Argues that British immigrants, including the Irish, found less nativism, less exclusion from important positions, no native-born hierarchy, and had more opportunity to lay the basis for their own society than their counterparts in the eastern United States.

134 Cannon, M. Hamlin. "Migration of English Mormons to America." AMERICAN HISTORICAL REVIEW 52 (1947): 436-55.

The story of the 30,000 British Mormons who emigrated to the United States, and ultimately to Utah, during the late 1830s to the 1860s when the first transcontinental railroad was completed.

135   Conway, Alan. "Welsh Emigration to the United States." In DISLOCATION AND EMIGRATION: THE SOCIAL BACKGROUND OF AMERICAN IMMIGRATION, edited by Donald Fleming and Bernard Bailyn, pp. 177-271. Perspectives in American History Series, vol. 7. Cambridge, Mass.: Charles Warren Center for Studies in American History, 1974.

Validates Brinley Thomas's thesis that "industrialization in Wales itself impeded a significant emigration movement from that country by providing an alternative to the United States much closer at hand."

136   _____, ed. THE WELSH IN AMERICA: LETTERS FROM THE IMMIGRANTS. Minneapolis: University of Minnesota Press, 1961. 341 p. Notes, bibliography, index.

A selection of nearly 200 nineteenth-century letters, many translated from Welsh, arranged by geographic region of settlement from New York to Oregon. Additional chapters deal with coal mining, the iron and steel industry, and the Civil War. Many letters were taken from Welsh newspapers and periodicals published by a variety of nonconformist denominations. There is a general introduction and shorter introductory comments before each section.

137   Cowan, Helen I. BRITISH EMIGRATION TO BRITISH NORTH AMERICA: THE FIRST HUNDRED YEARS. Toronto: University of Toronto Press, 1961. 321 p. Illustrations, appendices, notes, bibliography, index.

A substantial revision of her earlier volume which had covered the period from 1783 to 1837. She stresses the British policy of encouraging emigration to solve unemployment and the needs of migrants rather than the lure of the New World as major reasons for immigration to America.

138   Crary, Catherine S. "The Humble Immigrant and the American Dream: Some Case Histories, 1746-1776." MISSISSIPPI VALLEY HISTORICAL REVIEW 46 (1959): 46-66.

This study of appeals made to the British Crown by refugee loyalists who returned to England at the time of the Revolution indicates that most people of humble origin who migrated to America did indeed improve their economic and social status.

139   Cummings, Hubertis M. SCOTS BREED AND SUSQUEHANNA. Pittsburgh: University of Pittsburgh Press, 1964. 404 p. Notes, bibliography, index.

Contains twenty-five essays on various aspects of Scotch-Irish life in the Susquehanna Valley. Deals mostly with the political and military events in which they figured prominently.

140   Dickson, R.J.   ULSTER EMIGRATION TO COLONIAL AMERICA, 1718-1775. London: Routledge & Kegan Paul, 1966. 320 p. Maps, appendices, bibliography, index.

Traces the causes of Scotch-Irish migration from Ulster to the American colonies in the eighteenth century and examines the emigrants themselves, ports, agents, land promoters, governmental attitudes, and the voyage to and arrival in the colonies.

141   Dodd, Arthur H.   CHARACTER OF EARLY WELSH EMIGRATION TO THE UNITED STATES. Cardiff: University of Wales Press, 1953. 36 p. Footnotes.

An expansion of a lecture by Dodd on the geographic pattern of Welsh settlement in the United States from colonial days until 1840.

142   Dunaway, Wayland F.   SCOTCH-IRISH OF COLONIAL PENNSYLVANIA. Chapel Hill: University of North Carolina Press, 1944. 252 p. Bibliography, index.

The dominant reason for the immigration of over 250,000 Scotch-Irish Protestants during the eighteenth century was economic and the colony they most often chose was Pennsylvania. The author emphasizes their role in the government, religion, and education of Pennsylvania as well as their defense of the colony in the French and Indian War and the American Revolution.

143   Ellis, David Maldwyn.   "The Assimilation of the Welsh in Central New York." NEW YORK HISTORY 53 (1972): 299-333.

A study of Welsh settlement in upstate New York over a 175-year span in both rural and urban setting.

144   Erickson, Charlotte.   "Agrarian Myths of English Immigrants." In IN THE TREK OF THE IMMIGRANTS: ESSAYS PRESENTED TO CARL WITTKE, edited by O. Fritiof Ander, pp. 59-80. Rock Island, Ill.: Augustana College Library, 1964.

Based upon return letters of English immigrants, the author concludes that a large number of them in the 1830s and 1840s chose to become farmers in the United States, despite their mechanical skills, because they preferred the independence of land ownership to working for a wage.

145   _____.   INVISIBLE IMMIGRANTS: THE ADAPTATION OF BRITISH AND

SCOTTISH IMMIGRANTS IN NINETEENTH-CENTURY AMERICA. Coral Gables, Fla.: University of Miami Press, 1972. 131 p. Maps, illustrations, notes, index.

A collection of unpublished personal letters of twenty-five English and Scottish immigrant families during the nineteenth century with accompanying introductions by the author. She concludes that contemporary colonizing guidebooks and publications prompted few immigrants and contrary to popular opinion, those immigrants who came from Britain did not easily assimilate.

146 Fingerhut, Eugene R. "Assimilation of Immigrants on the Frontier of New York, 1764-1776." Ph.D. dissertation, Columbia University, 1962. 348 p.

Scots and English comprised the greatest number of immigrants to Charlotte County in the upper Hudson Valley and the Saratoga frontier. In both areas the relationship between New Englanders and newly arrived immigrants was often strained even though some immigrants rose to prominence with the coming of the Revolution.

147 Fiske, John. THE DUTCH AND QUAKER COLONIES IN AMERICA. Boston: Houghton Mifflin Co., 1903. 252 p. Illustrations, appendix, footnotes, index.

Part of a series of books by the prolific author designed to cover the history of colonial America. These two volumes, dealing with Dutch and Quaker settlement, begin with early explorations by the Dutch and include other immigrant groups which came to Pennsylvania and New York during the colonial period.

148 Ford, Henry Jones. THE SCOTCH-IRISH IN AMERICA. 1915. Reprint. New York: Arno Press, 1969. 540 p. Appendices, bibliography, index.

Study by a prominent political scientist. Details Scotch-Irish migration to colonial America, their spread through the frontier, their social and religious institutions, and their role in the American Revolution.

149 Gallaway, Lowell E., and Vedder, Richard K. "Emigration from the United Kingdom to the United States: 1860-1913." JOURNAL OF ECONOMIC HISTORY 31 (1971): 885-97.

Explains the volume of emigration from the United Kingdom to the United States in terms of "push" and "pull" hypotheses previously presented by Simon Kuznets, Ernest Rubin, and others.

150 Glasgow, Maude. SCOTCH-IRISH IN NORTHERN IRELAND AND IN THE

AMERICAN COLONIES. New York: G.P. Putnam's Sons, 1936. 345 p.
About one-fourth of the book covers the Scotch-Irish experience in America, including the post-colonial period.

151 Goodwin, M.W. DUTCH AND ENGLISH ON THE HUDSON. New
Haven, Conn.: Yale University Press, 1919. 230 p. Notes, bibliography, index.

Deals with the culture and society of the early Dutch settlers
in New Amsterdam and that of the English who replaced them
in New York after the naval wars of the mid-seventeenth century.

152 Graham, Ian Charles Cargill. COLONISTS FROM SCOTLAND: EMIGRA-
TION TO NORTH AMERICA, 1707-1783. Ithaca, N.Y.: Cornell University Press, 1956. 213 p. Appendix, bibliography, index.

Published dissertation which studies Scottish emigration from
the Union of the English and Scottish parliaments until the
Treaty of Paris and reveals that Scottish Presbyterians held
aloof from the Revolution. Lowland Scots tended to migrate
in groups and to mingle with older inhabitants along the sea-
board, while Highlanders founded their own communities on
the farming frontier of North Carolina and New York.

153 Gray, Malcolm. "Scottish Emigration: The Social Impact of Agrarian
Change in the Rural Lowlands, 1775-1875." In DISLOCATION AND
EMIGRATION: THE SOCIAL BACKGROUND OF AMERICAN IMMIGRA-
TION, edited by Donald Fleming and Bernard Bailyn, pp. 95-174. Per-
spectives in American History Series, vol. 7. Cambridge, Mass.: Charles
Warren Center for Studies in American History, 1974.

Argues that attractiveness of overseas emigration, as opposed
to internal migration, depended on geography: in parishes close
to growing towns there was much less pull than in more remote
areas where emigration offered better opportunity.

154 Green, Edward R.R., ed. ESSAYS IN SCOTCH-IRISH HISTORY. New
York: Humanities Press, 1969. 110 p. Illustrations, index.

Contains essays by Arthur Link on Woodrow Wilson's Presbyterian inheritance, Esmond Wright on Scottish influence on
U.S. education, Maldwyn Jones on Ulster emigration 1783-
1815, E. Estyn Evans on Scotch-Irish cultural adaptation in
the Old West, and by Green himself on Ulster emigrants'
letters.

155 Green, Samuel Swett. THE SCOTCH-IRISH IN AMERICA. Worcester,
Mass.: Press of Charles Hamilton, 1895. 37 p. Bibliography.

Brief, filiopietistic survey of Scotch-Irish settlement in colonial America.

156 Hanna, Charles A. THE SCOTCH-IRISH. New York and London: G.P. Putnam's Sons, 1902. 623 p. Maps, bibliography.

Traces the movement of Scots to Ireland and on to America. Strongly differentiates them from the English and attributes much in American culture and institutions normally regarded as English to the Scotch-Irish.

157 Hartmann, Edward G. AMERICANS FROM WALES. Boston: Christopher Publishing House, 1967. 291 p. Tables, appendix, notes, bibliography, index.

A history of Welsh immigration, especially in the nineteenth century, including their geographical distribution and occupations in America. Welsh were usually Baptists, Congregationalists, or Calvinists.

158 Heaton, Herbert. "Industrial Immigrant in United States, 1783-1812." AMERICAN PHILOSOPHICAL SOCIETY PROCEEDINGS 95 (1951): 519-27.

There was a continuous influx of industrial workers from Britain during this thirty year period. They contributed to the development of cotton manufacturing; the production of glass, metal, and paper; and the construction of machinery. British restriction on the exodus of artisans played no significant role in the size of immigration.

159 Jackson, W. Turrentine. THE ENTERPRISING SCOT; INVESTORS IN THE AMERICAN WEST AFTER 1873. Chicago: Aldine, 1968. 415 p. Illustrations, tables, notes, bibliography, index.

Concerned with economic history and the development of the American West by Scottish entrepreneurs, especially in the period from the depression of 1873 to 1921. Emphasizes Scottish investment in railroads, mining, and cattle raising.

160 Johnson, Stanley C. HISTORY OF EMIGRATION FROM UNITED KINGDOM TO NORTH AMERICA, 1763-1912. London: G. Routledge and Sons, 1913. 387 p. Appendices, footnotes, index.

Introductory chapters provide a historical survey followed by chapters on causes, transportation, reception, destination, and problems of immigrants.

161 Jones, Maldwyn Allen. "The Background to Emigration from Great Britain in the Nineteenth Century." In DISLOCATION AND EMIGRATION: THE SOCIAL BACKGROUND OF AMERICAN IMMIGRATION, edited by

Donald Fleming and Bernard Bailyn, pp. 3-92. Perspectives in American History Series, vol. 7. Cambridge, Mass.: Charles Warren Center for Studies in American History, 1974.

Sees nineteenth-century emigration in two patterns. Before 1870 people fled Great Britain to escape a loss of social status resulting from modernization of British economy. After the 1870s people came to America for economic advantage and were similar in motives, if not function, to the New Immigrants.

162 Leyburn, James G. THE SCOTCH-IRISH: A SOCIAL HISTORY. Chapel Hill: University of North Carolina Press, 1962. 337 p. Maps, notes, bibliography, index.

A historical account of the gradual development of Lowland Scots into Ulstermen and the modification of these Ulstermen and their institutions when they came, two hundred thousand strong, to the American colonies in the eighteenth century. The author believes that after the Revolution the Scotch-Irish ceased to remain a separate national stock.

163 Meyer, Duane Gilbert. "The Scottish Highlanders in North Carolina, 1733-1776." Ph.D. dissertation, University of Iowa, 1956. 297 p.

Explores three facets of the Scottish Highlanders: (1) reasons for and time of immigration, (2) the terms of settlement in the Cape Fear area, and (3) the reasons for their Loyalist sympathies at the time of the Revolution.

164 Myers, Albert Cook. IMMIGRATION OF THE IRISH QUAKERS INTO PENNSYLVANIA, 1682-1750. Swarthmore, Pa.: 1902. 276 p. Illustrations, appendix, bibliography, index.

Surveys development of the Quaker movement in Ireland, causes of migration to Pennsylvania, settlement patterns, institutions, and culture. Contains short biographies of prominent Irish-American Quakers.

165 Proper, Emberson E. COLONIAL IMMIGRATION LAWS. New York: Columbia University Press, 1900. 91 p.

Surveys immigration laws of thirteen colonies, their effort to promote or restrict immigration, the attitude of England toward migration, and the distribution and characteristics of colonial nationalities.

166 Robbins, Caroline. "The Rage for Going to America." PENNSYLVANIA HISTORY 28 (1961): 231-53.

Analyzes the appeal which the United States had for French and British refugees from the wars of the French Revolution

31

in the 1790s. Also discusses the process of their adjustment to American society and culture and their reactions to the conditions they found in the United States.

167 Rowse, A.L. THE COUSIN JACKS: THE CORNISH IN AMERICA. New York: Charles Scribner's Sons, 1969. 451 p. Appendix, index.

A historical treatment of Cornish immigration beginning first in Virginia and New England and from the colonies westward to the Pacific. Each state or region comprises a chapter with a concluding discussion on immigration in the twentieth century. Distinguishes the Cornish from English and Welsh and associates the former with mining.

168 Shepperson, George. "Writings in Scottish-American History: A Brief Survey." WILLIAM AND MARY QUARTERLY 11 (1954): 163-78.

Deals in part with the problem of finding and using source material on Scotch emigration to the United States, particularly during the colonial period.

169 Shepperson, Wilbur S. "British Backtrailers: Working Class Immigrants Return." In IN THE TREK OF THE IMMIGRANTS: ESSAYS PRESENTED TO CARL WITTKE, edited by O. Fritiof Ander, pp. 179-95. Rock Island, Ill.: Augustana College Library, 1964.

Investigates the cause for the return of 10,000 British immigrants to Great Britain in 1836. Attributes the large number to the U.S. depression and unemployment among mechanics, but more so to their inability to adjust to and assimilate their new environment.

170 _____. EMIGRATION AND DISENCHANTMENT: PORTRAITS OF ENGLISHMEN REPATRIATED FROM THE UNITED STATES. Norman: University of Oklahoma Press, 1965. 211 p. Notes, bibliography, index.

Based on a study of seventy-five British emigrants who came to America in the nineteenth century, this book concludes that these arrivals had greater difficulty adjusting to their new home than foreign-born immigrants who were unfamiliar with American customs and the English language. A high percentage of the emigrants he studied returned to Britain after their negative experiment in America.

171 Taylor, Philip A.M. EXPECTATIONS WESTWARD: THE MORMONS AND THE EMIGRATION OF THEIR BRITISH CONVERTS IN THE NINETEENTH CENTURY. Ithaca, N.Y.: Cornell University Press, 1956. 247 p. Illustrations, appendix, bibliography, index.

Examines the efforts of the Utah Mormons to proselytize in England and to induce their converts to settle in Utah between

1850 and 1890. Last third of the book traces the journey of
the immigrants across the Atlantic Ocean and across the United
States.

172 _____. "Why Did British Mormons Emigrate?" UTAH HISTORICAL
QUARTERLY 22 (1954): 249-70.

Weighs the evidence indicating that British Mormons emigrated
to the United States for religious reasons against those suggest-
ing movement for economic causes. Concludes that, despite
some conformity of immigration to business cycles, religious
motivation probably played a larger role than modern day nationalists would surmise.

173 Vale, Vivian. "English Settlers in Early Wisconsin: The British Temperance Emigration Society." BRITISH ASSOCIATION FOR AMERICAN
STUDIES BULLETIN 9 (1964): 24-31.

Describes the activities of the British Temperance Immigration
Society of Liverpool in buying land and establishing settlements
west of Madison in the 1840s. Although they achieved some
initial success in attracting Methodist immigrants from Yorkshire
and Lancaster, financial and legal difficulties eventually led
to failure.

174 Vedder, Richard K. "The Geographical Distribution of British and Irish
Emigrants to the United States after 1800." SCOTTISH JOURNAL OF
POLITICAL ECONOMICS 19 (1972): 19-35.

Validates the hypothesis that differences in income level
throughout the country were important in determining the settlement pattern of British immigrants to the United States after
1800.

175 Winther, Oscar. "The British in Oregon Country." PACIFIC NORTH-
WEST QUARTERLY 58 (1967): 179-87.

Argues that settlement of the Oregon boundary dispute in 1846
did not prevent Britons from migrating south of the line, to
the point where they constituted nearly 80 percent of the territory's population in 1850. Includes an appendix that details
place of origin, total number, and characteristics of British
employees of the Hudson Bay Company in 1846.

176 _____. "The English in Nebraska, 1857-1880." NEBRASKA HISTORY
48 (1967): 335-42.

Discusses the English people in Nebraska, the role of individuals in encouraging immigration, the efforts of the railroads
to sponsor and facilitate settlement, and immigrants' rate of
success and failure on the frontier.

177 _____. "English Migration to the American West, 1865-1900." HUNT-
INGTON LIBRARY QUARTERLY 27 (1964): 159-73.

> Identifies some 140,000 English immigrants to the trans-
> Mississippi West between 1965 and 1900 and attributes their
> motivation to the economic change in England, coupled with
> the promotional activities of U.S. railroads and other industries.

FRENCH, FRENCH CANADIAN, DUTCH, SWISS

178 Avery, Elizabeth Huntington. "Influence of French Immigration on the
Political History of the United States." Ph.D. dissertation, University
of Minnesota, 1895. 157 p.

> Discusses the impact of French political thought, as carried by
> both Huguenot and Catholic immigrants to the United States,
> upon American political thought and institutions. Contrasts
> the influence and experience of the two, attributing differ-
> ences to religious character, opportunity, and pace of assimi-
> lation.

179 Baird, Charles W. HISTORY OF THE HUGUENOT EMIGRATION. New
York: Dodd, Mead & Co., 1885. 328 p. Appendix.

> Chronicles the history of Huguenot persecutions in France
> which prompted migration to America and settlement through-
> out the English colonies.

180 Beers, Henry Putney. THE FRENCH IN NORTH AMERICA: A BIBLIO-
GRAPHICAL GUIDE TO FRENCH ARCHIVES, REPRODUCTIONS AND RE-
SEARCH MISSIONS. Baton Rouge: Louisiana State University Press,
1957. 413 p. Appendices, notes, bibliography, index.

> Chapters deal with the range of archives in France, the use
> of French archives by American historians, the relevant hold-
> ings on North America in French archives, and collections in
> America of reproductions of some of this archival data.

181 Bissell, Clifford H. "The French Language Press in California." CALI-
FORNIA HISTORICAL SOCIETY QUARTERLY 39 (1960): 219-62.

> Chronicles, in three parts, the history of the French language
> press in the Golden State from 1850 to post-1927. Discusses
> the activities of their founders, editorial policies, reasons for
> decline, and the bitter feuds among them for circulation.

182 Blick, Boris, and Grant, Roger H. "French Icarians in St. Louis." MIS-
SOURI HISTORICAL SOCIETY BULLETIN 30 (1973): 3-28.

> Based largely upon two 1859 issues of REVUE ICARIENNE,
> examines everyday life in the Utopian Socialist community

founded by French Icarians in St. Louis. Focuses on the economic life and constitution.

183 Caldwell, Norman Ward. THE FRENCH IN THE MISSISSIPPI VALLEY, 1740-1750. Illinois Studies in the Social Sciences, vol. 26. Urbana: University of Illinois Press, 1941. 113 p. Footnotes, bibliography, index.

After providing a description of the governmental system of New France, the author then focuses on population, industry, fur trade, and Indian relations during the decade.

184 Cometti, Elizabeth. "Swiss Immigration to West Virginia, 1864-1884: A Case Study." MISSISSIPPI VALLEY HISTORICAL REVIEW 47 (1960): 66-87.

Uses the experience of Swiss immigration to West Virginia to illustrate "a characteristic conflict of interests: on the one hand, the people of the state anxious to advance its prosperity; on the other, a legislature reluctant to provide funds and a few unscrupulous agents eager to appropriate whatever they could."

185 DeJong, Gerald F. THE DUTCH IN AMERICA. Boston: Twayne, 1975. 326 p. Illustrations, notes, bibliography, index.

Chronicles Dutch immigration from colonial times to the modern era with a special emphasis upon religious and language problems, contributions to American political life, and biographies of famous Dutch Americans.

186 Ducharme, Jacques. THE SHADOWS OF THE TREES: THE STORY OF THE FRENCH-CANADIANS IN NEW ENGLAND. New York: Harper & Brothers, 1943. 258 p. Bibliography.

An informal narrative of the French-Canadian settlements in New England with emphasis on the period of greatest immigration in the latter part of the nineteenth century.

187 Dufour, Perret. SWISS SETTLEMENT OF SWITZERLAND COUNTY, INDIANA. Indianapolis: Indiana Historical Commission, 1925. 446 p. Illustrations, appendix, index.

Originally written in 1876, this is a local history of Switzerland County during the nineteenth century, based mainly on the author's recollections. It was then edited for publication almost fifty years later.

188 THE DUTCH COMMUNITY IN AMERICA: AN ANNOTATED AND CLASSIFIED BIBLIOGRAPHICAL GUIDE. Burt Franklin Ethnic Bibliographical Guides. Edited by Francesco Cordasco and William W. Brickman. In preparation.

189 Faust, Albert Bernhardt. GUIDE TO THE MATERIALS FOR AMERICAN HISTORY IN SWISS AND AUSTRIAN ARCHIVES. Washington, D.C.: Carnegie Institute of Washington, 1916. 299 p. Index.

A descriptive inventory of manuscript and archival material from forty-six repositories in the various Swiss, German, Italian, and French cantons and the Austrian archives. Archival titles are listed in the native language, but the annotations are in English.

190 Hamon, E. LES CANADIENS-FRANCAIS DE LA NOUVELLE-ANGLETERRE. Quebec: N.S. Hardy, 1891. 483 p.

Discusses the magnitude and causes for French-Canadian emigration to New England and the efforts of the migrants to preserve their laws, customs, language, and religion.

191 Hirsch, Arthur H. THE HUGENOTS OF COLONIAL SOUTH CAROLINA. 1928. Reprint. Hamden, Conn.: Archon Books, 1962. 338 p. Illustrations, appendix, footnotes, bibliography, index.

Expansion of a dissertation which attempts "to disentangle from the network of colonial history the contributions made in Carolina by the French Protestants."

192 Lower, A.R.M. "New France in New England." NEW ENGLAND QUARTERLY 2 (1929): 278-95.

The story of French-Canadian immigration, stressing similarities with other immigrants as far as their common peasant background, but emphasizing differences as well. The major difference was that French-Canadian immigrants were more similar to Americans in culture and values than were European immigrants.

193 Lucas, Henry S. NETHERLANDS IN AMERICA; DUTCH IMMIGRATION TO THE UNITED STATES AND CANADA, 1789-1950. Ann Arbor: University of Michigan Press, 1955. 744 p. Maps, illustrations, appendices, notes, index.

Concludes that because of the relatively small size of their immigration and because the immigrants generally dispersed in their settlements and assimilated into the general population, the Dutch had relatively little impact on the history of immigration. Theirs is the story of settlement in the Midwest, church-building, and earning a living.

194 _____, ed. DUTCH IMMIGRANT MEMOIRS AND RELATED WRITINGS.

Vol. 1: 514 p. Vol. 2: 480 p. Assen, Netherlands: Van Gorcum, 1955. Illustrations, index.

A chronological arrangement of immigrant writings. Volume 1 covers Dutch immigration beginning in 1846 and deals with settlements in Michigan. Includes a chapter on American reaction to Dutch immigration. Volume 2 concentrates on Dutch immigration to Iowa, Wisconsin, Minnesota, and the Dakotas.

195 Magnan, Denis M.A. HISTOIRE DE LA RACE FRANCAISE AUX ETATS-UNIS. Paris: C. Amat, 1912. 356 p.

Mainly divided into three parts dealing respectively with the early exploration and settlement in the seventeenth century up to the French and Indian War; the period of the American Revolution through the early nineteenth century; and the patterns of immigration and settlement in the United States from French-speaking areas, especially Canada, during the remainder of the century.

196 Metraux, Guy Serge. "Social and Cultural Aspects of Swiss Immigration into the United States in the Nineteenth Century." Ph.D. dissertation, Yale University, 1949. 369 p.

Industrial and agricultural crises in Switzerland brought Swiss immigrants to the United States where farmers selected improved lands in the Midwest and skilled workers settled in New York, New Jersey, Connecticut, and Massachusetts. Although small, it was a highly organized movement.

197 Mulder, Arnold. AMERICANS FROM HOLLAND. Philadelphia: J.P. Lippincott Co., 1947. 320 p. Illustrations, footnotes, bibliography, index.

A chronological treatment of the Dutch in America from the time when they settled in the Hudson Valley in 1624, to the end of World War II, following the general pattern of settlement from New York to the Midwest and finally to the Northwest.

198 Pedea, Iris S. "Quebec to 'Little Canada': The Coming of the French Canadians to New England in the Nineteenth Century." NEW ENGLAND QUARTERLY 23 (1950): 365-80.

Describes the migration of the French Canadians from impoverished farms in Quebec province to New England mill towns prior to 1900. They brought with them their religion, schools, and traditions.

199 Picher, Robert L. "The Franco-Americans in Vermont." VERMONT HISTORY 28 (1960): 59-62.

Brief survey of French migration to Vermont from the seventeenth century to the present. Also discusses current French
place names and other reminders of their influence.

200   Pieters, Aleida J. A DUTCH SETTLEMENT IN MICHIGAN. Grand
Rapids, Mich.: Reformed Press, 1923. 207 p. Notes, bibliography,
index.

A Columbia University dissertation that describes the settlement in western Michigan in the 1840s of the Dutch, their
daily life, religious customs, education, and form of government. Devotes a chapter to the role of Albertus C. Van
Raalte, important in the early years of settlement.

201   Schelbert, Leo. "Swiss Migration to America: The Swiss Mennonites."
Ph.D. dissertation, Columbia University, 1966. 335 p.

The study considers first the Swiss background to emigration,
then proceeds to examine the patterns of settlement in America
by the Mennonites during the eighteenth and nineteenth century.

202   _____, ed. NEW GLARUS 1845-1970: THE MAKING OF A SWISS
AMERICAN TOWN. New Glarus, Wis.: Kommissions-verlag Tschudi
and Co., 1970. 239 p. Maps, illustrations, tables, appendix, notes,
bibliography.

Edited by the secretary of the Swiss-American Historical Association and published for the 125th anniversary of the founding of the German-Swiss community in southern Wisconsin.
Includes a register of the first immigrants and biographical
listings of sixty important Swiss Americans.

203   Schlarman, Joseph H. FROM QUEBEC TO NEW ORLEANS: FRENCH
IN AMERICA. Belleville, Ill.: Buechler Publishing Co., 1929. 596 p.

Deals with the discovery, exploration, and settlement of Canada and the Mississippi Valley by the French prior to the
American Revolution.

204   Smit, J.W., and Smit, Pamela, comps. and eds. THE DUTCH IN AMERICA
1609-1970: A CHRONOLOGY AND FACT BOOK. Dobbs Ferry, N.Y.:
Oceana, 1972. 116 p. Tables, bibliography, index.

Following the format of others in this series, this book begins
with a chronology of events involving the Dutch from colonial
times to the present. The last two-thirds of the book contains documents from the pre-twentieth-century period.

205   Van der Zee, Jacob. THE HOLLANDERS OF IOWA. Iowa City: State
Historical Society of Iowa, 1912. 368 p. Illustrations, appendices,

notes, bibliography, index.

Discusses the reasons for Dutch settlement in Iowa, their spread to various sections of the state, and their institutions, particularly the Dutch Reformed Church and affiliated schools on all educational levels.

206 Wabeke, Bertus, H. DUTCH EMIGRATION, 1624-1860, A SHORT HISTORY, 1944. Reprint. Freeport, N.Y.: Books for Libraries Press, 1970. 160 p.

Covers the causes for emigration, the settlement of New Netherlands, emigration to the British colonies in North America, Dutch involvement in the American Revolution, and the surge of Dutch immigration in the first half of the nineteenth century.

207 Walker, David B. POLITICS AND ETHNOCENTRISISM: THE CASE OF THE FRANCO-AMERICANS. Brunswick, Maine: Bureau for Research in Government, 1961. 48 p. Charts, footnotes.

A brief study of the political preferences of the Franco-Americans of Maine in elections from 1865 to 1960.

208 Yzenbaard, John H. "Dutch Settlement of Great Lakes Cities in the Mid-Nineteenth Century." INLAND SEAS 27 (1971): 18-27.

Dutch immigrants who left their country for economic and religious reasons settled in Holland, Michigan, but greater numbers went to Wisconsin where they became farmers or small businessmen.

GERMAN

209 Barry, Colman J. THE CATHOLIC CHURCH AND GERMAN AMERICANS. Milwaukee, Wis.: Bruce, 1953. 277 p. Appendices, sources, index.

Published dissertation dealing with the role of the Catholic church in leading splits within the German-American community and between the Church and other immigrant groups from the Civil War to World War I. Special emphasis on the drive for German national churches and on the impact of Americanization.

210 Bek, William Godfrey. THE GERMAN SETTLEMENT SOCIETY OF PHILADELPHIA AND ITS COLONY, HERMANN, MISSOURI. Philadelphia: Americana Germanica Press, 1907. 170 p.

This published dissertation describes the organization and growth of the society; the founding of its colony; its eventual separation; and its educational, political, economic, religious, social, and literary life.

211 Bell, Leland Virgil. "Anatomy of a Hate Movement: The German American Bund, 1936-1941." Ph.D. dissertation, West Virginia University, 1968. 281 p.

The story of the Nazi-inspired organization from its founding in Buffalo to the peak of its membership, when it numbered 8,500 members, to its final demise at the hands of Treasury Department agents who raided its national headquarters. Virulent anti-Semitism characterized much of the organization's racial thinking.

212 Benjamin, Gilbert Giddins. THE GERMANS IN TEXAS, A STUDY IN IMMIGRATION. Philadelphia: University of Pennsylvania Press, 1909. 161 p. Maps, bibliography.

Describes causes and magnitude of German migration to Texas and the economic and cultural life of the immigrants. Devotes a chapter to the relations among German Americans, slaves, and Indians.

213 Bergquist, James Manning. "The Political Attitudes of the German Immigrant in Illinois, 1848-1860." Ph.D. dissertation, Northwestern University, 1966. 463 p.

Stresses the role of Germans in Illinois politics where they had an important impact as Illinois's largest immigrant group. They successfully opposed nativist tendencies in the newly developing Republican party which they joined in the mid-1850s. They fit the general pattern of Northern Freesoil Jacksonians who shifted into the Republican party.

214 Bernheim, Gotthardt Dellman. HISTORY OF THE GERMAN SETTLEMENTS AND OF THE LUTHERAN CHURCH IN NORTH AND SOUTH CAROLINA, FROM THE EARLIEST PERIOD OF THE COLONIZATION OF THE DUTCH, GERMAN AND SWISS SETTLERS TO THE CLOSE OF THE FIRST HALF OF THE PRESENT CENTURY. Philadelphia: Lutheran Bookstore, 1872. 557 p. Illustrations.

Traces the development of the Lutheran church in the two states, from the colonial period to 1850, focusing on individual units, prominent leaders, and missionary societies. Concludes with an evaluation of the state of the church at mid-century.

215 Biesele, Rudolph Leopold. THE HISTORY OF THE GERMAN SETTLEMENTS IN TEXAS, 1831-1861. Austin, Tex.: Press of Von Boeckmann-Jones Co., 1930. 259 p. Illustrations.

Describes the work of the Society for the Protection of German Immigrants in Texas in attracting immigrants to the state. Looks at the key areas of settlements and discusses the political, social, and economic life of these communities.

216 Billigmeier, Robert Henry. AMERICAN FROM GERMANY: A STUDY IN CULTURAL DIVERSITY. Belmont, Calif.: Wadsworth, 1974. 177 p. Index.

A brief overview of German-American adjustment to life in the United States, with special emphasis on the Pennsylvania Germans and the impact of the anti-German hysteria of World War I.

217 Bittinger, Lucy F. THE GERMANS IN COLONIAL TIMES. 1901. Reprint. New York: Russell and Russell, 1968. 297 p. Appendix, bibliography.

Examines the migration of the various German pietistic religious sects to colonial America, their settlement patterns and institutions, and their role in the American Revolution.

218 Chambers, Theodore Frelinhuysen. THE EARLY GERMANS OF NEW JERSEY: THEIR HISTORY, CHURCHES AND GENEALOGIES. Dover, N.J.: Dover Printing Co., 1895. 667 p. Maps, illustrations, appendices, index.

Describes settlements of Moravian Germans in various Jersey towns, genealogies of prominent settlers and their families, and the churches they established.

219 Child, Clifton J. GERMAN-AMERICANS IN POLITICS: 1914-1917. Madison: University of Wisconsin Press, 1939. 193 p. Illustrations, bibliography.

Refers particularly to the German-American Alliance during World War I. The British author argues that the alliance was not an extension of the kaiser's foreign policy, but rather was an organization which developed out of the fight against prohibition and the pro-British position of President Wilson.

220 Conrad, Glenn R., ed. "The Germans in Louisiana in the Eighteenth Century." Translated by Rene LeConte. LOUISIANA HISTORY 8 (1967): 67-84.

Discusses the difficulties of determining the national origins and magnitude of immigration from German territories to French Louisiana in the eighteenth century. Concludes that German immigrants became quickly Gallicized and assimilated into the dominant society.

221 Conzen, Kathleen N. "The German Athens: Milwaukee and the Accomodations of Its Immigrants, 1830-1860." Ph.D. dissertation, University of Wisconsin, 1972. 512 p. Appendices, bibliography. To be published.

Details settlement and residence patterns, population and

socioeconomic characteristics, community organization, and political participation of Milwaukee's German population before the Civil War.

222 Cunz, Dieter. THE MARYLAND GERMANS. Princeton, N.J.: Princeton University Press, 1948. 476 p. Illustrations, appendix, footnotes, bibliography, index.

A history of the settlement in Maryland of German-speaking immigrants from central Europe from the colonial period until World War II. Successive waves of German immigrants, beginning with the first wave from 1730 to 1740 followed by a second after 1815, then again in the late 1840s and 1880s, account for the large German population of the state.

223 Davis-Dowie, Rachel, and Schweppe, Emma, eds. GERMANS IN AMERICAN LIFE. New York: Thomas Nelson and Sons, 1936. 180 p. Footnotes, bibliography.

A volume in the Building American Culture series. First half of the book is a brief chronological account, followed by topical chapters on how the German immigrant influenced education, science, art, music, literature, and economic life.

224 Desler, John H. THE SETTLEMENT OF THE GERMAN COAST OF LOUISIANA AND THE CREOLES OF GERMAN DESCENT. Philadelphia: Americana Germanica Press, 1909. 136 p. Illustrations.

Discusses German migration to Louisiana in the eighteenth century, and the relations of immigrants with the French government there. Much of the work focuses on the activities of prominent German-American families in the state.

225 Diamond, Sander A. THE NAZI MOVEMENT IN THE UNITED STATES, 1924-1941. Ithaca, N.Y.: Cornell University Press, 1974. 380 p. Illustrations, bibliography.

Based on a study of captured German documents and papers of the German-American Bund, the volume explores the relationship between the Nazi party and the Bund. Bund members were largely Germans who had immigrated to the United States in the 1920s, were skilled workers hard hit by the Depression, and were in constant fear of Jewish power in the United States.

226 Dobbert, G.A. "The Cincinnati Germans, 1870-1920; Disintegration of an Immigrant Community." BULLETIN OF THE CINCINNATI HISTORICAL SOCIETY 23 (1965): 229-42.

Describes the development of the German community in Cincinnati and its rapid disintegration under the pressures of Prohibition and Americanization set free by the First World War.

Argues that geographic dispersion and lack of cohesiveness
made them unable to resist outside pressure.

227 _____. "German-Americans between New and Old Fatherland, 1870-
1914." AMERICAN QUARTERLY 19 (1967): 663-80.

A study of German immigrant thought and behavior in Cincinnati, which explains the initial indifference of immigrants
during the first half of the period to events in Europe, and
the subsequent nationalism exhibited from the 1890s to 1914
in terms of immigration ecology rather than immigrant ideology.

228 Dorpalen, Andreas. "The Political Influence of the German Element in
Colonial America." PENNSYLVANIA HISTORY 6 (1939): 147-58; 221-
29.

Analyzes the political attitudes and behavior of the Pennsylvania Germans during the colonial and Revolutionary era.
Describes the gradual emancipation of German voters from
dictation by the Quaker party and their ambivalent attitude
toward the Revolution. Argues that, contrary to views of
Benjamin Franklin and others, Pennsylvania's Germans became
rapidly assimilated and acculturated.

229 Faust, Albert Bernhardt. GERMAN ELEMENT IN THE UNITED STATES.
Rev. ed. Vol. 1.: 526 p. Vol. 2.: 605 p. Boston: Houghton Mifflin
Co., 1927. Bibliography, index.

Details population figures, economic activity, political attitudes, contributions in education, theatre, literature, music,
religion, and recreational activities of German Americans.

230 Fox, Harry Clifford. GERMAN PRESBYTERIANISM IN THE UPPER MIS-
SISSIPPI VALLEY. Ypsilanti, Mich.: University Lithoprinters, 1942.
181 p. Appendices, notes, bibliography.

Traces the movement of German Presbyterians, aided by U.S.
Presbyterians, to the upper Mississippi Valley, also the founding of a theological seminary that later became the University
of Dubuque. Discusses the significance and influence of German Presbyterians in the region.

231 Fritsch, William A. GERMAN SETTLERS AND GERMAN SETTLEMENTS
IN INDIANA. Evansville, Ind.: 1915. 61 p.

A brief summary of early German settlement in Indiana, the
New Harmony community, Germans in the Civil War and after,
and contributions to the professions. The final chapter summarizes the principles of the German-American Alliance of
Indiana at the time of World War I.

232 Gibbons, Phebe H. PENNSYLVANIA DUTCH AND OTHER ESSAYS. 3d
      ed., rev. Philadelphia: J.B. Lippincott Co., 1882. 427 p.

      Essays on various immigrant groups in Pennsylvania, focusing
      on the Pennsylvania Dutch (Germans), Swiss, Afro-Americans,
      Welsh, Irish, English, and a variety of German religious sects,
      such as the Amish, Dunkers, Morovian Brethren, and Schwenk-
      felders.

233 Gingerich, Melvin. "The Reactions of the Russian Mennonite Immigrants
      of the 1870s to the American Frontier." MENNONITE QUARTERLY RE-
      VIEW 34 (1960): 135-44.

      Examines the migration of some 10,000 Germans to Kansas,
      Nebraska, Minnesota, and the Dakotas between 1873 and 1883.
      Discusses their reaction to the hardships of the frontier, their
      relations with Amerindians, and their response to the hostility
      of native-born Americans.

234 Gleason, Philip. THE CONSERVATIVE REFORMERS: AMERICAN CATH-
      OLICS AND THE SOCIAL ORDER. Notre Dame, Ind.: University of
      Notre Dame Press, 1968. 272 p. Notes, bibliography, index.

      Details the increasing involvement of midwestern German
      Catholics in social reform in the early twentieth century, pri-
      marily as a means of maintaining their cultural identity in the
      face of assimilationist pressures.

235 Graebner, Alan Niehaus. "The Acculturation of an Immigration Lutheran
      Church: The Lutheran Church-Missouri Synod, 1917-1929." Ph.D. dis-
      sertation, Columbia University, 1965. 398 p.

      A study of the gradual change in the conservative German
      Lutheran church--Missouri Synod--from an immigrant-based
      church which conducted most of its services in German, to a
      church which began to rely on native Americans for new mem-
      bership and which moved from rural areas to fast growing sub-
      urbs to win new converts.

236 Hawgood, John Arkas. THE TRAGEDY OF GERMAN-AMERICA: THE
      GERMANS IN THE UNITED STATES OF AMERICA DURING THE NINE-
      TEENTH CENTURY--AND AFTER. 1940. Reprint. New York: Arno
      Press, 1970. 310 p. Bibliographical notes, index.

      Analyzes the attempt to found "New Germanies" in Missouri,
      Texas, and Wisconsin, and the reasons for their failure to re-
      tain a hyphenated existence in a "Deutschtum."

237 Huebener, Theodore. THE GERMANS IN AMERICA. Philadelphia: Chil-
      ton Co., 1962. 168 p. Illustrations, bibliography, index.

      A brief chronological survey of German settlement in America

from colonial days to the end of World War II with emphasis
on the nineteenth century.

238 Iverson, Noel. GERMANIA, U.S.A.: SOCIAL CHANGE IN NEW ULM,
MINNESOTA. Minneapolis: University of Minnesota Press, 1966. 188 p.
Appendices, footnotes, bibliography, index.

The book "presents a fusion of ethnic and status community
analysis while at the same time it attempts to sharpen the distinction between class and status." The author does this by
showing "why the Turners founded Germania as an ethnic community in the first place and then proceeded to consolidate
their forces...emerging as the top status group of the community."

239 Johnson, Hildegard B. "The Location of German Immigrants in the Middle
West." ANNALS OF THE ASSOCIATION OF AMERICAN GEOGRAPHERS
41 (1951): 1-41.

Johnson's study of Germans in the second half of the nineteenth century reveals that they frequently settled directly on
the frontier, and that they often sought to perpetuate the
European pattern of village on American soil. The Germans
had a strong feeling of group coherence, and many who became farmers in America had not been peasants in their native
land.

240 Jordon, Terry G. GERMAN SEED IN TEXAS SOIL: IMMIGRANT FAR-
MERS IN NINETEENTH-CENTURY TEXAS. Austin: University of Texas
Press, 1966. 237 p. Maps, illustrations, tables, appendix, notes, index.

Using original census schedules for the second half of the nineteenth century for the eastern part of Texas, where German
immigrants tended to settle, Jordan shows that the new arrivals quickly adapted their farming methods to local conditions.
They farmed more intensively and invested more time and
money on farming than native Americans, but with no striking
results.

241 Juhnke, James C. A PEOPLE OF TWO KINGDOMS: THE POLITICAL
ACCULTURATION OF THE KANSAS MENNONITES. Newton, Kans.:
Faith and Life, 1975. 215 p. Illustrations, notes, bibliography, index.

Traces the evolution of the Mennonites from political participants to conscientious objectors and pacifists in World War I,
and their subsequent attempt to maintain a separate identity
by their staunch support of the Republican party. Sees their
behavior as Americanized nonconformity.

242 Keller, Phyllis. "German-America and the First World War." Ph.D.

dissertation, University of Pennsylvania, 1969. 489 p.

Moves from a description of the political and social conditions which shaped the German-American experience, "to a study of the ways in which it was perceived within the German-American community, and finally to an exploration of the responses of unusually sensitive individual German-Americans." He concludes that the crisis of the war made many Germans avoid ethnic nationalism and seek immediate assimilation.

243   Kerr, Thomas J. IV. "German-Americans and Neutrality in the 1916 Election." MID-AMERICA 43 (1961): 95-105.

Germany's efforts to use German Americans as a political club succeeded only in discrediting the German minority and increasing the distrust of their motives in 1916.

244   Klees, Frederic. THE PENNSYLVANIA DUTCH. New York: Macmillan Co., 1950. 451 p. Illustrations, selected bibliography.

Seventeenth- and eighteenth-century aspects of Dutch religion, folkways, arts, and work in Pennsylvania.

245   Knauss, James Owen. SOCIAL CONDITIONS AMONG THE PENNSYLVANIA GERMANS IN THE EIGHTEENTH CENTURY, AS REVEALED IN GERMAN NEWSPAPERS PUBLISHED IN AMERICA. Lancaster, Pa.: Press of the New Era Printing Co., 1922. 211 p. Appendices, bibliography.

Discusses German language newspapers and their publishers, religious life, charitable and humanitarian organizations, education, language, character traits, vocations, and political ideals of Pennsylvania Germans.

246   Knittle, Walter Allen. EARLY EIGHTEENTH CENTURY PALATINE EMIGRATION. Baltimore, Md.: Genealogical Publishing Co., 1965. 320 p. Illustrations, appendices, footnotes, bibliography, index.

This story of the Palatine migration from the Rhine Valley to England and then on to America is told in the context of the British Empire. The immigration policy was fostered by the British government to encourage the manufacture of naval stores.

247   Knoche, Carl Heinz. "The German Immigrant Press in Milwaukee." Ph.D. dissertation, Ohio State University, 1962. 302 p.

Explores the contradictory purposes of the German language press as a preserver of native culture in a foreign land and also as an Americanizing force easing the immigrant into assimilation. A chronological treatment with chapters on various publications according to ideology or ownership.

248 Kollmann, Wolfgang, and Marschalck, Peter. "German Emigration to the
United States." In DISLOCATION AND EMIGRATION: THE SOCIAL
BACKGROUND OF AMERICAN IMMIGRATION, edited by Donald Flem-
ing and Bernard Bailyn, pp. 499-554. Perspectives in American History
Series, vol. 7. Cambridge, Mass.: Charles Warren Center for Studies
in American History, 1974.

A largely statistical study of the pattern of emigration by geography, by type of employment, and by social background,
covering the nineteenth and twentieth centuries.

249 Kuhns, Levi Oscar. THE GERMAN AND SWISS SETTLEMENTS OF CO-
LONIAL PENNSYLVANIA: A STUDY OF THE SO-CALLED PENNSYL-
VANIA DUTCH. 1901. Reprint. New York: AMS Press, 1971.
268 p. Appendix, footnotes, bibliography, index.

Summarizes the seventeenth- and eighteenth-century settlement
of the German counties of Pennsylvania, including chapters on
manners and customs; language, literature, and education;
religious life; and the role of the Germans and Swiss in peace
and war.

250 Luebke, Frederick C. BONDS OF LOYALTY: GERMAN AMERICANS
DURING WORLD WAR I. Minorities in American History Series, edited
by Moses Rischin. DeKalb, Ill.: Northern Illinois University Press,
1974. 366 p. Illustrations, notes, bibliographical notes, index.

Sees World War I as "the traumatic climax of an ethno-cultural
struggle that long had festered just below the headlines."
The fact that German Americans were willing to use political
action to defend their life style meant that they would be in-
creasingly identified with the politics of Wilhelmine Germany.

251 _____. IMMIGRANTS AND POLITICS: THE GERMANS OF NEBRASKA,
1880-1900. Lincoln: University of Nebraska Press, 1969. 188 p. Appendices, bibliography, index.

Documents the primacy of ethnocultural factors in the voting
of German Americans in Nebraska, except for a brief flirtation with socioeconomic voting during the Populist era.

252 MacArthur, Mildred Sherwood. GERMANS IN COLORADO. 1917. Reprint. San Francisco: R and E Research Associates, 1972. 51 p. Notes.

A brief survey of German activities and influence in Colorado
from territorial times, especially in the economy and educational affairs. Primarily a discussion of the contributions of
outstanding individuals.

253 Massman, John Casper. "German Immigration to Minnesota, 1850-1890."
Ph.D. dissertation, University of Minnesota, 1966. 270 p.

After reviewing the causes of emigration, the author discusses "the promotional efforts and techniques utilized by settlers, missionaries, colonization groups, Minnesota's government and railroads to attract German settlers to Minnesota." He also covers the hazards of the Atlantic passage and development of German communities in the central and southeastern part of the state.

254 Mauelshagen, Carl. AMERICAN LUTHERANISM SURRENDERS TO THE FORCES OF CONSERVATISM. Athens: University of Georgia Press, 1936. 252 p. Notes, bibliography, index.

Published dissertation which discusses the struggle between evangelical American Lutheranism as carried over by immigrants from Saxony and contiguous states. Their concern for traditional beliefs and practices ultimately led to the creation of the Missouri Synod.

255 Nau, John F. THE GERMAN PEOPLE OF NEW ORLEANS, 1850-1900. Leiden, Netherlands: E.J. Brill, 1958. 154 p. Footnotes, bibliography.

Presents the social and economic history of the German immigrants in a city dominated by Spanish and French influences and with a climate radically different from Germany's.

256 Nelsen, Frank C. "The German-American Immigrants' Struggle." INTERNATIONAL REVIEW OF HISTORY AND POLITICAL SCIENCE 10 (1973): 37-49.

Details the efforts of three major groups of German immigrants --Catholics, Lutherans, and Forty-Eighters--to preserve their culture and religion through preservation of the language, parochial schools, and residential concentration in "das Deutschtum." Argues that they might have succeeded had it not been for both world wars.

257 Nelson, Clifford L. GERMAN-AMERICAN POLITICAL BEHAVIOR IN NEBRASKA AND WISCONSIN, 1916-1920. Lincoln: University of Nebraska, 1972. 114 p. Tables, notes, bibliography.

Analyzes the impact of World War I on the political behavior of German Americans with separate chapters on the elections of 1916, 1918, and 1920. The final chapter explores possible economic and religious factors affecting German voting patterns.

258 O'Connor, Richard. GERMAN-AMERICANS: AN INFORMAL HISTORY. Boston: Little, Brown and Co., 1968. 466 p. Notes, bibliography, index.

Popularly written account of German contributions to America and their reaction to the anti-German outbursts of both world wars.

259   Olson, Audrey Louise. "St. Louis Germans, 1850-1920: The Nature of an Immigrant Community and Its Relation to the Assimilation Process." Ph.D. dissertation, University of Kansas, 1970. 355 p.

Reveals that "the Germans did not settle in a close knit community in one section of the city; neither did they cling to the preservation of the language, nor were they affiliated with one particular church or political party." They did, however, maintain their social clubs for gemutlichkeit.

260   Overmoehle, Sr. M. Hedwigis. "The Anti-Clerical Activities of the Forth-Eighters in Wisconsin, 1848-1860: A Study in German-American Liberalism." Ph.D. dissertation, St. Louis University, 1941. 377 p.

Describes the religious phase of the German liberal-reform refugees to Wisconsin. As opponents of organized religion, they sought to exclude the Church from government and public life. Studies Wisconsin as the most German state in the Midwest.

261   Pochmann, Henry A., comp. BIBLIOGRAPHY OF GERMAN CULTURE IN AMERICA TO 1940. Edited by Arthur R. Schultz. Madison: University of Wisconsin Press, 1953. 483 p. Index.

Following introductory information about American depositories of source materials and German-American research associations, the book includes an exhaustive list of over 12,000 items alphabetically arranged by author.

262   _____. GERMAN CULTURE IN AMERICA: PHILOSOPHICAL AND LITERARY INFLUENCES, 1600-1900. Madison: University of Wisconsin Press, 1957. 865 p. Tables, notes, index.

Divided into two parts dealing respectively with German thought in America and German literary influences, with most material coming from the nineteenth century. Should be used in conjunction with his BIBLIOGRAPHY OF GERMAN CULTURE IN AMERICA TO 1940.

263   Rosengarten, Joseph George. THE GERMAN SOLDIER IN THE WARS OF THE UNITED STATES. 2d ed. Philadelphia: J.B. Lippincott Co., 1890. 298 p.

Discusses the role of German Americans in the nation's major wars, beginning with the French and Indian conflict and ending with the Civil War. Also describes many cultural contributions made by German Americans in the same period and their relations with other national groups.

264 Rothan, Emmet H. THE GERMAN CATHOLIC IMMIGRANT IN THE UNI-
TED STATES, 1830-1860. Washington, D.C.: Catholic University Press,
1946. 151 p. Bibliography, index.

Details the distribution of German Catholic immigrants throughout the United States before the Civil War, and focuses on
the efforts of the Catholic church to adjust to their culture
and needs.

265 Sallet, Richard. RUSSIAN-GERMAN SETTLEMENTS IN THE UNITED
STATES. Translated by Lavern J. Rippley and Armand Baver. Fargo:
North Dakota Institute for Regional Studies, 1974. 207 p. Maps, illus-
trations, tables, appendices, notes, index.

A monograph about German-speaking Russians who came to
the United States between 1870 and 1930. Although from
Russia, these immigrants were descendants of German minorities from the Volga, the Black Sea, Lithuania, and Volhy-
nia. These immigrants settled mainly in the Midwest and
in the West. First published in German in 1931.

266 Saul, Norman E. "The Migration of the Russian-Germans to Kansas."
KANSAS HISTORICAL QUARTERLY 40 (1974): 38-62.

Examines the reasons why Russian Germans fled from Russia,
why the majority of them settled in Kansas, the salient features of their settlement and reception, and their contributions
to Kansas history.

267 Schrader, Frederick Franklin. GERMANS IN THE MAKING OF AMERI-
CA. Boston: Stratford Co., 1924. 274 p. Footnotes, bibliography,
index.

Recounts German contributions to colonial settlement, the Revolution, westward expansion, and the Civil War. Concludes
with a chapter on German influence on literature, art, science,
and education.

268 _____. "1683-1920." New York: Concord Publishing Co., 1920.
258 p. Illustrations, index.

A former secretary of the Republican Congressional Committee
writes in defense of German people without justifying World
War I. He attacks Great Britain, the Espionage Act, and
"foreign propaganda in the public schools." Indicates the
depth of German-American reaction to ethnic slurs during the
war.

269 Schrott, Rev. Lambert. PIONEER GERMAN CATHOLICS IN THE
AMERICAN COLONIES (1734-1784). New York: U.S. Catholic Historical Society, 1933. 211 p. Bibliography.

This master's thesis was based on published sources. One chapter includes biographical sketches of ten German Catholic priests who were active in the middle colonies during the fifty years of this study.

270 Smith, Charles Henry. AN EPISODE IN THE SETTLING OF THE LAST FRONTIER, COMING OF RUSSIAN MENNONITES: 1874-1884. Berne, Ind.: Mennonite Book Concern, 1927. 296 p. Illustrations.

Using Mennonite periodicals, western newspapers, diaries, and interviews of the period, Smith traces the migration of the Mennonites of South Russia to Kansas, the Dakotas, Minnesota, Nebraska, and Manitoba, Canada.

271 _____. MENNONITE IMMIGRATION TO PENNSYLVANIA, 1929. Morristown, Pa.: Morristown Press, 1929. 412 p. Illustrations.

Chronicles German Mennonite migration to Pennsylvania, and explores their religious outlook, literature, music, and culture.

272 Stadler, Ernst A. "The German Settlement of St. Louis." MIDCONTINENT AMERICAN STUDIES JOURNAL 6 (1965): 16-27.

Discusses the leadership and development of German emigration to St. Louis; the establishment of German institutions; the reactionary nativist agitation of the 1840s and 1850s; and the educational, cultural, political, and economic contributions made by outstanding individuals within the German community.

273 Stourzh, Gerald. "Bibliographie der Deutschsprachigen Emigration in Den Vereinigten Staaten, 1933-1963. Geschichte und Politische Wissenschaft, Teil II und Nachtrag." JAHRBUCH FUR AMERIKASTUDIEN (West Germany) II (1966): 260-317.

Bibliography of scholarly works by German-speaking authors who migrated to the United States between 1933-63. Concerned especially with history and political science.

274 Weisert, John J. "Germans and the Southern Labor Shortage, 1865-1866." AMERICAN-GERMAN REVIEW 30 (1964): 29-31.

Recounts the largely futile efforts to attract German immigrants to Kentucky in 1865-66. The idea failed largely because opponents used the German press to warn of the dangerous and unsettled conditions and unhealthy climate that prevailed in the state.

275 Wenzlaff, Theodore C., ed. and trans. "The Russian Germans Come to the United States." NEBRASKA HISTORY 49 (1968): 379-99.

Contains a brief survey of Russian-German migration to Nebraska and the Dakotas, also translations of first hand accounts by nineteenth-century immigrants.

276 Wittke, Carl F. GERMAN-AMERICANS AND THE WORLD WAR (WITH SPECIAL EMPHASIS ON OHIO'S GERMAN-LANGUAGE PRESS). Columbus: Ohio State Archaeological and Historical Society, 1936. 223 p. Index.

Focusing largely on the German-American press, Wittke explores the attitude of German language papers toward World War I, American neutrality and entry, the election of 1916, wartime hysteria, President Wilson's peace efforts, and related subjects.

277 _____. THE GERMAN-LANGUAGE PRESS IN AMERICA. Lexington: University of Kentucky Press, 1957. 311 p. Notes, index.

Argues that from the first German language newspaper of colonial days until the 1950s, the most important function the German press served was to stabilize the German immigrant and ease his transformation from a German to an American.

278 _____. REFUGEES OF REVOLUTION: THE GERMAN FORTY-EIGHTERS IN AMERICA. Philadelphia: University of Pennsylvania Press, 1952. 384 p. Notes, index.

Monograph which begins with the German background to immigration in the 1840s and comprehensively treats the effect of the large influx of Germans on every important aspect of American politics and life for the next two decades.

279 Wolfe, Jonathan James. "Background of German Immigration." ARKANSAS HISTORICAL QUARTERLY 25 (1966): 151-82; 248-78.

First article stresses attempt by the state legislature and railroads to attract immigrants to Arkansas. Second emphasizes the positive role of the Catholic church in bringing immigrants to the area as being more successful than commercial agents.

280 Wood, Ralph, ed. THE PENNSYLVANIA GERMANS. Princeton, N.J.: Princeton University Press, 1942. 299 p. Appendix, bibliography, index.

Eight scholars discuss the Pennsylvania Dutch farmers, their religious sects, their education, literature and newspapers, and their role as soldiers. A final chapter deals with Pennsylvania Germans as seen by historian Richard H. Shryock.

281 Wust, Klaus. THE VIRGINIA GERMANS. Charlottesville: University Press of Virginia, 1969. 310 p. Notes, bibliographical notes, index.

Covers colonial settlement from 1714 to 1790, the early national period, and the period of "New German" immigration from the 1840s through World War II. Heaviest concentration is on the last half of the eighteenth century and first thirty years of the nineteenth century.

282 Zucker, A.E., ed. THE FORTY-EIGHTERS; POLITICAL REFUGEES OF THE GERMAN REVOLUTION OF 1848. New York: Columbia University Press, 1950. 379 p. Illustrations, appendix, bibliographical notes, index.

A topical presentation of the Forty-Eighters by different scholars. Except for a chapter on Carl Schurz, the remaining chapters deal with the Forty-Eighters as a specific immigrant group. A lengthy biographical dictionary of many of its leaders concludes the volume.

IRISH

283 Adams, William Forbes. IRELAND AND IRISH EMIGRATION TO THE NEW WORLD FROM 1815 TO THE FAMINE. New Haven, Conn.: Yale University Press, 1932. 444 p. Maps, appendix, bibliography.

A scholarly treatment of the million Irish immigrants who came to America during the period 1815 to 1845. It not only places the immigrants in the context of Irish history, but also shows the effects of Irish immigration on American institutions and life.

284 Birmingham, Stephen. REAL LACE: AMERICA'S IRISH RICH. New York: Harper and Row, 1973. 300 p. Illustrations, appendix, index.

Social and cultural look at the fortunes, recreations, and manners of the "first Irish families," the social and economic elite of the Irish Americans.

285 Blanshard, Paul. THE IRISH AND CATHOLIC POWER: AN AMERICAN INTERPRETATION. Boston: Beacon Press, 1953. 375 p. Appendix, notes, bibliography, index.

A study of "Irish Catholicism as a social and political force throughout the English-speaking world," written by the author of AMERICAN FREEDOM AND CATHOLIC POWER and COMMUNISM, DEMOCRACY, AND CATHOLIC POWER. All three books are critical of the Irish Catholic influence.

286 Broehl, Wayne G., Jr. THE MOLLY MAGUIRES. Cambridge, Mass.: Harvard University Press, 1964. 409 p. Illustrations, footnotes, index.

The history of an Irish secret society active in behalf of labor in the anthracite coal fields of eastern Pennsylvania during the 1870s.

287   Brown, Thomas N. IRISH-AMERICAN NATIONALISM, 1870-1890. Critical Periods of History Series. Philadelphia: J.B. Lippincott Co., 1966. 206 p. Notes, bibliography, index.

Analyzes the evolution of Irish-American nationalism in the two decades after the U.S. Civil War, especially the efforts of its proponents to influence events in Ireland.

288   Byrne, Stephen. IRISH EMIGRATION TO THE UNITED STATES. 1873. Reprint. New York: Arno Press, 1969. 165 p. Maps, charts, tables.

This study was meant to be of assistance to Irish immigrants in the United States. Byrne thinks that the immigrants mistakenly settled in the large cities along the East Coast instead of seeking the more sparsely inhabited West. Part 1 includes "information and directions of a general character respecting the prospects, duties, dangers and mistakes of emigrants." Part 2 provides information on the population and general resources of each state and territory, based on the 1870 census.

289   Calkin, Homer L. "The Irish in Iowa." PALIMPSEST 45 (1964): 33-96.

A series of eight articles dealing with the Irish homeland, the move to America, the settlement of the Iowa frontier, and the life, politics, and communities of the Irish in Iowa.

290   Clark, Dennis. THE IRISH IN PHILADELPHIA: TEN GENERATIONS OF URBAN EXPERIENCE. Philadelphia: Temple University Press, 1974. 246 p. Bibliography.

Analyzes the reasons why the Philadelphia Irish enjoyed better socioeconomic conditions and wielded less political influence than their counterparts in New York, Boston, or Chicago.

291   D'Arcy, William. FENIAN MOVEMENT IN UNITED STATES, 1858-1886. Washington, D.C.: Catholic University of America Press, 1947. 411 p. Bibliography, index.

Discusses the rise and fall of the Fenian movement to launch an invasion to free Ireland, from its training period during the U.S. Civil War to its defeat by the British in 1870.

292   Dewees, F.P. THE MOLLY MAGUIRES. Philadelphia: J.B. Lippincott Co., 1877. 358 p. Appendix.

Account by a contemporary lawyer which judges the Molly Maguires as a criminal conspiracy and praises the efforts of the Pinkertons to destroy them.

293   Duff, John B. THE IRISH IN THE UNITED STATES. Belmont, Calif.:
Wadsworth, 1971. 87 p. Illustrations, chart, sources.

A brief introduction to Irish immigration which synthesizes the
findings of numerous other studies and deals particularly with
religion, politics, and nationalism.

294   Ernst, Robert. IMMIGRANT LIFE IN NEW YORK CITY, 1825-1863. New
York: King's Crown Press, 1949. 331 p.

Describes the settlement patterns, economic life, institutions,
and political behavior of New York's pre-Civil War Irish and
German immigrants.

295   Esslinger, Dean R. "American, German and Irish Attitudes Toward Neutrality, 1914-1917: A Study of Catholic Minorities." CATHOLIC HIS-
TORICAL REVIEW 53 (1967): 194-216.

German and Irish Catholics tended to support the Central Powers less because of religious reasons than because the Irish re-
sented the political domination of the British, and the Germans did not want to fight friends and relatives in a European
war.

296   Gibson, Florence E. THE ATTITUDES OF THE NEW YORK IRISH TO-
WARD STATE AND NATIONAL AFFAIRS, 1848-1892. New York: Columbia University Press, 1951. 480 p. Footnotes, bibliography, index.

After initial chapters on immigration and early Irish leaders,
the author treats Irish reaction to the Know-Nothing movement,
the Tweed Ring, the Grant era, Grover Cleveland, and Tam-
many Hall.

297   Gitelman, Howard M. "The Waltham System and the Coming of the
Irish." LABOR HISTORY 8 (1967): 227-53.

Compares the Irish immigrant work force in Waltham with the
earlier Yankee laborers. Contends that the Irish helped destroy the "Waltham System" because of their different work
habits, lifestyle, and general cultural outlook.

298   Greeley, Andrew M. THAT MOST DISTRESSFUL NATION: THE TAMING
OF THE AMERICAN IRISH. Chicago: Quadrangle Books, 1972. 270 p.
Index.

Analyzes Irish attitudes, institutions, and behavior based largely
upon comparison with other ethnic groups. Focuses on the Irish
of Chicago's South Side.

299   Handlin, Oscar. BOSTON IMMIGRANTS, 1790-1880: A STUDY IN
ACCULTURATION, 1941. Reprint. Rev. and enl. New York: Athenoum,
1970. 230 p. Appendix, notes, index.

Intensive study of Irish immigration to Boston from 1790 to 1865. Concentrates upon economic and physical adjustment, anti-Irish prejudice, and the development of group consciousness and stability.

300   Kelly, Mary G. CATHOLIC IMMIGRANT COLONIZATION PROJECTS IN THE UNITED STATES, 1815-1860. New York: U.S. Catholic Historical Society, 1939. 272 p. Maps, bibliography.

A published dissertation which describes the efforts of the Catholic church to settle German and Irish Catholic immigrants in colonies in several midwestern states before the Civil War.

301   Levine, Edward M. THE IRISH AND THE IRISH POLITICIANS. Notre Dame, Ind.: University of Notre Dame Press, 1966. 208 p. Appendix, notes, index.

Analysis of Irish-American political culture and the role of politics in maintaining ethnic identity. Focuses especially on Chicago's Irish politicians.

302   MacDonald, Sr. M. Justille. HISTORY OF THE IRISH IN WISCONSIN IN THE NINETEENTH CENTURY. Washington, D.C.: Catholic University of America Press, 1954. 324 p. Maps, tables, appendix, footnotes, bibliography, index.

After outlining the factors accounting for Irish immigration to Wisconsin, this published dissertation discusses the location and occupations of the Irish across the state, their role in politics, and their religious and social life from territorial days to 1900.

303   Maginniss, Thomas Hobbs, Jr. THE IRISH CONTRIBUTION TO AMERICA'S INDEPENDENCE. Philadelphia: Doire Publishing Co., 1913. 140 p.

Written to prove that the Irish made significant contributions to the American Revolution. It provides information on reasons for Irish immigration, the Irish in Pennsylvania, and a lengthy final chapter on the Irish in the Revolutionary War, including lists of names of officers and soldiers.

304   Maguire, John Francis. THE IRISH IN AMERICA, 1868. Reprint. New York: Arno Press and New York Times, 1969. 624 p. Appendix.

Account written by prominent Irish member of Parliament in 1867 on the conditions of his compatriots in the United States. Heavy focus on the Catholic church and the Irish-American attitude toward England.

305   Man, Albon P., Jr. "The Irish in New York in the Early Eighteen-sixties." IRISH HISTORICAL STUDIES 7 (1950): 81-108.

Describes the deplorable condition of New York's Irish immigrants in the 1860s and attributes the "draft riots" to a variety of social deprivations, in addition to anger at conscription and job competition with blacks. Argues that many Irishmen were fearful of further black immigration and looked upon the riots and the war as a welcome respite from the boredom and squalor of slum life.

306 Niehaus, Earl F. THE IRISH IN NEW ORLEANS, 1800-1860. Baton Rouge: Louisiana State University Press, 1965. 194 p. Notes, index.

Explores the interaction of newly arrived Irish Catholics with the more established Creole Catholics. He shows that the Irish were a force for Americanizing the Catholic church in New Orleans. In addition he shows that when Irish and blacks competed for laboring jobs, the Irish usually won and thus contributed to the decline of urban slavery in the area.

307 O'Beirne, James. "Some Early Irish in Vermont." VERMONT HISTORY 28 (1960): 63-72.

Deals with history of Irish immigrants in Vermont prior to the exodus induced by the great Irish famine of the 1840s. Focuses mostly on their role as indentured servants and on their efforts to defend themselves against prejudice.

308 O'Brien, Michael Joseph. A HIDDEN PHASE OF AMERICAN HISTORY; IRELAND'S PART IN AMERICA'S STRUGGLE FOR LIBERTY. New York: Devin-Adair Co., 1919. 533 p. Illustrations, appendix, index.

Details the help given to the American revolutionists by Ireland and by Irish immigrants to the United States. Argues that many so-called Scotch-Irish were really Irish and that the latter constituted a much larger portion of the American population than recognized by the 1790 census.

309 O'Grady, Joseph P. HOW THE IRISH BECAME AMERICANS. New York: Twayne, 1973. 190 p. Notes, glossary, bibliographic essays, index.

Surveys Irish immigration from the colonial period until the 1920s, with emphasis on the nineteenth century. Because the author believes "that minority groups in America function as successful pressure groups only when they possess a cause around which they can rally their people," he concentrates on the influence of the Anglo-Irish struggle.

310 Potter, George W. TO THE GOLDEN DOOR: THE STORY OF THE IRISH IN IRELAND AND AMERICA. Boston: Little, Brown and Co., 1960. 630 p. Illustrations, index.

Popular account of the causes of Irish immigration, the journey

overseas, and adjustment to American life up to the outbreak
of the Civil War.

311 Quigley, Hugh. THE IRISH RACE IN CALIFORNIA AND ON THE PACIF-
IC COAST. San Francisco: A. Roman and Co., 1878. 548 p. Illustrations.

Much of this work deals with challenges to the evolutionary
theory of race, but it contains valuable information about the
numbers and settlement patterns of Irish immigrants to the West
Coast in the nineteenth century.

312 Schrier, Arnold. IRELAND AND THE AMERICAN EMIGRATION, 1850-
1900. Minneapolis: University of Minnesota Press, 1958. 156 p. Appendix, notes, bibliography, index.

Published dissertation which discusses the reasons for Irish migration to the United States and its consequences for both
countries. Based upon emigrant letters, newspapers, official
reports of U.S. and British governments, and interviews conducted by the Irish Folklore Commission.

313 Shannon, William Vincent. THE AMERICAN IRISH. 2d ed., rev. New
York: Macmillan Co., 1966. 438 p. Notes, index.

Concentrates on Irish-American activities in politics, religion,
entertainment, literature, athletics, and law enforcement.
Concludes with an assessment of the "Irishness" of Joseph R.
McCarthy and John F. Kennedy.

314 Vinyard, Jo Ellen. "Inland Urban Immigrants: The Detroit Irish, 1850."
MICHIGAN HISTORY 57 (1973): 121-39.

Using census data and case studies of individuals and families,
the author reconstructs a profile of the Irish in Detroit in the
mid-nineteenth century. Although the majority were unskilled
laborers, a few had progressed into middle class business and
professional status.

315 Walsh, Francis Robert. "The 'Boston Pilot': A Newspaper for the Irish
Immigrant, 1829-1908." Ph.D. dissertation, Boston University, 1968.
305 p.

A history of the oldest Catholic journal in America and of the
oldest continuing newspaper in Boston. Provides information
on Irish reaction to abolitionism, the Civil War, nativism, reform, blacks, and other immigrant groups.

316 Weisz, Howard Ralph. "Irish-American and Italian-American Educational
Views and Activities, 1870-1900: A Comparison." Ph.D. dissertation,
Columbia University, 1968. 477 p.

A study of Irish attitudes toward education in the United States, and the Irish immigrant dilemma: supporting public schools and losing Catholic education, or supporting sectarian schools and being considered unpatriotic. In contrast, later arriving Italian immigrants generally accepted the already well-developed public school system.

317 Williams, T.D., and Edwards, R.D., eds. THE GREAT FAMINE; STUDIES IN IRISH HISTORY, 1845-1952. Dublin: Browne and Nolan, 1956. 517 p. Maps, Illustrations.

A collection of essays by different authors dealing with historical and social developments in Ireland during the famine. While the opening essay offers an overview of Ireland on the eve of the famine, the rest explore agriculture, political background, organization and administration of relief, medical history of the famine, and culminate in an examination of the Irish immigration to the United States and to the British colonies. The book also includes an account of the famine in Irish oral tradition and an extensive bibliography.

318 Willigan, Walter L. "A Bibliography of the Irish American Press, 1691-1835." Ph.D. dissertation, Fordham University, 1934. 71 p.

A chronological listing of books, pamphlets, essays, almanacs, newspapers, hymns, and plays written by Irish Americans between 1691 and 1817.

319 Wittke, Carl F. THE IRISH IN AMERICA. Baton Rouge: Louisiana State University Press, 1956. 294 p. Bibliography, index.

Surveys the Irish-American experience, culture and institutions, relations with other ethnic groups, economic activities, political behavior, and efforts to influence events in the Old Country.

320 Woodham-Smith, Cecil. THE GREAT HUNGER: IRELAND 1845-1849. New York: Harper & Row, 1962. 510 p. Illustrations.

Details the devastating impact of the potato blight upon Ireland as a cause for large scale emigration to the United States. Details also British policy, financial aid from kinsmen in America, and the horrors of the voyage to the United States.

SCANDINAVIANS (DANES, FINNS, NORWEGIANS, SWEDES)

321 Aho, Gustaf A. "History of the First Finnish Lutherans in Northern Ohio and the National Evangelical Lutheran Church." CONCORDIA HISTORICAL INSTITUTE QUARTERLY 40 (1967): 3-8.

Focuses on the evolution of the National Evangelical Lutheran church among Finnish Americans in Ohio, and the eventual schism that occurred largely out of doctrinal disputes.

322 Ander, Oscar Fritiof. CULTURAL HERITAGE OF SWEDISH IMMIGRANTS: SELECTED REFERENCES. Rock Island, Ill.: Augustana College Library, 1956. 192 p.

Compilation of original sources on Swedish immigration. Topics include a bibliography of bibliographies, Swedish background materials, American books, general contributions to American life, church and education, literature, art, music, theatre, newspapers, periodicals, and archives.

323 _____. "Some Factors in the Americanization of the Swedish Immigrant, 1850-1890." ILLINOIS STATE HISTORICAL SOCIETY JOURNAL 26 (1933-1934): 136-50.

Discusses the role of the church and press in Americanizing Swedish immigrants.

324 Andersen, Arlow William. IMMIGRANT TAKES HIS STAND: THE NOR-WEGIAN-AMERICAN PRESS AND PUBLIC AFFAIRS, 1847-1872. Northfield, Minn.: Norwegian American Historical Association, 1953. 176 p. Bibliography, index.

A study of editorial opinion on political, social, and diplomatic developments from 1847-72, in more than twenty publications from Illinois, Minnesota, and Wisconsin. The author concludes that except in a few instances, such as the issue of public education, the press reflected the conservatism of most Norwegian immigrants.

325 _____. THE NORWEGIAN-AMERICANS. Boston: Twayne, 1975. 274 p. Illustrations, notes, bibliography, index.

Follows Norwegian immigrants from their homeland to the upper Midwest, and analyzes their economic adjustment, participation in public life, establishment of a unique culture, and its religious, educational, and social ramifications.

326 Anderson, Rasmus B. THE FIRST CHAPTER OF NORWEGIAN IMMIGRATION (1821-1840): ITS CAUSES AND RESULTS. WITH AN INTRODUCTION ON THE SERVICES RENDERED BY THE SCANDINAVIANS TO THE WORLD AND TO AMERICA. Madison, Wis.: 1896. 476 p. Illustrations.

Deals with the magnitude and causes of the first two decades of Norwegian immigration, and its settlement pattern, including colonies in Texas. Latter part of the book focuses on outstanding individuals and on religious activity among the immigrants.

327 Babcock, Kendrick C. THE SCANDINAVIAN ELEMENT IN THE UNITED STATES. 1914. Reprint. New York: Arno Press, 1969. 205 p. Appendices, index.

Examines the causes of Norwegian, Swedish, and Danish immigration, settlement patterns, and economic, religious, intellectual, social, and political life in the United States.

328 Beijbom, Ulf. SWEDES IN CHICAGO: A DEMOGRAPHIC AND SOCIAL STUDY OF THE 1846-1880 IMMIGRATION. Chicago: Chicago Historical Society and STUDIA HISTORIA UPSALIENSIA, 1973. 381 p. Appendix, footnotes, bibliography, index.

Tries to evaluate Swedish immigrant interaction with other immigrant groups, to determine whether Chicago was merely a stopping off point for immigrants, to locate Swedish immigrants on the socioeconomic ladder, and to see how Swedish-American organizations served the immigrant.

329 Benson, Adolph B., and Hedin, Naboth. AMERICANS FROM SWEDEN. Philadelphia: J.B. Lippincott Co., 1950. 448 p. Bibliography, index.

Based on available published sources in the United States and in Sweden. Surveys the historical background, religious life, education, and the role of Swedes in the trades and professions.

330 _____, eds. SWEDES IN AMERICA, 1638-1938. New Haven, Conn.: Yale University Press, 1938. 614 p. Illustrations.

Published in conjunction with the tercentenary of the Swedish settlements on the Delaware. Contains contributions from nearly forty authors dealing with the social and intellectual side of prominent Swedes and Swedish societies in America.

331 Bergendoff, Conrad. "The Swedish Immigrant and the American Way." SWEDISH PIONEER HISTORY QUARTERLY 19 (1968): 143-57.

Disputes the melting pot theory as applied to nineteenth-century Swedish immigrants, especially those who settled in urban, industrial areas. Contends that they were often discouraged, remained largely apolitical, and frequently returned to Sweden. Sees only the existence of Swedish newspapers and periodicals as ameliorating factors in their lives.

332 Bergmann, Leola Nelson. "The Norwegians in Iowa." PALIMPSEST 40 (1959): 289-368.

A special nationality edition with six articles by Bergmann on the process of immigration, settlement, occupations, church and school organization, the press, and politics of Norwegians in Iowa.

333 Bjork, Kenneth O. SAGA IN STEEL AND CONCRETE: NORWEGIAN
ENGINEERS IN AMERICA. Northfield, Minn.: Norwegian-American
Historical Association, 1947. 504 p. Illustrations, footnotes, index.

The greatest influx of Norwegians came in the period from
1880 to 1930, and many of these brought technical skills which
were important for an industrializing nation which needed sky-
scrapers, bridges, tunnels, and machinery. The final chapter
discusses the social philosophy of these immigrant engineers.

334 _____. WEST OF THE GREAT DIVIDE: NORWEGIAN MIGRATION TO
THE PACIFIC COAST, 1847-1893. Northfield, Minn.: Norwegian- '
American Historical Association, 1958. 671 p. Illustrations, footnotes,
index.

The migration of Norwegians both from Europe and the American Midwest to the Pacific Coast beginning with the California Gold Rush, and ending with the settlement of the Pacific
Northwest.

335 Blegen, Theodore C. NORWEGIAN MIGRATION TO AMERICA, 1825-
1860. 1931. Reprint. New York: Arno Press, 1969. 413 p. Index.

A published dissertation which gives the classic account of
pre-Civil War Norwegian immigration, relying almost exclusively on letters from immigrants, guidebooks, songs, and poems
for original source material.

336 _____, ed. LAND OF THEIR CHOICE: THE IMMIGRANTS WRITE HOME.
Minneapolis: University of Minnesota Press, 1955. 446 p. Index.

Collection of hundreds of "American letters" written by Scandinavian immigrants to relatives back home describing the journey, the difficulties of resettlement, and conditions existing
in a wide variety of American cities.

337 Capps, Finis Herbert. FROM ISOLATIONISM TO INVOLVEMENT: THE
SWEDISH IMMIGRANT PRESS IN AMERICA, 1914-1945. Chicago: Swedish Pioneer Historical Society, 1966. 238 p. Tables, notes, bibliographical notes, index.

This published dissertation is a study of the attitude of the
Swedish immigrant press toward American foreign policy from
1914 to 1945. During that time Swedish publications dropped
from nearly 350 to less than 20 by the close of the period.
Not only did the number decline, but most of the remaining
publications were in the English language.

338 Chrisman, Noel J. "Ethnic Influence on Urban Groups: The Danish-
Americans." Ph.D. dissertation, University of California at Berkeley,
1966. 211 p.

Based upon research among Danish Americans in the San Francisco area, this dissertation concludes that, even in the ab-
sence of cultural unity and structural cohesion, Danish
Americans have maintained a sense of ethnic identity through
membership in voluntary associations.

339 Christensen, Thomas P. HISTORY OF DANES IN IOWA. Solvang, Calif.:
Dansk Folkesamfund, 1952. 282 p. Illustrations, appendices, notes,
references, bibliography, index.

A dissertation which first provides a background of nineteenth-
century Denmark and the pattern of emigration and then focuses on Danish churches, schools, press, and organizations
in Iowa.

340 Clay, Jehu Curtis. ANNALS OF THE SWEDES ON THE DELAWARE.
4th ed. Chicago: John Ericsson Memorial Committee, 1938. 232 p.
Illustrations, appendix, notes, memoranda.

Originally published in 1834 by a man of Swedish ancestry
and based mainly on translated manuscript collections. Covers
from the seventeenth to the nineteenth century.

341 Dahlie, Jorgen. "A Social History of Scandinavian Immigration, Washington State, 1895-1910." Ph.D. dissertation, Washington State University, 1967. 194 p.

Scandinavians comprised the largest number of immigrants to
the state during the period, and they experienced no significant cultural shock because they successfully combined their
traditions with American culture.

342 De Besche, Hubert. "The Sweden of the Immigrants and the Sweden of
Today." SWEDISH PIONEER HISTORICAL QUARTERLY 16 (1965): 47-
55.

Contends that 1.3 million Swedes left their homeland because
of a dwindling supply of farm acreage there and a superabun-
dance in the United States. Concludes that eventual industrialization enabled those who remained behind to achieve one
of the highest standards of living in the world, but notes that
those who came to America also generally prospered.

343 Dowie, James I. PRAIRIE GRASS DIVIDING. Rock Island, Ill.: Augustana Historical Society, 1959. 262 p. Appendix, notes, index.

The story of Swedish Lutheran immigrants settling in the Platte
Valley, Nebraska, in the second half of the nineteenth century. Dowie describes the establishment of the Nebraska Conference of the Augustana Lutheran church and of Luther College. S.G. Larson, Martin Noyd, and S.M. Hill are given
special attention.

344 Dowie, James I., and Espelie, Ernest M. THE SWEDISH IMMIGRANT
COMMUNITY IN TRANSITION: ESSAYS IN HONOR OF DR. CONRAD
BERGENDOFF. Rock Island, Ill.: Augustana Historical Society, 1963.
246 p. Illustrations, notes, bibliography, index.

A festschrift by fourteen authors honoring the former president
of Augustana College. The essays discuss the early Swedish
Lutheran church and the later organization of the Augustana
Synod at Rock Island, Illinois, by E.P. Esbjorn.

345 Ehn, Erik. "The Swedes in Wisconsin: Concerning Source Material on
the Study of Early Swedish Immigration to Wisconsin." SWEDISH PIO-
NEER HISTORICAL QUARTERLY 19 (1968): 116-29.

Generally focuses on the magnitude of Swedish migration to
Wisconsin from 1850 to 1910. Notes that the presence of
earlier Swedish settlers became the largest single factor attracting later immigrants.

346 Flom, George T. A HISTORY OF NORWEGIAN IMMIGRATION INTO
THE UNITED STATES. Iowa City, Iowa: 1909. 407 p. Appendices,
footnotes, index.

Traces Norwegian immigration to America from 1825 until 1848.
Certain chapters appeared in modified form in the IOWA
JOURNAL OF HISTORY AND POLITICS as "The Scandinavian
Factor in the American Population," and "The Coming of the
Norwegians to Iowa." He also covers Norwegian settlements
in Illinois and Wisconsin, on a county-by-county basis.

347 Fonkalsrud, Alfred O., and Stevenson, Beatrice. THE SCANDINAVIAN
AMERICAN. Minneapolis: K.C. Holter Publishing Co., 1915. 167 p.

Discusses the actual and potential impact of Scandinavian immigrants to the United States on the economy, politics, literature, religion, and the arts. Concludes with a consideration
of their favorable influence in the "Great Race."

348 Furer, Howard B., comp. and ed. THE SCANDINAVIANS IN AMERICA
986-1970: A CHRONOLOGY AND FACT BOOK. Dobbs Ferry, N.Y.:
Oceana Publications, 1972. 138 p. Bibliography, index.

Contains a chronology of Norwegian, Swedish, and Danish immigration and a collection of excerpts from letters, diaries,
pamphlets, newspapers, and other documents.

349 Gjerset, Knut, trans. "An Account of the Norwegian Settlers in North
America." WISCONSIN MAGAZINE OF HISTORY 8 (1924): 77-88.

A translation from a report of Consul General Adam Loven-
skjold to the Norwegian government, dated October 15, 1847,

describing his visit during the preceding summer to the Norwegian settlements in the western districts of the United States.

350   Guterman, Stanley S. "The Americanization of Norwegian Immigrants: A Study in Historical Sociology." SOCIOLOGY AND SOCIAL RESEARCH 52 (1968): 252-70.

Concentrates on the differences between immigrants settling the rural and urban areas during the nineteenth century to determine their degree of acculturation.

351   Harvey, Dorothy Mayo. "The Swedes in Vermont." VERMONT HISTORY 28 (1960): 39-58.

Deals with the details of Swedish immigration to Vermont, patterns of settlement, occupational placement, and contributions to the state.

352   Haugen, Einar. THE NORWEGIAN LANGUAGE IN AMERICA: A STUDY IN BILINGUAL BEHAVIOR. 2 vols in 1. 2d ed. Bloomington: Indiana University Press, 1969. 699 p. Maps, tables, appendices, footnotes, index.

Composed of two volumes, THE BILINGUAL COMMUNITY and THE AMERICAN DIALECTS OF NORWEGIANS. This book treats language as a social phenomenon of interest to both historians and sociologists. It is also intended as a "paradigmatic analysis of a bilingual community in dynamic linguistic transition." The first volume contains more historical information on immigration than the second.

353   Havighurst, Walter. UPPER MISSISSIPPI, A WILDERNESS SAGA. New York: Farrar and Rinehart, 1937. 269 p. Illustrations, index.

Relates the story of Norwegians coming to the upper Midwest to farm the land and harvest the timber, and includes "actual happenings, traditions and folktales, little known outside the Scandinavian-American communities."

354   Hoglund, A. William. "Finnish Immigrant Farmers in New York, 1910-1960." In IN THE TREK OF THE IMMIGRANTS: ESSAYS PRESENTED TO CARL WITTKE, edited by O. Fritiof Ander, pp. 141-55. Rock Island, Ill.: Augustana College Library, 1964.

Describes the efforts of promoters in central upstate New York to attract Finnish immigrants from Michigan, Wyoming, Pennsylvania, Minnesota, and Ohio to run the farms abandoned by earlier settlers. The first generation performed well in dairy and chicken farming but the second generation generally abandoned agriculture and allowed their churches and cooperative societies to decline.

355 _____. FINNISH IMMIGRANTS IN AMERICA, 1880-1920. Madison: University of Wisconsin Press, 1960. 213 p. Illustrations, notes, sources, index.

Concentrates on Finnish organizations "which pursued different ideals and aspirations for a better and happier life...how their heritage from Finland was reshaped in America...[and] the immigrants' reassessment of their organizational endeavors after a generation of effort." Sees 1920 as the end of an era in their "organized search for paradise."

356 Hokanson, Nels Magnus. SWEDISH IMMIGRANTS IN LINCOLN'S TIME. New York: Harper & Brothers, 1942. 259 p. Illustrations, appendices, notes, bibliography, index.

A detailed study of Swedish settlement in the Midwest--especially Illinois--in the mid-nineteenth century, and the Swedish support for Lincoln, including chapters on the immigrants' role in the army and navy on both sides of the Civil War.

357 Hvidt, Kristian. FLIGHT TO AMERICA: THE SOCIAL BACKGROUND OF 300,000 DANISH EMIGRANTS. New York: Academic Press, 1975. 214 p. Illustrations, references, index.

Originally a dissertation at the University of Copenhagen. The author uses registry records from 1868 to 1914 to analyze the demographic and socioeconomic characteristics of Danish emigrants and the causes for their migration. He also compares his data with that for other Scandinavian countries.

358 _____. "Mass Emigration from Denmark to the United States, 1868-1914." AMERICAN STUDIES IN SCANDINAVIA 9 (1972): 3-30.

Based on a statistical analysis of 287,000 Danish emigrants during the period, the article provides a profile of the age, sex, geographical background, occupation, and destination of the emigrants. Special emphasis is on the late nineteenth century.

359 Jalkanen, Ralph J., ed. FINNS IN NORTH AMERICA: A SOCIAL SYMPOSIUM. Hancock: Michigan State University Press, 1969. 224 p. Notes.

A series of fifteen different articles covering Finnish emigration to America, the founding of a Finnish community, the growth of Suomi College, Finnish-American culture, religious life among the Lutheran Finns, and social problems and ethnic self-consciousness.

360 Janson, Florence Edith. BACKGROUND OF SWEDISH IMMIGRATION, 1840-1930. 1931. Reprint. New York: Arno Press, 1970. 517 p.

Tables, appendices, footnotes, bibliography, index.

A study of the causes of Swedish immigration, with emphasis
on economic, social, religious, and political conditions in
Sweden that caused migration to the United States. Originally
a dissertation.

361   Kolehmainen, John I. THE FINNS IN AMERICA: A BIBLIOGRAPHICAL
GUIDE TO THEIR HISTORY. Hancock, Mich.: Finnish American Historical Library, 1947. 141 p.

An extensive list of English and foreign language sources arranged under these topics: emigration, settlement, employment,
religion, temperance, labor, newspapers and periodicals, education, literature and the arts, and observations on immigrant
life.

362   _____. "The Inimitable Marxists: The Finnish Immigrant Socialists."
MICHIGAN HISTORY 36 (1952): 395-405.

Traces the development of the Finnish Socialist movement in
the United States, noting its economic efforts, but focusing
on its troubled relations with the American Socialist party,
an organization denigrated for its conservatism by the Finnish
immigrants.

363   _____. "Soumalaiset Amerikassa: Asutus Ja Tyoolot." TURUN HIS-
TORIALLINEN ARKISTO 19 (1967): 257-68.

"The Finns in America: Settlement and Employment" describes
how job opportunities in mining, shipping docks, Columbia
River fishing, lumbering, domestic service, factory work, and
farming outweigh geographical preference as a cause of Finnish settlement patterns In the United States during the late
nineteenth and early twentieth centuries.

364   Kolehmainen, John I., and Hill, George W. HAVEN IN THE WOODS:
THE STORY OF THE FINNS IN WISCONSIN. Madison: State Historical Society of Wisconsin, 1951. 177 p. Appendix, footnotes, bibliographical note, index.

The Finns, who never amounted to more than 7,000 immigrants
in the twentieth century, settled mainly in the depleted "cut-
over" in northern Wisconsin. After some background on emigration from Finland, the volume provides sketches of immigrant communities, a discussion of farming, and a description
of immigrant institutions. Kolehmainen wrote the chapters on
emigration, geographical and occupational distribution of Finns,
and their religious, cultural, and social life. George W.
Hill wrote the material on logging and agriculture.

365 Kukkonen, Walter J. "The Evangelical Movement of Finland in America."
CONCORDIA HISTORICAL INSTITUTIONS QUARTERLY 42 (1969): 119-
32.

Describes the efforts of Finnish Lutheran immigrants to adjust
to the evangelical movement without leaving the church.
Forming their own national church, they sought to maintain
connections with evangelicalism in the Old Country by founding a Gospel Society.

366 Lindberg, John S. THE BACKGROUND OF SWEDISH EMIGRATION TO
THE UNITED STATES. 1930. Reprint. New York: Jerome S. Ozer,
1971. 272 p. Index.

Discusses the personal and national causes for Swedish migration, its character and pattern, regulation by the homeland,
remigration to Sweden, and the reasons for the cessation of
emigration.

367 Lindmark, Sture. "The Census of 1930 and the Swedes in the United
States." SWEDISH PIONEER HISTORICAL QUARTERLY 16 (1965): 216-
32.

Describes the changes in geographic distribution and occupations of Swedish immigrants between 1880 and 1950. Finds a
significant shift after 1900 from the rural areas of the Midwest to the industrial cities of the Northeast and a corresponding change from rural to urban employment. Also notes significant reimmigration to Sweden during the Great Depression.

368 _____. "End of the Great Migration: Decline, Restriction, and Press
Reaction, 1929-1932." SWEDISH PIONEER HISTORICAL QUARTERLY
20 (1969): 25-41.

Although most Swedish immigration to the United States ended
before the quota laws of the 1920s, the Swedish-American
press reacted strongly. The author feels that the Depression,
even more than the quota laws, reduced immigration in the
1930s.

369 _____. SWEDISH AMERICA, 1914-1932: STUDIES IN ETHNICITY WITH
EMPHASIS ON ILLINOIS AND MINNESOTA. Uppsala, Sweden: Scandinavian University Books, 1971. 360 p. Tables, appendices, footnotes,
bibliography, index.

Seeks to determine to what extent Swedish immigrants sought
to preserve their language, churches, organizations, and
foreign language press. Concludes Swedes assimilated no more
quickly than most other immigrant groups from Europe.

370 Lindquist, Emory. "Appraisals of Sweden and America By Swedish Emi-

grants: The Testimony of Letters in Emigrationsutredningen." SWEDISH PIONEER HISTORICAL QUARTERLY 17 (1966): 78-95.

Based upon letters written by Swedish immigrants, attributes their immigration to class distinctions, voting restrictions, lack of a democratic spirit in their loveland, the quest for religious freedom in the face of the established church, and protests against compulsory military training.

371 _____. "The Swedish Immigrant and Life in Kansas." KANSAS HISTORICAL QUARTERLY 29 (1963): 1-24.

A former president of Bethany College, founded by Lutheran Swedes, discusses Swedish immigration and settlement during the second half of the nineteenth century. Covers their political affiliations, occupations, education, and religion. Sees Swedish immigrants being attracted to Kansas by railroads, immigration companies, Swedish land speculation, the state bureau of immigration, and letters from earlier migrants.

372 Ljungmark, Lars. FOR SALE--MINNESOTA: ORGANIZED PROMOTION OF SCANDINAVIAN IMMIGRATION, 1866-1873. Stockholm: Scandinavian University Books, 1971. 304 p. Appendices, bibliography, index.

Translated from Swedish. Discusses the "push-pull" causes of Swedish migration to Minnesota, focusing on the promotional efforts of both the state board of immigration and the major railroads.

373 Lovoll, Odd Sverre. A FOLK EPIC: THE BYGDELAG IN AMERICA. Boston: Twayne, Norwegian-American Historical Association, 1975. 326 p. Illustrations, appendix, notes, bibliography, index.

Focuses on the BYDELAG, a society of Norwegian Americans from a particular region or village in the old country as a means of preserving cultural heritage and fostering ethnic consciousness.

374 Mattson, Hans. REMINISCENCES: THE STORY OF AN EMIGRANT. St. Paul, Minn.: D.D. Merrill Co., 1891. 314 p. Illustrations.

Memoir by the author, a Swedish immigrant who later became U.S. Consul General to India. Deals with his early life in Sweden, his immigration, his work with other Swedish immigrants, and his travels. Contains many comparisons of life in the two countries.

375 Mulder, William. HOMEWARD TO ZION: THE MORMON MIGRATION FROM SCANDINAVIA. Minneapolis: University of Minnesota Press, 1957. 375 p. Notes, sources, index.

Discusses the arrival in Utah of some 30,000 Mormon immi-

grants from Norway, Sweden, and Denmark during the period
1850-1905.

376 Myhrman, Anders. "Finlandssvenska Immigranter I Amerika" [Swedish-
speaking Finnish immigrants in America]. HISTORISKA OCH LITTERATUR-
HISTORISKA STUDIER 41 (1966): 261-83.

Concentrates on the period from 1885 to 1929 and emphasizes
the role of sickness, insurance, and temperance organizations,
the order of Runeberg, and different religious congregations.

377 Nelson, Helge. SWEDES AND THE SWEDISH SETTLEMENTS IN NORTH
AMERICA. Vol. 1. 383 p. Maps, illustrations, tables, graphs, ap-
pendix, bibliography, index. Vol. 2. 73 p. Atlas. New York: A.
Bonnier, 1943.

These volumes, written by a professor of geography at Lund
University, Sweden, provide a geographical explanation for
the pattern of Swedish settlement in North America, but con-
centrate much attention on the Swedes in Minnesota and Illinois. Minnesota in particular attracted those who hoped to
find in their new country the climate and topography of their
mother country.

378 Nelson, Olaf N., ed. HISTORY OF THE SCANDINAVIANS AND SUC-
CESSFUL SCANDINAVIANS IN THE UNITED STATES. Vol. 1. 643 p.
Bibliography. Vol. 2. 498 p. Illustrations, bibliography. Minneapo-
lis: O.N. Nelson and Co., 1900.

Compilation of works by numerous Scandinavian-American authors about nearly all aspects of Scandinavian life in America,
especially religion and education. Much of the material consists of brief biographies of prominent Scandinavians in the
United States.

379 Norwegian-American Historical Association. NORWEGIAN AMERICAN
STUDIES AND RECORDS. Northfield, Minn.: 1926-- .

Each volume in this continuing series is a collection of essays,
translated letters, and bibliographies on a wide range of topics.
Volumes are not organized around a theme. Those with specific relevance to immigration have been noted in the individual volume annotations. Annotated bibliographies of recent
publications are found in each volume, beginning with volume
5.

380 _____. Vol. 1, 1926. Theodore C. Blegen, ed. 175 p.

Six articles, many of which are translations of contemporary
writers, including information on health and medical practices
among the early settlers, Norwegian Quakers, Norwegians in

the West, Bishop Jacob Newmann, and Carl F. Solberg.

381 _____. Vol. 2, 1927. Theodore C. Blegen, ed. 137 p.

Six articles, including ones on Norwegian language and literature in American universities, Norwegian-American church history, and the Norwegian pioneer in American scholarship.

382 _____. Vol. 3, 1928. Theodore C. Blegen, ed. 150 p.

Nine articles, including ones on Sjur J. Haaeim, Hans Barlien, Ole S. Gjerset, Icelandic communities in America, and
American Emigration Societies of the 1840s and 1850s.

383 _____. Vol. 4, 1929. Theodore C. Blegen, ed. 150 p.

Eight articles, including ones on "The Mind of the Scandinavian Immigrant," and "Immigration and Social Amelioration."

384 _____. Vol. 5, 1930. Theodore C. Blegen, ed. 152 p.

Eight articles, including translations of articles and letters
dealing with immigrant women on the frontier, the trip from
New York to Wisconsin, Norwegian-American fiction, and
the founding of St. Olaf College.

385 _____. Vol. 6, 1931. Theodore C. Blegen, ed. 191 p.

A dozen articles on various pioneer settlements and promoters,
and immigration to America before the Civil War.

386 _____. Vol. 7, 1933. Theodore C. Blegen, ed. 139 p.

Six articles, two of which are on O.E. Rolvaag, and another
about a pioneer pastor's wife. A third deals with how to
search for Norwegian-American records.

387 _____. Vol. 8, 1934. Theodore C. Blegen, ed. 176 p.

Ten articles ranging from immigration, Norwegian Americans,
and Wisconsin politics, to EMIGRANTEN and the election of
1852.

388 _____. Vol. 9, 1936. Theodore C. Blegen, ed. 131 p.

Nine articles, including Marcus L. Hansen's "Immigration and
Puritanism," and Laurence M. Larson's "Collection and Pre-
servation of Sources." Other articles deal with settlements in
Iowa, Illinois, and Minnesota.

389 _____. Vol. 13, 1943. Theodore C. Blegen, ed. 203 p.

Ten articles, some of which are related to the settling of the trans-Mississippi West. Other articles deal with Norwegian and Swedish immigration (1870), and materials in the National Archives relating to Scandinavian countries.

390 _____. Vol. 14, 1944. Theodore C. Blegen, ed. 264 p.

Nearly a dozen articles, including "A Migration of Skills," "When America Called for Immigrants," and Norwegian immigration in the 1840s.

391 _____. Vol. 15, 1949. Theodore C. Blegen, ed. 238 p.

Ten articles, several on social and cultural aspects of Norwegian Americans. Also biographical sketches of Julius Baumann, Kristian Prestgard, Erik Petersen, and an essay on "Scandinavia, Wisconsin."

392 _____. Vol. 16, 1950. Theodore C. Blegen, ed. 218 p.

Six articles dealing with Norwegian settlements in the Far West and Alaska.

393 _____. Vol. 17, 1952. Theodore C. Blegen, ed. 185 p.

Eight articles, including ones by Einar Haugen, Kenneth Bjork, Franklin D. Scott, and Blegen. Some deal with assimilation and ethnicity.

394 _____. Vol. 18, 1954. Theodore C. Blegen, ed. 252 p.

Eight articles, including those by Haugen on "Norwegian Migration to America," Paul Knaplund on Rasmus B. Anderson, and Peter A. Munch on "Segregation and Assimilation of Norwegian Settlements in Wisconsin."

395 _____. Vol. 19, 1956. Theodore C. Blegen, ed. 218 p.

Eight articles which include Blegen's "The Immigrant Image of America," Oystein Ore's "Norwegian Emigrants with University Training, 1830–1880," and Clarence A. Glasrud's "Boyesen and the Norwegian Immigration."

396 _____. Vol. 20, 1959. Theodore C. Blegen, ed. 246 p.

Twelve articles including ones on Henrik Ibsen in America, settlements in Texas and Alaska, and a review of Norwegian studies in American institutions of higher learning.

397 _____. Vol. 21, 1962. Kenneth O. Bjork, ed. 311 p.

Ten articles including ones on Scandinavian immigrant writers, the Americanization of Norwegians, and the communitarian background of Norwegian immigration.

398 _____. Vol. 22, 1965. Kenneth O. Bjork, ed. 255 p.

Eight articles dealing with the following topics: a pioneer artist and his masterpiece, Kristofer Jonson's lecture tour, two men of Old Waupaca, pioneering in Montova, seven American letters to Valdres, music for youth in an emerging church, and the independent historical society.

399 _____. Vol. 23, 1967. Carlton C. Qualey, ed. 256 p.

Eight articles, half of which are letters and memoirs, while three others deal with social and literary history. "The Norwegian Immigrant and His Church" was read before the 1965 meeting of the American Historical Association.

400 _____. Vol. 24, 1970. Kenneth O. Bjork, ed. 300 p.

Nine articles, most of which relate to specific individuals, except for "The Norwegian Press in North Dakota" and "Norwegians in New York."

401 _____. Vol. 25, 1972. Kenneth O. Bjork, ed. 293 p.

Ten articles including "Norway's Organized Response to Emigration," "From Norwegian State Church to American Free Church," and "The 1842 Immigrants from Norway."

402 _____. Vol. 26, 1974. Kenneth O. Bjork, ed. 269 p.

Twelve articles including: Scandinavian migration to the Canadian prairie provinces, the story of Peder Anderson, emigration from Lend Parish to America, Georg Svendrup and the Augsburg plan of education, the school controversy among Norwegian immigrants, and Norwegians learning English.

403 Nyholm, Paul C. THE AMERICANIZATION OF THE DANISH CHURCHES. Minneapolis: Augsburg Publishing House, 1963. 480 p. Illustrations, tables.

Analyzes the eventual adjustment of the Danish church to the American environment, particularly in the use of the English language, the training of the clergy, church services, congregational life, and participation in American political, social, and cultural life.

404 Olson, John Alden. "Proselytism, Immigration and Settlement of Foreign
     Converts to the Mormon Culture in Zion." JOURNAL OF THE WEST 6
     (1967): 189-204.

     Discusses the efforts of Mormon leaders to attract British arti-
     sans and mechanics and Scandinavian farmers to Utah in order
     to maintain the church's economic self-sufficiency. Also
     analyzes the reasons for the decline of this inflow after 1900
     and its stabilizing effect on "Zion in the Wilderness."

405 Olsson, Nils William. SWEDISH PASSENGER ARRIVALS IN NEW YORK,
     1820-1850. Chicago: Swedish Pioneer Historical Society Press, 1967.
     392 p. Illustrations, addenda, footnotes, index.

     A chronological arrangement of passenger arrivals giving name,
     age, sex, and occupation, plus detailed biographical notes
     on many of the passengers. Of particular use to genealogists.

406 Qualey, Carlton C. NORWEGIAN SETTLEMENT IN THE UNITED STATES.
     Northfield, Minn.: Norwegian-American Historical Association, 1938.
     285 p. Maps, illustrations, appendix, bibliography.

     Covers the movement of the immigrants from Europe to the East
     Coast and subsequent inland migrations to the Midwest, espe-
     cially in the period following the Civil War. In some respects
     it is an extension of Blegen's NORWEGIAN MIGRATION TO
     AMERICA, 1825-1860.

407 Quigley, John Michael. "An Economic Model of Swedish Emigration."
     QUARTERLY JOURNAL OF ECONOMICS 86 (1972): 111-26.

     Argues that poor economic conditions in Sweden provided more
     "push" than demand conditions in the United States in prompt-
     ing emigration from Sweden in the nineteenth century.

408 Rohne, John Magus. NORWEGIAN-AMERICAN LUTHERANISM UP TO
     1872. New York: Macmillan Co., 1926. 271 p. Footnotes, bibliog-
     raphy, index.

     A dissertation, written for a Doctor of Theology degree, with
     a detailed table of contents. Discusses the historical back-
     ground to immigration and settlement with particular attention
     to education and religion during the nineteenth century in the
     Midwest.

409 THE SCANDINAVIAN COMMUNITY IN AMERICA: AN ANNOTATED
     AND CLASSIFIED BIBLIOGRAPHICAL GUIDE. Burt Franklin Ethnic Bib-
     liographical Guides. Edited by Francesco Cordasco and William W.
     Brickman. In preparation.

410 Scott, Franklin D. "Literature in Periodicals of Protest of Swedish Ameri-

ca." SWEDISH PIONEER HISTORICAL QUARTERLY 16 (1965): 193-215.

Examines Swedish-American protest articles written between 1860 and 1959, especially those written by Socialist-influenced workers from 1915 to 1929. These periodicals stressed the evils of materialism and the need for intellectual pursuits, but their proliferation declined in the late twenties due to as-similation and acculturation.

411   Skard, Sigmund, and Wasser, Henry H., eds. AMERICANA NORVEGICA: NORWEGIAN CONTRIBUTIONS TO AMERICAN STUDIES. Vol. 2. Philadelphia: University of Pennsylvania Press, 1966. 340 p. Notes.

A publication of the American Institute of the University of Oslo, edited by the institute's founder, Sigmund Skard. Most of the essays are written by a younger generation of scholars, many of whom were students of Skard, who analyze various aspects of America, including its literature, religion, educa-tion, history, and politics.

412   Skardal, Dorothy Burton. THE DIVIDED HEART: SCANDINAVIAN IM-MIGRANT EXPERIENCE THROUGH LITERARY SOURCES. Lincoln: Uni-versity of Nebraska Press, 1974. 393 p. Notes, bibliography, index.

Develops various themes arising out of a reading of Scandina-vian-American literature, including theories of cultural adjust-ment, economic and social success, changes in immigrant in-stitutions, and alterations in their value.

413   Smith, Timothy L. "Religious Denominations as Ethnic Communities: A Regional Case Study." CHURCH HISTORY 35 (1966): 207-26.

Analyzes the relationship between religious and social institu-tions and ethnic identity among Finnish and Slovenian immi-grants in the Lake Superior mining region. The Finns used Socialist, temperance, and religious organizations to maintain identity in the first generation, but competition and ideologi-cal division caused most of the second generation to cultivate an American identity through education and economic achieve-ment.

414   Stephenson, George M. "Background of the Beginnings of Swedish Immi-gration, 1850-1875." AMERICAN HISTORICAL REVIEW 31 (1926): 708-23.

Explains why Swedish immigration began in earnest in the 1850s and why it swelled to such a degree that some native Swedes feared that their country would be depopulated. Much of the answer, he feels, lies in the frontier which offered the immigrant tremendous potential success.

415 _____. THE RELIGIOUS ASPECTS OF SWEDISH IMMIGRATIONS; A
STUDY OF IMMIGRANT CHURCHES. Minneapolis: University of Minnesota Press, 1932. 542 p. Illustrations, bibliography, index.

Emphasizes the role of religion in Swedish immigration, but
also provides information about immigrant community life,
journalism, and the rapid acculturation of Swedes in America.

416 Wefald, Jon Michael. "From Peasant Ideals to the Reform State: A Study
of Norwegian Attitudes Toward Reform in the American Middle West,
1890-1917." Ph.D. dissertation, University of Michigan, 1965. 196 p.

From analyzing Norwegian-American newspapers, debates and
voting records of Norwegians in Congress, and some election
statistics, the author concludes that on reform issues such as
the Hepburn Act, Mann-Elkins Act, Underwood Tariff, Federal
Reserve Act, and the Clayton Anti-Trust Act Norwegians supported progressive reforms.

417 Westin, Gunnar. "Background of Swedish Immigration, 1840-1850." In
SWEDISH IMMIGRANT COMMUNITY IN TRANSITION: ESSAYS IN
HONOR OF DR. CONRAD BERGENDOFF, edited by J. Iverne Dowie
and Ernest M. Espelie, pp. 19-30. Rock Island, Ill.: Augustana Historical Society, 1963.

Attributes Swedish immigration to a variety of factors, including lack of political power or social security, Methodist and
Baptist religious dissatisfaction with the established Lutheran
church, the tales of Swedish sailors, and "American Letters"
from earlier settlers.

Chapter 3

NEW IMMIGRATION

GENERAL

418 Appel, John J., ed. THE NEW IMMIGRATION. New York: Pitman Publishing Corp., 1971. 215 p. Bibliographical essay.

Compilation of essays on various aspects of the New Immigration, focusing on the problems involved in arrival and adjustment, the building of ethnic institutions, and the debate over restriction from eight different perspectives.

419 Bromwell, William J. HISTORY OF IMMIGRATION TO THE UNITED STATES. 1856. Reprint. New York: Arno Press, 1969. 225 p. Tables.

Almost completely a set of tables giving the number, sex, age, occupation, and country of birth for immigrants from 1819 to 1855. Information taken from the Annual Reports on Immigration, Passenger Abstracts, and custom house records.

420 Hutchinson, Edward P., special ed. "The New Immigration." THE ANNALS OF THE AMERICAN ACADEMY OF POLITICAL AND SOCIAL SCIENCE 367 (1966): 1-249.

Issue divided into three sections with a general introduction by the editor. Section 1 deals with "Characteristics of the New Immigration" and includes articles on demography, national origins, the immigrant worker, the migration of professionals, World War II refugees, migration between the United States and Canada, and a European view of immigration. Section 2 covers "Administration of the Immigration Laws" and includes five articles mainly of a technical nature. Section 3 is on "Recent Legislative Action," and includes information on the McCarran-Walter Act of 1952 as amended to 1965, and an article by Senator Edward Kennedy describing efforts to change the quota system by the 1965 Immigration Act.

421 Roberts, Peter. THE NEW IMMIGRATION. 1912. Reprint. New York:

Arno Press, 1970. 386 p. Illustrations.

Examines various facets of community life and culture of immigrants from southeastern Europe with some sympathy and understanding, but concludes with a strong argument for assimilation
and acculturation efforts by native American organizations.

422   Shriver, William P. IMMIGRANT FORCES: FACTORS IN THE NEW
DEMOCRACY. 1913. Reprint. New York: Jerome S. Ozer, 1971.
277 p. Illustrations, appendices, footnotes, index.

Studies the New Immigrants who came in the late nineteenth
century, their problems, adjustments, and religious influences.

422a Vecoli, Rudolph J. "The Immigration Studies Collection of the University
of Minnesota." AMERICAN ARCHIVIST 32 (1969): 139-45.

Discusses the need for and problems inherent in building an
immigration studies collection. Includes sampling of Minnesota
collection. Collection consists largely of material on southern
and eastern European immigrants.

ITALIANS

423   Albini, Joseph L. THE AMERICAN MAFIA: GENESIS OF A LEGEND.
New York: Appleton-Century-Crofts, 1971. 354 p. References, bibliography, indices.

Part of the publisher's series in sociology. Describes the development and functional aspects of criminal syndicates in the
United States with particular attention to New York and Italians.

424   Amfitheatrof, E. THE CHILDREN OF COLUMBUS: AN INFORMAL HIS-
TORY OF THE ITALIANS IN THE NEW WORLD. Totowa, N.J.: Row-
man and Littlefield, 1973. 371 p. Sources, references, index.

A popular survey of Italian immigration which touches only
lightly on the period before the Civil War and emphasizes the
new immigration of the late nineteenth century up through the
Depression years. Concludes with a chapter on well-known
contemporary citizens of Italian ancestry.

425   Anderson, Nels. "The Social Antecedents of a Slum: A Developmental
Study of the East Harlem Area of Manhattan Island, New York City."
Ph.D. dissertation, New York University, 1930. 205 p.

Describes the evolution of the Italian-American community in
the East Harlem section of New York City.

426 Baily, Samuel L. "The Italians and the Development of Organized Labor in Argentina, Brazil and the United States, 1880-1914." JOURNAL OF SOCIAL HISTORY 3 (1969-70): 123-34.

Provides some tentative answers to the questions of why Italian immigrants in Argentina and Brazil were among the leaders in organizing and developing the labor movement whereas in the United States they were almost completely excluded from the movement.

427 Bianco, Carla. THE TWO ROSETOS. Bloomington: Indiana University Press, 1975. 234 p. Illustrations, bibliography.

Chronicles the migration of an entire village in southern Italy to Pennsylvania and efforts to keep much of their culture, folklore, and dialect intact.

428 Bohme, Frederick G. "The Italians in New Mexico." NEW MEXICO HISTORICAL REVIEW 33 (1959): 98-116.

Based on his dissertation of the same title which sees the immigration of Italians as important, not because of their small number, but because they represented a bridge between Anglo-Saxon and Hispanic cultures.

429 Bosi, Alfredo. CINQUANTI'ANNI DI VITA ITALIANA IN AMERICA. New York: Bagnasco Press, 1921. 530 p. Illustrations.

Contains reminiscences and narratives of life in America by early twentieth-century Italian immigrants and visitors.

430 Briggs, John Walker. "Italians in Italy and America: A Study of Change within Continuity for Immigrants to Three American Cities, 1890-1930." Ph.D. dissertation, University of Minnesota, 1972. 382 p.

A study of Italians in Utica and Rochester, New York, and Kansas City, Missouri, which indicates the points of similarity between these immigrants and their host society, especially "bourgeois values such as individual advancement through hard work, thrift, education, property acquisition, and autonomy in their occupational and economic life."

431 Capponi, Guido. "Italy and Italians in Early American Periodicals (1741-1830)." Ph.D. dissertation, University of Wisconsin, 1958. 467 p.

Attempts "to record the nature and extent of early American interest in Italy and its literature," and describes the change in attitude from initial ignorance and lack of concern in the eighteenth century to an expanded interest in the early nineteenth century because of American travel abroad and the emerging nationalism of Italy.

432 Caroli, Betty Boyd. ITALIAN REPATRIATION FROM THE UNITED STATES, 1900-1914. New York: Center for Migration Studies, 1974. 117 p. Maps, tables, notes, bibliography.

Based largely upon Italian sources and interviews with repatriates, analyzes the causes and effects of the 1.5 million Italian immigrants who returned to their native land in these years. Notes that the Italian government encouraged temporary emigration before World War I, but that most migrants left and returned for their own reasons.

433 Caselli, Ron. "Making It in America--The Italian Experience." SOCIAL STUDIES 64 (1973): 147-53.

Argues that the only way the Italians made it in America was through relinquishing their ethnic heritage to embrace assimilation. Calls for newer ethnic groups to bring their culture with them as new programs open up for minorities and opportunities increase.

434 Child, Irvin L. ITALIAN OR AMERICAN? THE SECOND GENERATION IN CONFLICT. New York: Russell and Russell, 1943. 206 p. References, index.

A psychology dissertation published as a sequel to Phyllis H. Williams's SOUTH ITALIAN FOLKWAYS IN EUROPE AND AMERICA. It is a study of second generation Italians in New Haven, Connecticut, in the process of acculturation.

435 Cordasco, Francesco [M.]. THE ITALIAN-AMERICAN EXPERIENCE: AN ANNOTATED AND CLASSIFIED BIBLIOGRAPHICAL GUIDE, WITH SELECTED PUBLICATIONS OF THE CAST ITALIANA EDUCATIONAL BUREAU. Burt Franklin Ethnic Biographical Guide Series, edited by Francesco Cordasco and William W. Brickman. New York: Burt Franklin, 1974. 179 p. Appendix, index.

Contains a list of bibliographies and archives and a bibliography of works dealing with Italian immigration to America, general and regional studies, and analyses of Italian social, political, and economic structure and institutions. Appendix contains four short essays on the Cosa Italian Educational Bureau, the Italians in America, and population and occupational patterns of Italian Americans in New York City.

436 _____. ITALIANS IN THE UNITED STATES: A BIBLIOGRAPHY OF REPORTS, TEXTS, CRITICAL STUDIES AND RELATED MATERIALS. New York: Oriole Editions, 1972. 137 p. Illustrations.

An unannotated compilation designed to present a sufficient representation of Italian-American literature to afford both orientation and resources for further study. Includes a preliminary checklist of novels written in English dealing with the Italian-American experience.

437   Cordasco, Francesco [M.], and Bucchioni, Eugene. THE ITALIANS: SOCIAL BACKGROUNDS OF AN AMERICAN GROUP. Clifton, N.J.: Augustus M. Kelley, 1974. 598 p. Illustrations, bibliography.

Contains sources dealing with various aspects of the Italian-American experience between 1880 and 1940, including sections on emigration communities, responses to American life, employment, health, social needs, and the education experience of Italian children in American schools.

438   Covello, Leonard. THE SOCIAL BACKGROUND OF THE ITALO-AMERICAN SCHOOL CHILD. Leiden, Netherlands: E.J. Brill, 1967. 488 p. Tables, appendices, footnotes, bibliography.

Subtitled: "A Study of the Southern Italian Family Mores and Their Effect on the School Situation in Italy and America." First written as a dissertation in 1944, this study provides a historical background for the author's technical analysis and also gives attention to the process of assimilation and cultural independence which Italians faced.

439   Cunningham, George E. "The Italian, a Hindrance to White Solidarity in Louisiana, 1890-1898." JOURNAL OF NEGRO HISTORY 50 (1965): 22-36.

Demonstrates that anti-Italian discrimination, including lynchings, caused the newcomers to identify for a time with the state's Negroes, combining with the Populists to defeat a disfranchisement amendment. Eventually the New Orleans political machine succeeded in guaranteeing Italian exemption from disfranchisement and the immigrants joined the older white citizens in the anti-Negro consensus.

440   DeConde, Alexander. HALF BITTER, HALF SWEET: AN EXCURSION INTO ITALIAN-AMERICAN HISTORY. New York: Charles Scribner's Sons, 1971. 386 p. Bibliographical essay, index.

Explores the bittersweet relationship between Italian and American peoples, institutions, and cultures in both the Old World and the New. Strong emphasis on foreign relations contacts between the two.

441   Diggins, John P. "The Italo-American Anti-Fascist Opposition." JOURNAL OF AMERICAN HISTORY 54 (1967): 579-98.

Details efforts of Italo-Americans, labor leaders, radicals, and intellectuals to form an anti-Fascist front in the 1920s and their failure to arouse American support.

442   _____. MUSSOLINI AND FASCISM: THE VIEW FROM AMERICA. Princeton, N.J.: Princeton University Press, 1972. 524 p. Illustra-

tions, footnotes, bibliographical notes, index.

Studies the values which underlay attitudes toward fascism, analyzes the symbols and images of Mussolini, delineates opinion by economic, political, and religious groups, investigates the role of the press in forming public opinion, and presents the view of administrations in Washington.

443   Federal Writers' Project. THE ITALIANS OF NEW YORK. 1938. Reprint. New York: Arno Press, 1969. 241 p. Illustrations, bibliography, index.

Surveys the causes of immigration and accompanying problems of social adjustment, then topically treats Italian-American religious life, civic and social life, as well as their influence in the professions, business, and industry.

444   Fenton, Edwin. IMMIGRANTS AND UNIONS, A CASE STUDY: ITALIANS AND AMERICAN LABOR, 1870-1920. 1958. Reprint. New York: Arno Press, 1975. 630 p. Bibliography.

A published dissertation which investigates the interaction between Italian immigrants and the American labor movement ranging from the craft union to socialism and anarchism. Argues that union activity led to assimilation into political and social life and that the immigrants forced unions to alter their programs and tactics.

445   _____. "Italians in the Labor Movement." PENNSYLVANIA MAGAZINE OF HISTORY AND BIOGRAPHY 26 (1959): 133-48.

Argues that Italian laborers in Pennsylvania, given sufficient bargaining power, organized rapidly and well. Challenges labor historians to abandon belief in the opinions of contemporary labor leaders and to examine the facts carefully.

446   Ferroni, Charles D. "The Italians in Cleveland: A Study in Assimilation." Ph.D. dissertation, Kent State University, 1969. 292 p.

A study of four institutions--churches, organizations, public schools, and settlement houses--to determine the degree of assimilation since the 1920s. Sees World War II as a watershed because from that time forward intermarriages increased, Italian communities became more decentralized, and there was widespread acceptance of Italians as loyal citizens.

447   Fiore, Alphonse Thomas. "History of Italian Immigration in Nebraska." Ph.D. dissertation, University of Nebraska, 1942. 79 p.

Discusses the reasons for migration from South Italy (Calabria) to Nebraska and for settlement in Omaha and Lincoln. Analyzes immigrants' efforts to preserve their culture and their economic and political progress in both communities.

448   Foerster, Robert F. THE ITALIAN EMIGRATION OF OUR TIMES. Cambridge, Mass.: Harvard University Press, 1919. 528 p. Appendix, bibliography, index.

Detailed examinations of the causes of Italian emigration to the United States, Latin America, Europe, and North Africa. Much less treatment given to Italian experience in the United States. Very critical of Italian policy toward immigration and suggests international conference.

449   Gallo, Patrick J. ETHNIC ALIENATION: THE ITALIAN-AMERICANS. Rutherford, N.J.: Fairleigh Dickinson University Press, 1974. 254 p. Tables, notes, bibliography, index.

A study, based largely on interviews of Italians in urban New Jersey, "to determine whether the American political system tends to neutralize or sharpen an ethnic group's sense of exclusion from the dominant roles, values and institutions, and result in types of behavior that differentiate them from native whites."

450   Gambino, Richard. BLOOD OF MY BLOOD; THE DILEMMA OF THE ITALIAN AMERICANS. New York: Doubleday, 1974. 342 p. Index.

Interprets Italian-American outlooks toward work, sex and sex roles, family, religion, education, politics, and the Mafia. Examines "what it means to be Italian-American in today's United States."

451   Gans, Herbert. THE URBAN VILLAGERS: GROUP AND CLASS IN THE LIFE OF ITALIAN-AMERICANS. Glencoe, Ill.: Free Press, 1962. 335 p. Appendix, bibliography, indices.

Studies the Italian-American community of Boston's West End with respect to its internal social structure and its relation to the wider urban community.

452   Gilkey, George R. "The United States and Italy: Migration and Repatriation." JOURNAL OF DEVELOPING AREAS 2 (1967): 23-36.

Investigates the progress of those immigrants from southern Italy and Sicily who came to the United States to earn money and return to the homeland. Concludes that the migration of these "Americans" had only a palliative effect on Italy's economic problems and returned relatively few benefits to the individual repatriate compared to his paesani who remained in America.

453   Glanz, Rudolf. JEW AND ITALIAN: HISTORIC GROUP RELATIONS

AND THE NEW IMMIGRATION (1881-1924). New York: Ktav Publishing House, 1971. 232 p. Notes, index.

Stresses the cooperation between Jews and Italians in which Jews instructed the new immigrants not only in specific trades but also in the value of unionization. Although the study is not restricted to New York, much of Glanz's work concentrates on organizational activities in the city.

454   Harney, Robert F. "The Padrone and Immigrant." CANADIAN REVIEW OF AMERICAN STUDIES 5 (1974): 101-17.

Examines the contradictions and misconceptions that have prevented contemporaries and modern day scholars from a realistic understanding of the role played by the padrone in Italian and other Mediterranean immigrant communities. Argues that the padrone was both patron and exploiter and an often necessary middle man between the ethnic and host societies.

455   Iorizzo, Luciano John. "Italian Immigration and the Impact of the Padrone System." Ph.D. dissertation, Syracuse University, 1966. 256 p.

Details the role of the padroni from the 1880s to World War I. They were often middlemen who advanced their countrymen steamship fares, housed and fed them temporarily, acted as their interpreters, and operated as labor agents and bankers to the New Immigrant.

456   Iorizzo, Luciano John, and Mondello, Salvatore. THE ITALIAN AMERICANS. New York: Twayne, 1971. 217 p. Tables, notes, bibliography, index.

Surveys the varieties of the Italian-American experience on farms, and in small towns and large cities in the areas of politics, occupations, crime, religion, and reaction to Mussolini.

457   "The Italian Experience in Emigration." INTERNATIONAL MIGRATION REVIEW 1 (1967): 1-113.

All articles in this issue deal with this general topic. Articles are by Herbert Gans, G. Lucrezio Monticelli, Joseph Vlikonja, Humbert Nelli, Samuel Baily, Francesco Cerase, and Antonio Perotti.

458   Juliani, Richard N. "The Social Organization of Immigration: The Italians, in Philadelphia." Ph.D. dissertation, University of Pennsylvania, 1971. 262 p.

Examines the social organization of immigration, based upon taped interviews with Italian-born male immigrants who entered the United States between 1894 and 1924. Finds that the

Italians in Philadelphia passed through an adventurer phase, a
padroni stage, and a paesani one, each different in the character of the migrants, their intentions and motives, and the
social processes and relations which prevailed.

459   LaGumina, Salvatore J., ed. WOP! A DOCUMENTARY HISTORY OF
      ANTI-ITALIAN DISCRIMINATION IN THE UNITED STATES. San Fran-
      cisco: Straight Arrow, 1973. 319 p. Illustrations, tables, notes, bib-
      liography.

      Explores the historical evolution of anti-Italian prejudice in
      the United States from the mid-nineteenth century to post
      World War II. Original sources with commentary by the edi-
      tor.

460   LoGatto, Anthony F., comp. and ed. THE ITALIANS IN AMERICA,
      1492-1972: A CHRONOLOGY & FACT BOOK. Ethnic Chronology
      Series. Dobbs Ferry, N.Y.: Oceana, 1972. 149 p. Illustrations, ap-
      pendices, bibliography, index.

      Begins with a chronological listing of events involving Italians
      from Columbus to the present. The remainder of the book is
      divided between a selection of documents paralleling the
      chronology and a series of eight appendices listing the contri-
      butions of Italians in contemporary America.

461   Lopreato, Joseph. ITALIAN AMERICANS. New York: Random House,
      1970. 204 p. Bibliography.

      Investigates patterns of Italian settlement in the United States,
      the impact of immigration on social institutions and intergroup
      relations, and the process of assimilation and achievement.

462   Mangano, Antonio. SONS OF ITALY; A SOCIAL AND RELIGIOUS
      STUDY OF THE ITALIANS IN AMERICA. New York: Missionary Edu-
      cation Movement of the United States and Canada, 1917. 234 p. Il-
      lustrations, bibliography.

      Deals primarily with the work of the Protestant evangelical
      churches in the United States in assimilating and acculturating
      Italian immigrants. The author was an Italian immigrant who
      became a Baptist minister and taught Italian studies at Colgate
      University.

463   Mariano, John Horace. THE ITALIAN CONTRIBUTION TO AMERICAN
      DEMOCRACY. Introduction by the Honorable F.H. LaGuardia. Boston:
      Christopher Publishing House, 1921. 317 p. Illustrations, bibliography.

      Deals largely with socioeconomic and demographic conditions
      of New York City Italians, their psychological traits, and their
      various social and professional organizations. Last section dis-

cusses the process of assimilation and acculturation, based largely upon responses from questionnaires.

464 Martellone, Anna Maria. UNA LITTLE ITALY NELL'ATENE D'AMERICA: LA COMMUNITA ITALIANA DI BOSTON DAL 1880 al 1920. Naples: Guida Editori, 1973. 597 p. Tables, appendix, notes, index.

The story of Boston's "Little Italy" in the North End where Italians displaced the earlier immigrant Irish. The account includes information about occupations, housing conditions, religion, ethnic conflicts, and cultural and social activities in the district.

465 Mondello, Salvatore. "The Italian Immigrant in Urban America, 1880-1920, as Reported in the Contemporary Periodical Press." Ph.D. dissertation, New York University, 1960. 266 p.

Periodical literature on the Italian immigrants was greatest during the 1900-1920 period which also corresponded to the greatest influx of Italians. While magazine writers tried to popularize the Americanizing process they succeeded merely in isolating the immigrants, popularizing racist sentiments, and supporting restrictive immigration legislation.

466 _____. "Italian Migration to the United States as Reported in American Magazines, 1880-1920." SOCIAL SCIENCE 39 (1964): 131-42.

Reviews the attitude toward Italian immigration expressed in American periodicals and finds that the periodicals generally attributed immigration to the miserable conditions in southern Italy and the expectation of socioeconomic betterment. Most magazines regarded the migration as a benefit to Italy and a detriment to the United States.

467 _____. "The Magazine 'Charities' and the Italian Immigrants, 1903-1914." JOURNALISM QUARTERLY 44 (1967): 91-98.

Discusses the interaction between social reformers from the magazine CHARITIES (later the SURVEY) and Italian immigrants during the Progressive era. Contends that the reformers displayed real empathy for the immigrants' plight, but greatly limited their own effectiveness because they regarded the Italians as a "social problem" and stressed "Americanization."

468 Moquin, Wayne, and Van Doren, Charles, eds. A DOCUMENTARY HISTORY OF THE ITALIAN AMERICANS. New York: Praeger, 1974. 443 p. Illustrations, bibliography, index.

Collection of documents on Italian-American interaction from Columbus through Vince Lombardi. Organized around: the age of discovery, the period of mass migration, making a living,

organized crime and the Italian American, anti-Italian discrimination, and the emergence of the Italian American.

469   Musmanno, Michael A. THE STORY OF THE ITALIANS IN AMERICA.
New York: Doubleday, 1965. 300 p. Maps, illustrations.

An advocate's overview of Italian-American successes in the
United States.

470   Nelli, Humbert S. ITALIANS IN CHICAGO, 1880-1930: A STUDY IN
ETHNIC MOBILITY. New York: Oxford, 1970. 244 p. Maps, tables,
notes, bibliographic essay, index.

An intensive study of Chicago's Italian community up to the
Great Depression. Deals especially with settlement patterns,
economic and political life, community institutions, crime,
and assimilation.

471   _____. "Italians in Urban America: A Study in Ethnic Adjustment."
INTERNATIONAL MIGRATION REVIEW 1 (1967): 38-55.

Insists that Italian-Americans' strong community ties and group
consciousness were not part of their cultural heritage, but
rather developed out of a need for survival and security in
urban America.

472   Pisani, Lawrence Frank. THE ITALIAN IN AMERICA: A SOCIAL STUDY
AND HISTORY. New York: Exposition Press, 1957. 293 p. Bibliography, index.

Sociologist and son of Italian immigrants writes a topical treatment of Italian Americans, stressing their role in labor, religion, arts and sciences, and the urban scene. A concluding
chapter briefly discusses the impact of Italians on America.

473   Pozzetta, George E. "The Italian Immigrant Press of New York City:
The Early Years, 1880-1915." JOURNAL OF ETHNIC STUDIES 1 (1973):
32-46.

Discusses the role of a variety of Italian language newspapers
in aiding the new arrivals with information and, in some cases,
in exploiting them.

474   _____. "The Italians of New York City, 1890-1914." Ph.D. dissertation, University of North Carolina at Chapel Hill, 1971. 433 p.

Examines the "southern Italian backgrounds, causes of immigration, city settlement patterns, urban crime and Italians, the
political, economic and religious adjustments of Italians and
the new-world ethnic community" to "ascertain the impact of
an American urban environment upon immigrants possessing an
alien, rural culture...."

475 Rolle, Andrew F. THE AMERICAN ITALIANS: THEIR HISTORY AND CULTURE. Belmont, Calif.: Wadsworth, 1972. 122 p. Index.

A brief survey of Italian immigration from colonial times to the present. Gives special emphasis to Italians in the American West and those who antedated the mass migration after 1890.

476 _____. THE IMMIGRANT UPRAISED: ITALIAN ADVENTURERS AND COLONISTS IN AN EXPANDING AMERICA. Norman: University of Oklahoma Press, 1968. 338 p. Appendices, bibliography, index.

Focuses on those Italian immigrants who generally arrived before the mass migration and settled in the West. Concludes that they assimilated and prospered, while retaining much of their old world culture.

477 _____. "The Italian Moves Westward." MONTANA: THE MAGAZINE OF WESTERN HISTORY 16 (1966): 13-24.

Discusses Italian immigration to Montana in the person of Jesuit missionaries, businessmen, and miners. Finds few Italians engaged in agriculture or ranching.

478 Rose, Philip M. THE ITALIANS IN AMERICA: THE ITALIAN AMERICAN EXPERIENCE. 1922. Reprint. New York: Arno Press, 1975. 155 p. Appendices, bibliography, index.

This book, written by the pastor of the First Italian Congregational Church of Hartford, Connecticut, attributes the difficulties of Italian immigrants to their Catholic faith and "socialistic" tendencies. Sees sympathetic work among them by Protestant churches as the most mutually beneficial approach.

479 Scarpaci, Jean. "Italian Immigrants in Louisiana's Sugar Parishes: Recruitment, Labor Conditions and Community Relations, 1880-1910." Ph.D. dissertation, Rutgers University, 1972.

Discusses the efforts of Louisiana sugar planters to attract 16,000 to 80,000 Sicilian laborers as field hands. Notes that most did not remain long in Louisiana and that those who did worked in retail and agriculturally related occupations, largely maintaining their group cohesiveness and ethnic identity into the twentieth century.

480 Schiavo, Giovanni. ITALIANS IN AMERICA BEFORE THE CIVIL WAR. New York: Virgo Press, under the auspices of the Italian Historical Society, 1934. 399 p. Synoptic table, appendices, bibliography.

Although not arranged in a strictly chronological framework, the book discusses the role of Italians in discovering and exploring the New World and includes examples of Italians in

the seventeenth century. The last half of the book deals with
the period 1800 to 1860 and illustrates the variety of Italian
immigrants who came during that period.

481 _____. THE ITALIANS IN CHICAGO, A STUDY IN AMERICANIZA-
TION. Chicago: Italian American Publishing Co., 1928. 207 p. Illustrations.

Examines all phases of Italian-American life in Chicago, especially immigrants who lived in strictly "American" neighborhoods and prospered in business or the professions.

482 Sheridan, Frank J. ITALIAN, SLAVIC AND HUNGARIAN UNSKILLED
IMMIGRANT LABORERS IN THE UNITED STATES. 1907. Reprint. New
York: Jerome S. Ozer, 1971. Pp. 403-86. Tables.

Part of Ozer's "American Immigration Library." A study of
"immigrant laborers and their selection of certain states for
special industrial activity, the demand for their services, their
wages, their methods and costs of living compared with American standards and costs of living, and their segregated system
of living and employment and its effect upon them and upon
their assimilation."

483 Stella, Antonio. SOME ASPECTS OF ITALIAN IMMIGRATION TO THE
UNITED STATES. New York: G.P. Putnam's Sons, 1924. 124 p. Illustrations, tables, appendix, footnotes, bibliography.

Written by a defender of Italian immigration in a period of
popular calls for immigration restriction, this study makes use
of census data and other government publications. This is
the published version of remarks the author presented to the
New York Society of Medical Jurisprudence on "the relation
of the immigrant to public health and the welfare of the nation generally."

484 Tait, Joseph Wilfrid. SOME ASPECTS OF THE EFFECT OF THE DOMI-
NANT AMERICAN CULTURE UPON CHILDREN OF ITALIAN-BORN
PARENTS. 1942. Reprint. Clifton, N.J.: Augustus M. Kelley, 1972.
74 p. Tables, appendices, footnotes, bibliography.

Based on tests and questionnaires of some 2,000 eleven- to
fifteen-year-old students along the East Coast. This book
hypothesizes that Italian children have a better adjustment,
lesser degree of inferiority, and more emotional stability the
less they associate with American-born children.

485 Tomasi, Lydio F. THE ITALIAN AMERICAN FAMILY. Staten Island, N.Y.:
Center for Migration Studies, 1972. 43 p. Tables, notes, figures.

Traces the evolution of the Italian-American family through

its first three generations and discusses the interaction between the individual, the family, and society.

486 _____, ed. THE ITALIAN IN AMERICA: THE PROGRESSIVE VIEW, 1891-1914. New York: Center for Migration Studies, 1972. 221 p. Maps, illustrations, tables, notes.

Collection of articles, largely by settlement house workers, originally published in journals of social work, on a wide variety of aspects of Italian-American life.

487 Tomasi, Mari. "The Italian Story in Vermont." VERMONT HISTORY 28 (1960): 73-87.

Notes, with many individual examples, that Italian immigrants to Vermont were mostly stonecutters and sculptors from northern Italy who came to work in the state's quarries. Discusses their problems of adjustment and relationship with earlier settlers.

488 Tomasi, Silvano M. THE ITALIANS IN AMERICA. Occasional Paper. New York: Istituto Italiano di Cultura, 1971. 6 p.

Bibliographical essay on sources for the study of Italian emigration and the Italian-American experience.

489 _____. PIETY AND POWER: THE ROLE OF ITALIAN PARISHES IN THE NEW YORK METROPOLITAN AREA (1880-1930). Staten Island, N.Y.: Center for Migration Studies, 1975. 185 p. Bibliography.

Deals with the background of Italian immigrants, varying interpretations of their American experience, and with the role played by the Italian national parish as an institution to help them cope with the urban environment.

490 Tomasi, Silvano M., and Engel, Madeline H., eds. THE ITALIAN EXPERIENCE IN THE UNITED STATES. Staten Island, N.Y.: Center for Migration Studies, 1970. 239 p. Footnotes, bibliography.

Collection of studies by ten scholars on the settlement patterns, institutions, political activity, religion, and return migration of Italian Americans. A selected bibliography follows each article.

491 U.S. Bureau of Labor. THE ITALIANS IN CHICAGO. Prepared under the direction of Carroll D. Wright, Commissioner of Labor. Washington, D.C.: Government Printing Office, 1897. 403 p.

Statistical tables dealing with social and economic conditions of Chicago Italians, including their literacy, school attendance, birth rates, wages, hours and conditions of labor, and voting frequency.

492   Vecoli, Rudolph J. "Chicago's Italians Prior to World War I: A Study
       of Their Social and Economic Adjustment." Ph.D. dissertation, University
       of Wisconsin, 1963. 495 p.

       Concludes that although Chicago generally welcomed immi-
       grants, Italians were the object of discrimination, especially
       by organized labor. These early twentieth-century Italians
       were peasants from southern Italy and were thus poorly suited
       for life in an urban center. Few were employed in Chicago's
       industries, but many worked on railroad construction.

493   _____. "The Contadini in Chicago: A Critique of THE UPROOTED."
       JOURNAL OF AMERICAN HISTORY 51 (1964): 404-17.

       Utilizes experience of Chicago's Sicilian Americans to dispute
       notion that New Immigrants were decimated by urban-indus-
       trial life. Argues that the cultural heritage of the rural south-
       ern Italian immigrants was successfully resistant to pressures
       for assimilation in Chicago.

494   Whyte, William F. STREET CORNER SOCIETY: SOCIAL STRUCTURE OF
       AN ITALIAN SLUM. Chicago: University of Chicago Press, 1955.
       278 p. Illustrations, index.

       Classic sociological investigation of "Cornerville," the Italian
       section of "Eastern City," which focuses on the structure and
       behavior of street gangs and their preparation for careers in
       the rackets and politics.

495   Williams, Phyllis H. SOUTH ITALIAN FOLKWAYS IN EUROPE AND
       AMERICA: A HANDBOOK FOR SOCIAL WORKERS, VISITING NURSES,
       SCHOOL TEACHERS AND PHYSICIANS. New Haven, Conn.: Yale
       University Press, 1938. 216 p. Illustrations, footnotes, index.

       This "is a pragmatically structured handbook of comparative
       social anthropology which presents a detailed overview of south
       Italian cultural attributes in capsuled areas of social behavior
       and interaction (Employment, Housing, Marriage and the Fami-
       ly, Education, etc.), and then relates these to the American
       society to which they had been transplanted."

496   Yans-McLaughlin, Virginia. "A Flexible Tradition: South Italian Immi-
       grants Confront a New Work Experience." JOURNAL OF SOCIAL HIS-
       TORY 7 (1974): 429-45.

       Argues that the factory system in New York canneries and
       other businesses had a much less devastating effect upon south-
       ern Italian culture, and especially family relationships, than
       is usually alleged. Asserts that canneries permitted families
       to work together and that homework also permitted continuance
       of that tradition.

497 _____. "Patterns of Work and Family Organization: Buffalo's Italians."
JOURNAL OF INTER-DISCIPLINARY HISTORY 5 (1971): 299-314.

Based upon an investigation of female occupational patterns
and family organization among Buffalo's Italian Americans between 1900 and 1930, from which the author concludes that
working wives did not necessarily alter family power arrange-
ments or disrupt the traditional family. Concludes that gen-
eralization of the impact of female labor upon family arrange-
ments must be qualified by class, ethnic and religious background, region, and city.

JEWS

498 Berman, Hyman. "A Cursory View of the Jewish Labor Movement: An
Historiographical Survey." AMERICAN JEWISH HISTORICAL QUARTERLY
52 (1962): 79-97.

Sees the Jewish labor movement as part of the total ethnocultural adjustment to the American environment and argues for
new histories of its components "through the eyes of the worker."

499 Berman, Myron. "The Attitude of American Jewry Towards East European Jewish Immigration, 1881-1914." Ph.D. dissertation, Columbia
University, 1963. 585 p.

The three parts of this dissertation deal successively with the
American-Jewish community's reaction to East European Jewish
immigration, the reaction to nativism and immigration restriction, and the institutions created by the older Jewish community to encourage assimilation of the new Jewish arrivals.

500 Bernheimer, Charles Seligman. RUSSIAN JEWS IN THE UNITED STATES.
Philadelphia and Chicago: J.C. Winston Co., 1905. 415 p. Maps,
reading list, index.

Collection of pieces by several authors analyzing the Russian-
Jewish communities in New York, Philadelphia, and Chicago
with respect to philanthropy, economy, religion, education,
politics, amusements, health and sanitation, and the law.

501 Birmingham, Stephen. "OUR CROWD"; THE GREAT JEWISH FAMILIES
OF NEW YORK. New York: Harper & Row, 1967. 404 p. Illustrations, genealogy tables, facsimile.

Details the social history of the great German-Jewish banking
families of New York City from their arrival in the United
States in the 1830s to their dispersal in the post-World War II
years.

502   Blau, Joseph L., and Baron, Salo W., eds. THE JEWS OF THE UNITED STATES, 1790-1840: A DOCUMENTARY HISTORY. 3 vols. New York: Columbia University Press, 1963. 1,034 p. Notes, index.

Over 300 documents arranged chronologically in three volumes, with introductions to each document and general introductions to each major section: "The Place of the Jews in American Life," "Economic Life," "The Family and Social Life," "The First Jews in American Politics," "Stirrings of Cultural Activity," "The Strains of Religious Adjustment," "Christian and Jew," "Widening Geographic Horizons" and "American Jews and World Jewry."

503   Breck, Allen duPont. THE CENTENNIAL HISTORY OF THE JEWS OF COLORADO, 1859-1959. Denver: University of Denver, 1960. 360 p. Illustrations, appendices, notes, sources, index.

In 1954 the Jewish Tercentenary Committee of Colorado suggested the writing of a history of the Jews in the Rocky Mountain Region. Breck wrote the volume for Colorado. It is a chronological treatment, beginning with territorial settlement in the 1850s, through statehood and ending in 1959. German Jews and Eastern European Jews receive special treatment. Most of the fifty-one illustrations are of individual Jews who figure prominently in the story.

504   Brody, David. "American Jewry, the Refugees and Immigration Restriction, 1932-1942." PUBLICATIONS OF THE AMERICAN JEWISH HISTORICAL SOCIETY 45 (1956): 219-47.

Attempts "to define the Jewish attitudes and efforts concerned with American restrictive policy from 1932 to 1942...[and]... to uncover the causes behind the positions taken."

505   Chyet, Stanley F. "The Political Rights of the Jews in the United States, 1776-1840." AMERICAN JEWISH ARCHIVES 10 (1958): 14-75.

Explores the changing attitudes of various American states toward the rights of Jews and compares the realities to the actual statements in state constitutions and bills of rights.

506   Cogan, Sara G., comp. THE JEWS OF SAN FRANCISCO & THE GREATER BAY AREA, 1849-1919: AN ANNOTATED BIBLIOGRAPHY. Foreword by Moses Rischin. Western Jewish Americana Series, publication 2. Berkeley, Calif.: Western Jewish History Center, Judah L. Magnes Memorial Museum, 1973. 127 p. Index.

A selective and annotated bibliography which includes primary material from 1849 to 1919 and secondary material without restriction and totals over 600 entries. Geographically, the book includes material from Alameda, Contra Costa, Marin, San Mateo, Santa Clara, and Sonoma Counties.

507 Cohen, George. THE JEW IN THE MAKING OF AMERICA. Boston: Stratford Co., 1924. 274 p. Tables, index.

Chapters cover Jewish contributions to America's wars, economic life, theater, literature, music, art, science, public, and religious life. Final chapter deals with the psychology of the Jew.

508 Cross, Robert D. "Some Reflections on Jewish Immigration." AMERICAN JEWISH HISTORICAL QUARTERLY 56 (1966): 143-50.

Argues for studying Jewish immigration as the product of centuries of history as a self-conscious minority rather than as the creation of a few outstanding individuals.

509 Davis, Moshe, and Meyer, Isidore S., eds. THE WRITING OF AMERICAN JEWISH HISTORY. New York: American Jewish Historical Society, 1957. 464 p. Footnotes, index.

A series of essays and discussions of the Conference of Historians on the Writing of American Jewish History in 1954 organized around four general topics: local and regional history, economic history, immigration, and biography. Immigration essays were written by Robert Ernst, Arthur Mann, Clement Mihanovich, John O'Grady, Harry Rosenfield, and Bernard Weinryb.

510 Dinnerstein, Leonard. THE LEO FRANK CASE. New York: Columbia University Press, 1970. 248 p. Illustrations, appendices, notes, bibliography, index.

The celebrated case of Leo Frank, a northern Jewish industrialist who was convicted of murdering a thirteen-year-old working girl in Georgia in the pre-World War I period. Author sees this case as representative of the fear and reactions of rural Protestant Southerners to the industrialization and urbanization of their region.

511 Dinnerstein, Leonard, and Palsson, Mary Dale, eds. JEWS IN THE SOUTH. Baton Rouge: Louisiana State University Press, 1973. 392 p. Footnotes, bibliographical essay.

A series of essays arranged in five chronological sections chosen "to show the problems encountered by the Jews, their successes, what they thought about their life in this region and what other Southerners thought about them."

512 Edidin, Ben M. JEWISH COMMUNITY LIFE IN AMERICA. New York: Hebrew Publishing Co., 1947. 282 p. Charts, graphs, references, selected bibliography, index.

A contemporary survey, with some historical background to Jewish group life: "its structure and composition, its agencies, institutions and organizations, its activities and functions, its needs and problems, and its purposes and aspirations."

513 Eisenstadt, Shmuel Noah. THE ABSORPTION OF IMMIGRANTS: A COMPARATIVE STUDY BASED MAINLY ON THE JEWISH COMMUNITY IN PALESTINE AND THE STATE OF ISRAEL. London: Routledge & Kegan Paul, 1954. 275 p. Footnotes, bibliography, index.

A monograph with a twofold purpose: to analyze the process of absorption of successive waves of immigration into Palestine and Israel and secondly, "to provide a systematic sociological framework for the analysis of migration and the absorption of immigrants in modern societies." His analysis of case studies of modern migration includes some material on the United States.

514 Elovitz, Mark H. A CENTURY OF JEWISH LIFE IN DIXIE: THE BIRMINGHAM EXPERIENCE. Birmingham: University of Alabama Press, 1974. 258 p. Appendices, notes, sources, index.

Recounts the formation and evolution of the city's synagogues, enumerates the accomplishments of prominent Jewish civic and religious leaders, and discusses the contributions Jews have made to the cultural and economic development of the city from 1871 to 1971. Written by a rabbi and historian.

515 Epstein, Melech. JEWISH LABOR IN U.S.A.: AN INDUSTRIAL, POLITICAL AND CULTURAL HISTORY OF THE JEWISH LABOR MOVEMENT, 1882-1952. New York: Ktav Publishing House, 1969. 457 p.

Author sees three features of Jewish labor: (1) its veterans were "militant adherents of radical beliefs"; (2) "ideological and political beginnings preceded industrial organization"; and (3) "young intellectuals had a decisive part in its formative stages."

516 ESSAYS IN AMERICAN JEWISH HISTORY, TO COMMEMORATE THE TENTH ANNIVERSARY OF THE FOUNDING OF THE AMERICAN JEWISH ARCHIVES UNDER THE DIRECTION OF JACOB RADER MARCUS. Publications of the American Jewish Archives, no. 5. Cincinnati: American Jewish Archives, 1958. 538 p. Illustrations, notes, index.

Relevant essays deal with Jewish assimilation in the United States before 1840, German-Jewish emigration after 1815, and a synthesis of American-Jewish history along with annotated documents on different aspects of Jewish history. A bibliography of Jacob R. Marcus's writings is included.

517 Feingold, Henry L. ZION IN AMERICA: THE JEWISH EXPERIENCE FROM COLONIAL TIMES TO THE PRESENT. New York: Twayne, 1974. 375 p. Notes, bibliography, index.

Chronicles the Jewish experience in America since colonial times, concentrating upon economic and political assimilation, religious adaptation and change, and intergroup and intragroup relations. Little emphasis upon cultural questions.

518   Freund, Miriam K. "Each Man's Country: A Nation of Immigrants." AMERICAN JEWISH HISTORICAL QUARTERLY 55 (1965): 137-49.

Surveys Jewish immigration to the United States over the past three centuries. Describes the melting pot model and emphasizes the notion of pluralism as the keystone of American ideals.

519   Friedman, Lee M. PILGRIMS IN A NEW LAND. Philadelphia: Jewish Publication Society of America, 1948. 471 p. Illustrations, notes, bibliography, index.

A selective history of Jews in America from colonial days to the twentieth century. It includes some information on the process of adjustment and the role of Jews in American economic life.

520   Fuchs, Lawrence H. THE POLITICAL BEHAVIOR OF AMERICAN JEWS. Glencoe, Ill.: Free Press, 1956. 204 p. Methodological note, bibliographical notes, index.

Explores the reasons for political behavior and styles of Jews, their liberalism, Democratic affiliation, internationalism, flirtation with socialism and other minor parties, and their proclivity toward ticket splitting.

521   Gerstein, Arnold Aaron. "The American Reform Rabbi and the East European Jewish Immigrant, 1890-1922." Ph.D. dissertation, University of Minnesota, 1971. 488 p.

Investigates "the urban ethnic conflict between a Jewish haute bourgeois class, the Reform Clergy and the East European immigrant elite." This latter group, comprised of Conservative, Orthodox, Socialist, and Yiddish-speaking Jews actively opposed assimilation efforts by older Jewish Americans who were mainly of German descent.

522   Glanz, Rudolf. THE GERMAN JEW IN AMERICA: AN ANNOTATED BIBLIOGRAPHY. New York: Hebrew Union College, 1968. 192 p. Pamphlets, articles.

Contains material about German Jews and their relation to the German-American community organized under five major headings: immigration and acculturation to American life, their place in the German-American community, their independent existence as Jews, biographies of prominent members, and comparison with the achievements of other immigrant groups.

523 _____. JEWS OF CALIFORNIA: FROM THE DISCOVERY OF GOLD
UNTIL 1880. New York: Rudolf Glanz and the Southern California
Jewish Historical Society, 1960. 188 p. Notes, index.

Discusses motives for Jewish immigration to California in the
period 1848-1880 and assesses their cultural, political, and
economic contributions to the state.

524 Glazer, Nathan. AMERICAN JUDAISM. Chicago: University of Chicago Press, 1960. 150 p. Appendices, notes, suggested reading, important dates, index.

Traces historical evolution of Judaism from colonial Sephardim,
through German reformers and conservatives, down to eastern
European Orthodox and their interaction to form the present
American Judaism.

525 Golden, Harry L., and Rywell, Martin. JEWS IN AMERICAN HISTORY:
THEIR CONTRIBUTION TO THE UNITED STATES OF AMERICA. Charlotte, N.C.: Henry Lewis Martin Co., 1950. 498 p. Resources, bibliography, index.

Essentially a biographical directory of prominent Jews in
America who have established a name in the sciences, humanities, politics, and professions.

526 Goldstein, Judith. "Ethnic Politics: The American Jewish Committee as
Lobbyist, 1915-1917." AMERICAN JEWISH HISTORICAL QUARTERLY 65
(1975): 36-58.

Contends that the American Jewish Committee, outraged by
Russian pogroms, sought to influence American foreign policy
and to prevent the passage of the 1917 Literacy Test Act.
Feels that they were frustrated by America's fear about the
postwar world.

527 _____. "The Politics of Ethnic Pressure: The American Jewish Committee as Lobbyist, 1906-1917." Ph.D. dissertation, Columbia University,
1972. 358 p.

Emphasizes that although German Jews in America consistently
excluded Russian Jews from the American Jewish Committee,
"the historical record reveals that the leaders of the AJC
used their impressive financial resources, their social status
and the resulting access to men in government to try to solve
the Jewish problem in Russia and to fight the restrictionist
movement in the United States."

528 Goodman, Abram V. AMERICAN OVERTURE. Philadelphia: Jewish
Publication Society of America, 1947. 264 p. Illustrations, notes, bibliography, index.

A published dissertation which traces the struggle of American Jews for equal rights during the colonial period and celebrates its recognition, at least in principle, by the Constitution. Sees America as pushed and pulled between the contrasting forces of tribal fanaticism and neighborly understanding, which accounted for ambivalent attitudes toward minorities.

529   Goren, Arthur A. NEW YORK JEWS AND THE QUEST FOR COMMUNI-
      TY: THE KEHILLAH EXPERIMENT, 1908-1922. New York: Columbia
      University Press, 1970. 361 p. Notes, note on sources, bibliography,
      index.

      A study of Jewish immigrants' attempts both to maintain their
      ethnic integrity and at the same time to integrate into the
      larger social setting. Goren focuses on the rise and decline
      of the New York Kehillah (community) during the second
      decade of the twentieth century.

530   Gorenstein, Arthur. "A Portrait of Ethnic Politics." AMERICAN JEWISH
      HISTORICAL QUARTERLY 50 (1961): 202-38.

      Argues that the eventual success of the Socialists on New
      York's lower East Side flowed from their gradual recognition
      of and identification with the peculiar ethnic interests of the
      district's inhabitants.

531   Gottlieb, Moshe. "The Anti-Nazi Boycott Movement in the American
      Jewish Community, 1933-1941." Ph.D. dissertation, Brandeis University,
      1967. 547 p.

      Analyzes "the ideological issues involved in the boycott move-
      ment, the divisions and alignments it produced in the American
      Jewish community and the pressure tactics that it employed
      against recalcitrant offenders." The Non-Sectarian Anti-Nazi
      League to Champion Human Rights and the Joint Boycott Coun-
      cil were America's principal boycott organizations.

532   Grinstein, Hyman B. RISE OF JEWISH COMMUNITY OF NEW YORK,
      1654-1860. Philadelphia: Jewish Publication Society of America, 1945.
      645 p. Illustrations, appendix, notes, bibliography, index.

      Primarily concerned with the institutions, religion, and cul-
      ture of the Jews of New York City and "with the social, phil-
      anthropic and other activities which grew out of their living
      together in a Jewish community." Although the study covers
      from colonial times to the Civil War, most of the book is
      devoted to the second quarter of the nineteenth century.

533   Guttmann, Allen. THE JEWISH WRITER IN AMERICA: ASSIMILATION
      AND THE CRISIS OF IDENTITY. New York: Oxford University Press,

1971. 256 p. Notes, supplementary bibliography, index.
After an introduction which defines terms and surveys the history of Jews in America, turns to a discussion of prominent Jewish writers from the 1880s to the present, treating the works and influence of nearly two dozen writers from Emma Lazarus to Saul Bellow.

534 Handlin, Oscar. ADVENTURE IN FREEDOM: THREE HUNDRED YEARS OF JEWISH LIFE IN AMERICA. New York: McGraw-Hill, 1954. 262 p. Illustrations, glossary, bibliography, index.

Surveys Jewish life in America from 1654 to 1954, with emphasis on communal life and reaction to persistent anti-Semitism.

535 Higham, John. "Social Discrimination Against Jews in America, 1830-1930." PUBLICATIONS OF THE AMERICAN JEWISH HISTORICAL SOCIETY 47 (1957): 1-33.

Attempts to answer such questions as why and when discrimination has increased, how discrimination against other minorities is similar to or different from the Jewish experience, and what role intellectual and political doctrines have played in social discrimination.

536 Hirschler, Eric E., ed. JEWS FROM GERMANY IN THE UNITED STATES. New York: Farrar, Straus and Co., 1955. 182 p. Appendices, notes.

A compilation of five articles on German Jews in America by Selma Stern-Taeubler, Eric E. Hirshler, Bernard D. Weinryb, Adolf Kober, and Albert H. Friedlander. Essays of particular interest deal with immigration and the cultural contributions of German Jews.

537 Jacobs, Joseph. THE JEWISH PRESS IN AMERICA. New York: Joseph Jacobs Organization, 1970. 140 p.

Annotated bibliography of the Jewish press in the United States and Canada. Includes analysis of U.S. market for Jewish products, history of Jewish press, and Yiddish-English dictionary.

538 Janowsky, Oscar I., ed. THE AMERICAN JEW: A REAPPRAISAL. Philadelphia: Jewish Publication Society of America, 1964. 468 p. Notes, bibliography, index.

Chapters written by nearly two dozen authors who attempt to identify American Jewry, "to explain how it became what it is today and how it functions through its institutions and services; to analyze the special features which distinguish it as a group in demographic, economic and social patterns, in religion and education, in currents of thought and cultural expression, in philanthropic motivation and in conceptions and efforts to further its continuance and welfare."

539 Joseph, Samuel. JEWISH IMMIGRATION TO THE UNITED STATES FROM 1881-1910. 1914. Reprint. New York: Arno Press, 1969. 209 p. Statistical tables, footnotes, bibliography.

A political science dissertation at Columbia University which is largely a statistical and comparative study of the "causes of Jewish emigration from Eastern Europe, the course of Jewish immigration to the United States and the most important social qualities of the Jewish immigrants...."

540 Karp, Abraham J., ed. THE JEWISH EXPERIENCE IN AMERICA: SE-LECTED STUDIES FROM THE PUBLICATIONS OF THE AMERICAN JEWISH HISTORICAL SOCIETY. Vol. 1: THE COLONIAL PERIOD. 455 p. Footnotes, index. Vol. 2: THE EARLY REPUBLIC. 399 p. Illustrations, footnotes, index. Vol. 3: THE EMERGING COMMUNITY. 417 p. Illustrations, footnotes, index. Vol. 4: THE ERA OF IMMIGRATION. 422 p. Illustrations, footnotes, index. Vol. 5: AT HOME IN AMERI-CA. 440 p. Illustrations, footnotes, index. New York: KTAV, 1969.

A selection of chronologically arranged articles taken from the fifty-seven volumes of the PUBLICATIONS OF THE AMERICAN JEWISH HISTORICAL SOCIETY and the AMERICAN JEWISH HISTORICAL QUARTERLY and with a general introduction to each volume by the editor. Although the quality of the articles is uneven, there are relevant articles in each volume, especially volumes 4 and 5.

541 Kligsberg, Moses. "Jewish Immigrants in Business; A Sociological Study." AMERICAN JEWISH HISTORICAL QUARTERLY 56 (1967): 283-311.

Case histories of three turn-of-the-century Eastern European Jewish immigrants who were successful in business. Concludes that the Yiddishkeit manifested in transmitted folkways, mores, and living styles, and their desire to rise in the world and pass an improved status on to their children were the driving forces in their material success.

542 Korn, Bertram Wallace. AMERICAN JEWRY AND THE CIVIL WAR. Philadelphia: Jewish Publication Society of America, 1951. 331 p. Illustrations, notes, bibliography, index.

Studies Jewish support for the war effort, North and South; the attitudes of Jewish leaders on slavery, secession, war, prejudice against Jews; and the influence of the war experiences on the Jewish community.

543 _____. EVENTFUL YEARS AND EXPERIENCES: NINETEENTH CEN-

TURY AMERICAN JEWISH HISTORY. Cincinnati: American Jewish Archives, 1954. 249 p. Notes, index.

Deals primarily with the Jews in the middle of the nineteenth century, including the Jewish "forty-eighters," the Know-Nothing movement, the establishment of the first American Jewish Theological Seminary, and Jewish welfare activities during the Spanish-American War.

544 Kramer, Judith R., and Leventmen, Seymour. CHILDREN OF THE GILDED GHETTO: CONFLICT RESOLUTIONS OF THREE GENERATIONS OF AMERICAN JEWS. New Haven, Conn.: Yale University Press, 1961. 228 p. Tables, footnotes, bibliography, index.

A sociological study of the Jewish community of a midwestern city as representative of the minority situation of American Jews. It samples 100 individuals from each of three generations to determine their class, status, and conflicts within the dominant culture. Contends that Jews have moved from an ethnic to a status-oriented community because of occupational advancement.

545 Kramer, William M., and Stern, Norton B. "Anti-Semitism and the Jewish Image in the Early West." WESTERN STATES JEWISH HISTORICAL QUARTERLY 6 (1974): 129-40.

Describes examples of anti-Semitism in the early West, especially in newspaper accounts, but concludes that frontier democracy and fellowship among white people tended to minimize its impact.

546 Learsi, Rufus [Israel Goldberg]. THE JEWS IN AMERICA: A HISTORY. Cleveland: World Publishing Co., 1954. 382 p. Illustrations, bibliographical notes, index.

A chronological history from colonial times to the present with emphasis on the period from 1880.

547 Lebeson, Anita L. JEWISH PIONEERS IN AMERICA, 1492-1848. New York: Brentano's, 1931. 372 p. Illustrations, notes, bibliography.

A Jewish Book Club selection intended for the general reader. Focuses primarily on the pre-Revolutionary period and includes material on the founding of the earliest congregations, the movement west with the frontier, and the role of the Jew in commerce.

548 Levinger, Rabbi Lee J. A HISTORY OF THE JEWS IN THE UNITED STATES. Cincinnati: Union of American Hebrew Congregations, Department of Synagogue and School Extension, 1930. 543 p. Illustrations, bibliography.

A high school text for use in Jewish religious schools. Based
on secondary sources, covering the range of the Jewish experience in America.

549   Marcus, Jacob Rader. EARLY AMERICAN JEWRY: THE JEWS OF NEW
YORK, NEW ENGLAND AND CANADA, 1649-1794. Philadelphia:
Jewish Publication Society of America, 1951-1952. 301 p. Illustrations,
notes, index.

First of a projected two-volume study of early Jewish life
during the Sephardic period, when Spanish-Portuguese Jews
settled in America. Based on personal letters and petitions.

550   _____, ed. AMERICAN JEWRY: DOCUMENTS, EIGHTEENTH CEN-
TURY. Publications of the American Jewish Archives, no. 3. Cincinnati: Hebrew Union College Press, 1959. 492 p. Index.

Divided into four topical sections: personal life, religious life,
the general community, and commerce and trade. Makes extensive use of unpublished manuscripts.

551   _____. THE COLONIAL AMERICAN JEW: 1492-1776. 3 vols. Detroit: Wayne State University Press, 1970. 1,650 p. Illustrations,
notes, bibliographical notes, index.

Eight major sections comprise these volumes: "a sketch of the
Near Eastern and European Jewish backgrounds; the Jewish
settlements in Spain, South America, Mexico and the West
Indies; the settlements in New Netherland; the settlements in
British North America; the legal and political status of Jews
in British North America; the economic activities of Jews in
North America; religion, social welfare and education in the
lives of North American Jews; and a description and assessment of the relationship of Jews to the larger North American
community."

552   _____. CRITICAL STUDIES IN AMERICAN JEWISH HISTORY: SE-
LECTED ARTICLES FROM AMERICAN JEWISH ARCHIVES. 3 vols. New
York: KTAV Publishing House, 1971. 296 p., 260 p., 373 p.

Thirty-six articles selected from the past twenty years of
AMERICAN JEWISH ARCHIVES. The first two volumes con-
centrate on the pre-twentieth-century period. Many articles
are biographical or religious, but others deal with the Jew
as immigrant, reformer, and as the object of discrimination.

553   _____. JEWISH AMERICANA. Monographs of the American Jewish
Archives, no. 1. Cincinnati: American Jewish Archives, 1954. 115 p.
Index.

"A catalogue of books and articles by Jews or relating to them printed in the United States from the earliest days to 1850 and found in the library of the Hebrew Union College-Jewish Institute of Religion in Cincinnati." Intended as a supplement to A.S.W. Rosenbach's AN AMERICAN JEWISH BIBLIOGRA-PHY. Includes 227 entries, almost exclusively from the nineteenth century.

554 Meltzer, Milton. REMEMBER THE DAYS: A SHORT HISTORY OF THE JEWISH AMERICAN. Garden City, N.Y.: Doubleday and Co., 1974. 114 p. Index.

Traces the waves of Jewish immigration from colonial times to the present, residential and occupational patterns, self-help organizations, and reactions to prejudice and discrimination. Speculates on the future of Jewish Americans and their relation to Zionism.

555 Neuringer, Sheldon Morris. "American Jewry and United States Immigration Policy, 1881-1953." Ph.D. dissertation, University of Wisconsin, 1969. 491 p.

Describes the Jewish response (1) to the arrival of East European Jews and accompanying attempts to control the flow; (2) to the use of literacy tests; (3) to quota legislation; (4) to efforts to admit refugees from Nazi Germany; (5) to the question of displaced persons; and (6) to efforts to modify the quota system in the early 1950s.

556 Panitz, Esther L. "In Defense of the Jewish Immigrant, 1891-1924." AMERICAN JEWISH HISTORICAL QUARTERLY 55 (1965): 57-97.

Shows that at the time the United States moved toward a restrictionist policy, prominent Jewish leaders, such as Simon Wolf, Max Kohler, and Louis Marshall, tried to eliminate or modify quotas and restrictionist legislation.

557 _____. "Polarity of Jewish Attitudes to Immigration." AMERICAN JEWISH HISTORICAL QUARTERLY 53 (1963): 99-130.

Uses letters, communications, and other documents to illustrate the opposition of official German-Jewish organizations in America toward Eastern European Jewish immigrants until outside antipathy to all Jews united the two groups.

558 Peters, Madison C. JEWS IN AMERICA: A SHORT STORY OF THEIR PART IN THE BUILDING OF THE REPUBLIC. Philadelphia: John C. Winston Co., 1905. 138 p. Illustrations.

Mainly a survey of Jewish contributions to American politics, finance, arts, sciences, and defense of the United States in war. Concludes with a discussion of Jewish characteristics and anti-Semitism.

559 Plaut, W. Gunther. JEWS IN MINNESOTA: THE FIRST SEVENTY-FIVE
YEARS. American Jewish Communal Histories, vol. 3. New York:
American Jewish Historical Society, 1959. 347 p. Appendices, notes,
glossary, sources, index.

Deals with Minnesota from pioneering days until the 1920s.
A few selected subjects, such as anti-Semitism, extend beyond
the 1920s. The interaction between "old" and "new" Jewish
immigrants is developed.

560 Pool, David de Sola. PORTRAITS ETCHED IN STONE: EARLY JEWISH
SETTLERS, 1682-1831. New York: Columbia University Press, 1952.
543 p. Appendices, footnotes, glossary, bibliography, index.

Contains a history of the Chatham Square Cemetery of New
York and biographies of 179 people buried there.

561 Rappaport, Joseph. "Jewish Immigrants and World War I: A Study of
American Yiddish Press Reactions." Ph.D. dissertation, Columbia University, 1950. 455 p.

Indicates that because many of the New Immigrants were from
Russia and had maintained ties with relatives, they saw Tsarist
Russia as the enemy in World War I. This attitude changed
after America's entry into the war, the revolutions in Russia,
the Balfour Declaration, and the Treaty of Brest-Litovsk.

562 Reissner, H.G. "The German-American Jews (1800-1850)." LEO BAECK
INSTITUTE YEARBOOK 10 (1965): 57-116.

Describes growth of the Jewish community in the United States
from 15,000 to 50,000 between 1790-1880, largely through the
influx of German immigrants. Discusses their economic, religious, and fraternal activities and provides an extensive list
of names and an up-to-date bibliography.

563 Rischin, Moses. INVENTORY OF AMERICAN JEWISH HISTORY. Cambridge, Mass.: Harvard University Press, 1954. 66 p. Footnotes, index.

A critical inventory of books, articles, and other publications,
including foreign language sources, organized in two parts:
sources of American-Jewish history followed by a chronological and topical arrangement of literature in the field.

564 _____. THE PROMISED CITY: NEW YORK'S JEWS, 1870-1914. Cambridge, Mass.: Harvard University Press, 1962. 342 p. Illustrations,
bibliography.

Traces the evolution of New York's Jewish community between
the Civil War and World War I, stressing the integration of

the Russian Jews, the growth of reform Judaism, and involvement in politics and labor unions.

565 Rockaway, Robert A. "Anti-Semitism in an American City: Detroit, 1850-1914." AMERICAN JEWISH HISTORICAL QUARTERLY 64 (1974): 42-53.

Contends that the anti-Semitism that emerged in Detroit in the 1920s and 1930s, led by Henry Ford and Father Coughlin, had its roots in the nineteenth century. Argues that it was different from that manifested in other U.S. cities and less sinister than that in Europe, but sufficiently virulent to cause anxiety among the city's Jews.

566 _____. "Ethnic Conflict in an Urban Environment: the German and Russian Jew in Detroit, 1881-1914." AMERICAN JEWISH HISTORICAL QUARTERLY 60 (1970): 133-50.

Discusses the conflict between German Jews who immigrated to the United States in the nineteenth century and the Russian Jews who immigrated later. Although the former group felt some obligation to assist the new immigrants, as the number of recent immigrants swelled, tensions between the two groups increased.

567 _____. "From Americanization to Jewish Americanism: The Jew of Detroit, 1850-1914." Ph.D. dissertation, University of Michigan, 1970. 258 p.

Analyzes the contrasting impulses of Detroit's Jews who sought to become fully Americanized at the same time they tried to perpetuate their ancient traditions. Describes the internal conflict between the older German Jews and the newer East European Jewish Immigrants.

568 Rose, Peter I. THE GHETTO AND BEYOND: ESSAYS ON JEWISH LIFE IN AMERICA. New York: Random House, 1969. 504 p. Notes.

Over twenty-five articles, most of which were previously published, dealing with the persistence of Jewish culture in America, Jewish involvement in politics, and relations with Protestants and blacks.

569 Rosenbach, Abraham S.W. AN AMERICAN JEWISH BIBLIOGRAPHY: BEING A LIST OF BOOKS AND PAMPHLETS BY JEWS OR RELATING TO THEM PRINTED IN THE UNITED STATES FROM THE ESTABLISHMENT OF THE PRESS IN THE COLONIES UNTIL 1850. Baltimore, Md.: American Jewish Historical Society and Lord Baltimore Press, 1926. 500 p. List of members, index.

An annotated bibliography of a wide variety of writings ranging from novels to dictionaries to religious tracts.

570   Rosenbloom, Joseph R.   BIOGRAPHICAL DICTIONARY OF EARLY AMERI-
       CAN JEWS THROUGH 1800.   Lexington: University of Kentucky Press,
       1960.   175 p.

       Brief biographical information about "most Jews who lived in
       America during the late seventeenth, the eighteenth, and early
       nineteenth centuries."   Purports to include "every person iden-
       tifiable as a Jew in America before 1800."

571   Shapiro, Yonathan.   LEADERSHIP OF THE AMERICAN ZIONIST ORGANI-
       ZATION 1897-1930.   Urbana: University of Illinois Press, 1971.   295 p.
       Footnotes, bibliography, index.

       A study of Zionism from the founding of the Federation of
       American Zionists in New York to the emergence of Palestin-
       ianism as the official ideology of the American Zionist Or-
       ganization by 1930.

572   Sherman, Charles Bezalel.   THE JEW WITHIN AMERICAN SOCIETY: A
       STUDY IN ETHNIC INDIVIDUALITY.   Detroit: Wayne State University
       Press, 1961.   261 p.   Tables, notes, bibliography, index.

       Concentrates on what he considers the most important period
       of American-Jewish history, the period from the 1880s to the
       present.   Stresses the unique role of Jews who have integrated
       within American society, yet retained their ethnic individuality.

573   Strauss, Herbert.   "The Immigration and Acculturation of the German Jew
       in the United States of America."   LEO BAECK INSTITUTE YEARBOOK
       16 (1971):   63-94.

       Shows that German Jews who fled Nazi Germany in the 1930s
       and came to America were quickly absorbed into American-
       Jewish society because both the new immigrant and the domi-
       nant American attitude was anti-Nazi and to a certain degree,
       anti-German.

574   Switchkow, Louis J., and Gartner, Lloyd P.   THE HISTORY OF THE
       JEWS OF MILWAUKEE.   Philadelphia: Jewish Publications Society of
       America, 1963.   355 p.   Appendix, notes, bibliography, index.

       Surveys the evolution of Milwaukee's Jewish community from
       its 1844 foundation to 1950, with emphasis on its institutions
       and interaction with the wider urban environment.

575   Szajkowksi, Zosa.   "The Attitude of American Jews to Refugees from
       Germany in the 1930s."   AMERICAN JEWISH HISTORICAL QUARTERLY
       51 (1971):   101-43.

       Compares and contrasts the work of the National Refugee Ser-
       vice and the Hebrew Immigrant Aid Society with Christian

and nonsectarian organizations. Shows that many of the plans pioneered by the NRS were later incorporated in immigration regulations.

576 Tumin, Melvin M. AN INVENTORY AND APPRAISAL OF RESEARCH ON AMERICAN ANTI-SEMITISM. New York: Freedom Books, 1961. 185 p. Notes.

A "series of digests of researches, theories and hypotheses about anti-Semitism in America." Essentially a series of thirteen detailed evaluative annotated bibliographical essays.

577 Wechman, Robert J., and Zielonka, David M. THE EAGER IMMIGRANTS: A SURVEY OF THE LIFE AND AMERICANIZATION OF JEWISH IMMI-GRANTS TO THE UNITED STATES. Champaign, Ill.: Stipes Publishing Co., 1972. 103 p. Notes, selected bibliography, index.

A chronological survey of Jewish immigration to American periodized into four units: (1) the Sephardic period--the seventeenth and eighteenth centuries, (2) the German period--1776-1880, (3) the East European period--1880-1920, and (4) the American period--1920-present.

578 Weisbord, Robert G., and Stein, Arthur. BITTERSWEET ENCOUNTER: THE AFRO-AMERICAN AND THE AMERICAN JEW. Westport, Conn.: Negro Universities Press, 1970. 242 p. Notes, bibliography, index.

Emphasizes black reactions to Jews rather than Jewish attitude toward blacks. Challenges the idea that blacks are particularly anti-Semitic by placing the black-Jewish confrontation of the 1960s in the context of the ghetto experience. There, blacks' direct experience is with the Jewish merchant whom the blacks see as representative of white exploitation.

579 Weyl, Nathaniel. THE JEW IN AMERICAN POLITICS. New Rochelle, N.Y.: Arlington House, 1968. 375 p. Bibliographical references, notes.

Notes that Jewish voters, despite their generally high education, income, and status, display overwhelmingly liberal to radical political attitudes and behavior.

580 Wolf, Edwin II, and Whiteman, Maxwell. HISTORY OF JEWS OF PHILA-DELPHIA FROM COLONIAL TIMES TO THE AGE OF JACKSON. Philadelphia: Jewish Publication Society of America, 1956. 534 p. Illustrations, notes, index.

Largely the story of individual Jews in Philadelphia during a period when they "were neither a sizable element in the city nor a decisive influence on its history."

POLES

581   Andrews, Theodore. POLISH NATIONAL CHURCH IN AMERICA AND POLAND. London: S.P.C.K., 1953. 117 p. Appendices, notes, bibliography.

An investigation of the origins, nature, expansion, doctrine, worship, and organization of the Polish National Catholic church in America, as well as its relations with the homeland and with other churches in the United States, by an Anglican priest.

582   Bolek, Francis. WHO'S WHO IN POLISH AMERICA: A BIOGRAPHICAL DIRECTORY OF POLISH AMERICAN LEADERS AND DISTINGUISHED POLES RESIDENT IN AMERICA. 1943. Reprint. New York: Arno Press, 1970. 581 p.

Contains brief biographical sketches of some 5,000 prominent Polish Americans and Poles. Also arranges them by geographic location and profession and includes a nationwide list of Polish-American organizations.

583   Brozek, Andrzej. "The Roots of Polish Migration to Texas." POLISH AMERICAN STUDIES 30 (1973): 20-35.

Investigates the oldest Polish settlements in the United States formed by emigrants from Silesia in the 1840s. Discusses the causes of their migration, their journey and settlement, and the reasons for the ending of the movement.

584   Fox, Paul. THE POLES IN AMERICA. 1922. Reprint. New York: Arno Press, 1970. 143 p. Illustrations, footnotes, brief bibliography, index.

A brief history of Poland, Polish immigration to America, and the economic and social conditions of the immigrants. Written by a Presbyterian pastor to "help America to appreciate...the spiritual wealth...of New Americans."

585   _____. THE POLISH NATIONAL CATHOLIC CHURCH. Scranton, Pa.: School of Christian Living, 1955. 146 p. Appendices.

Discusses the Church's rise and growth, the causes of its break with Rome and its essential characteristics. Appendices contain the Church's creed, mass, constitution, and parish directory.

586   Gerson, Louis L. THE AMERICAN POLES. Belmont, Calif.: Wadsworth. In preparation.

587 _____ . WOODROW WILSON AND THE REBIRTH OF POLAND, 1914-
1920: A STUDY IN THE INFLUENCE ON AMERICAN POLICY OF
MINORITY GROUPS OF FOREIGN ORIGIN. Hamden, Conn.: Archon,
1972. 139 p. Tables, appendix, notes, bibliographical essay, index.

Deals largely with the efforts of Polish Americans to influence
Wilson to bring about the recreation of Poland at the Ver-
sailles Conference and the president's rocky relations with them.

588 Golab, Carol Ann. "The Polish Communities of Philadelphia, 1870-1920:
Immigration Distribution and Adaptation in Urban America." Ph.D. dissertation, University of Pennsylvania, 1971. 480 p.

Views "immigrant adaptation as a function of spatial distribution." Seeks to explain why Philadelphia had a smaller percentage of immigrants than other northern cities.

589 Greene, Victor R. FOR GOD AND COUNTRY: THE RISE OF POLISH
AND LITHUANIAN NATIONAL CONSCIOUSNESS IN AMERICA. Madison: State Historical Society of Wisconsin, 1976. 202 p. Illustrations,
bibliography, index.

Analyzes the rise of ethnic consciousness among Polish and
Lithuanian immigrants, especially in Chicago. Deals largely
with their efforts to achieve recognition within the Catholic
church, and their attainment of a dual identity as ethnics
and Americans.

590 Irons, Peter H. "'The Test is Poland': Polish Americans and the Origins
of the Cold War." POLISH AMERICAN STUDIES 30 (1973): 5-63.

Focuses on the political composition and attitudes of Polish
Americans within the Catholic church, the labor movement,
and the Democratic party; their attempts to influence the
foreign policy of the Roosevelt and Truman administrations
toward the homeland; and the probable effects of their efforts
on U.S. actions.

591 Kantowicz, Edward. "The Emergence of the Polish-Democratic Vote in
Chicago." POLISH AMERICAN STUDIES 29 (1972): 67-80.

Text of a paper delivered before the Polish American Historical Association in New York City on December 27, 1971.
Argues that the affinity of Poles for the Democratic party
long antedates 1928 and usually approximated 70 percent.
On pages 81-85 Victor Greene presents a generally favorable
commentary but questions the validity of Kantowicz's statistics and cautions that political affiliation differs from political sensitivity.

592 Lerski, Jerzy J. POLISH CHAPTER IN JACKSONIAN AMERICA: THE

UNITED STATES AND THE POLISH EXILES OF 1831. Madison: University of Wisconsin Press, 1958. 242 p. Appendices, notes, bibliography, index.

Narrates "the saga of the Polish exiles who were welcomed in the United States as heroes of universal freedom" and describes "the deep interest and understanding of Europe shown by the leading intellectuals of Jacksonian America and their stand for the cause of enslaved Poland as though it were their own." A published dissertation.

593 Lichten, Joseph L. "Polish Americans and American Jews: Some Issues which Unite and Divide." POLISH REVIEW 18 (1973): 52-62.

Discusses the confusion over the meaning of the word "ethnic" and its relation to religious grouping, especially as applied to Polish Jews in America. Analyzes the reasons for conflict between Jews and other Polish Americans and suggests possible remedies to promote greater understanding between the two communities.

594 Madaj, M.J. "The Polish Community--A Ghetto?" POLISH AMERICAN STUDIES 25 (1968): 65-71.

Sees "the Polish city settlements as cultural communities rather than ghettos." Surveys Polish immigration to America during the nineteenth century, stressing the importance of the Polish Roman Catholic Union and the Polish National Alliance.

595 Monzell, Thomas I. "The Catholic Church and the Americanization of the Polish Immigrant." POLISH AMERICAN STUDIES 26 (1969): 1-15.

Sees Catholic efforts to organize national parishes and parochial schools for new and second generation immigrants as an attempt to preserve Polish customs and heritage while teaching American attitudes and habits. The Catholic church thus Americanized immigrant Poles.

596 Parot, Joseph. "Ethnic versus Black Metropolis: The Origins of Polish-Black Housing Tensions in Chicago." POLISH AMERICAN STUDIES 29 (1972): 5-33.

Discusses the reaction of Chicago's POLONIA to black incursions. Argues that Poles were reluctant to leave their neighborhoods because they sought to preserve cultural identity and traditions and that they moved slowly across the city rather than fleeing in panic. On pages 34-39 Rudolph Vecoli presents a generally favorable commentary on Parot's paper.

597 Pienkos, Donald. "Dimensions of Ethnicity: A Preliminary Report on the Milwaukee Polish American Population." POLISH AMERICAN STUDIES

30 (1973): 5-19.

Insists that the alleged biogtry and racism of white ethnics is due in large measure to a failure to differentiate between social class characteristics and ethnic proclivities. Studies five dimensions of ethnicity among Milwaukee's Polish Americans and finds wide variations in identification with their Polish heritage.

598 Pliszke, Stanley R. "The Polish American Community and the Rebirth of Poland." POLISH AMERICAN STUDIES 26 (1969): 41-60.

A discussion of the efforts of Polish Americans on behalf of a new Polish state formed at the end of World War I. Gives special attention to the Detroit convention of 1918 which Pliszka sees as the key to the movement.

599 Roucek, Joseph S. POLES IN THE UNITED STATES OF AMERICA. Gdynia, Poland: Blatic Institute, 1937. 64 p. Appendices, notes, tables, bibliography.

Briefly surveys the occupational distributions, demography, organizations, religion, education, press, politics, culture, and problems of assimilation of Polish immigrants.

600 Sandberg, Neil C. "The Changing Polish American." POLISH AMERICAN STUDIES 31 (1974): 5-13.

Surveys the Polish-American community in Los Angeles and concludes that sense of ethnic identification varies with length of residence, social class, and degree of Catholic religious identification. Sandberg feels that current trends such as the resurgence of ethnicity and the mobility of southern California life may significantly affect his findings.

601 Starczewska, Maria. "The Historical Geography of the Oldest Polish Settlement in the United States." POLISH REVIEW 12 (1967): 11-40.

Describes the founding of the oldest Polish settlement in the United States in Panna Moria, Texas, in 1854. Details the Old World background and the social and political organization of the first Polonia.

602 Thomas, William I., and Znaniecki, Florian. THE POLISH PEASANT IN EUROPE AND AMERICA 1918. 1927. Reprint. 2 vols. New York: Dover, 1958. 2,250 p. Index.

Classic sociological study of the Polish peasant in his native land and the difficulties of his adjustment to American life. Stresses social disorganization as manifested in marital and family problems, juvenile delinquency, violence, and sexual immorality. First volume contains almost 800 pages of selections from the correspondence of Polish peasants.

603 Thurner, Arthur W. "Polish Americans in Chicago Politics, 1890-1930." POLISH AMERICAN STUDIES 28 (1971): 20-42.

Discusses the evolution of ethnic politics among Chicago's Polish Americans. Concludes that Poles have never achieved the material benefits and status from political activity to which their numbers entitled them, largely because of Irish domination of the Democratic party.

604 Wepsiec, Jan. POLISH AMERICAN SERIAL PUBLICATIONS, 1842-1966: AN ANNOTATED BIBLIOGRAPHY. Chicago, 1968. 191 p. Bibliography, index.

A compilation of serial publications about Poles either in the United States or Poland, written in English or Polish but published in the United States. This extensive bibliography includes subject, place of publication, and editor-in-chief indices as well as 1,200 entries.

605 Wytrwal, Joseph A. POLES IN AMERICAN HISTORY AND TRADITION. Detroit: Endurance Press, 1969. 485 p. Maps, notes, bibliography, index.

A revised and updated version of the author's AMERICA'S POLISH HERITAGE: A SOCIAL HISTORY OF THE POLES IN AMERICA (1961). The book provides numerous biographical sketches of Polish Americans from colonial times to the present and in all professions and trades. Wytrwal's discussion of the causes for emigration and his treatment of the Polish Roman Catholic Union and Polish National Alliance were eliminated from the revision.

SLAVS (CZECH, RUSSIAN, SLOVAK, UKRAINIAN, SOUTH SLAVS)

606 Ardan, Ivan. "The Ruthenians in America." CHARITIES 13 (1904-5): 245-52.

Discusses briefly, economic, political, and religious causes of Ruthenian (Ukrainian) immigration. Also deals with economic, fraternal, and religious adjustment to life in the United States.

607 Balch, Emily Greene. OUR SLAVIC FELLOW CITIZEN. 1910. Reprint. New York: Arno Press, 1969. 428 p. Bibliography, index.

Based on the author's investigation of European conditions and of Slavic enclaves in the United States. Concludes with plea for understanding and assimilation of Slavs.

608 Byington, Margaret F. HOMESTEAD: THE HOUSEHOLDS OF A MILL
     TOWN. 1910. Reprint. New York: Arno Press, 1969. 292 p. Il-
     lustrations, tables, appendices, index.

     Concerned largely with the interaction between the English-
     speaking population and Slavic laborers in Homestead, a steel
     mill town adjacent to Pittsburgh. Compares their standard of
     living, family, and organizational life and discusses the ways
     in which a company town limits the role played by the family.

609 Cada, Joseph. CZECH-AMERICAN CATHOLICS, 1850-1920. Chicago:
     Center for Slav Culture, 1964. 124 p. Bibliography.

     A brief presentation of the establishment of the Catholic church
     among immigrant Czechs in America, drawn mainly from printed
     sources and covering the period from 1850 to World War I.

610 Capek, Thomas. CZECHS IN AMERICA. 1920. Reprint. New York:
     Arno Press, 1969. 293 p. Illustrations, appendix, index.

     Pioneering study by prominent Czech Americans detailing set-
     tlement and occupational patterns, political and military activ-
     ities, education and language, and fraternal and religious or-
     ganizations.

611 Chmelar, Johann. "The Austrian Emigration, 1900-1914." In DISLOCA-
     TION AND EMIGRATION: THE SOCIAL BACKGROUND OF AMERICAN
     IMMIGRATION, edited by Donald Fleming and Bernard Bailyn, pp. 275-
     378. Perspectives in American History Series, vol. 7. Cambridge, Mass.:
     Charles Warren Center for Studies in American History, 1974.

     Shows that Austro-Hungarian emigration in the early twentieth
     century was a mass movement of the agrarian proletariat, main-
     ly from the area around Galicia and Bukovina inhabited by
     Slovenes and Croats. The poor economic condition of the
     eastern and southern regions of Austria accounted for the exo-
     dus.

612 Chyz, Yaroslav J. THE UKRAINIAN IMMIGRANTS IN THE UNITED
     STATES. Scranton, Pa.: Ukrainian Workingmen's Association, 1940. 32 p.
     Notes.

     A brief survey of the Ukrainians in America, their churches,
     newspapers, fraternal organizations, cultural life, occupations,
     and geographic distribution.

613 Chyz, Yaroslav J., and Roucek, Joseph S. "Russians in the United
     States." SLAVONIC REVIEW 17 (1939): 638-58.

     Discusses the causes and magnitude of Russian migration to
     America and the difficulty of separating Russian immigrants

from other Slavic immigrants. Also deals briefly with their
religious and political organizations, periodicals, occupational
and residential distribution, and influence on American culture.

614   Claghorn, Kate Holloday. "Slavs, Magyars and Some Others in the New
       Immigration." CHARITIES 13 (1904-5): 199-205.

       Discusses the ethnic and linguistic makeup of the eastern
       European immigration to the United States, the causes of mi-
       gration, and economic and educational characteristics.

615   Davis, Jerome. THE RUSSIAN IMMIGRANT. 1922. Reprint. New
       York: Arno Press, 1969. 219 p. Appendix, footnotes, bibliography.

       A sociological treatment of Russian immigrants, surveying their
       pattern of migration, economic settlement, and religious and
       educational mores. Includes an appendix on conditions in
       Russia in the 1920s. A published dissertation.

616   _____. THE RUSSIANS AND RUTHENIANS IN AMERICA; BOLSHEVIKS
       OR BROTHERS? New York: George H. Doran Co., 1922. 155 p. Il-
       lustrations, appendices, index.

       Deals with the causes of migration, economic and social con-
       ditions, educational forces, and religious practices of Russian
       and Ruthenian (Ukrainian) immigrants. Makes recommendations
       for U.S. treatment of these groups.

617   Day, George M. THE RUSSIANS IN HOLLYWOOD: A STUDY IN CUL-
       TURE CONFLICT. Los Angeles: University of Southern California Press,
       1934. 102 p. Bibliography.

       Deals with the adjustment to life in southern California of
       some 1,500 anti-Communist Russian refugees who were largely
       aristocrats and professionals. Focuses mainly on the conflict
       between Russian and American culture which also provoked
       divisions within the immigrant community itself.

618   Gazi, Stjepan. CROATIAN IMMIGRATION TO ALLEGHENY COUNTY:
       1882-1914. Pittsburgh: Croatian Fraternal Union, 1956. 55 p.

       Deals with the causes of Croatian migration to the United
       States and Allegheny County, Pennsylvania, occupational and
       residential patterns, religious life, and the creation of the
       Croatian Society of the United States.

619   Govorchin, Gerald G. AMERICANS FROM YUGOSLAVIA. Gaines-
       ville: University of Florida Press, 1961. 352 p. Maps, illustrations,
       appendix, notes, index.

A survey of South Slav immigrants: why they came, where
they settled, what they did, and how they interacted with
American culture from colonial times to the twentieth century,
with emphasis on the period from 1880 to 1920.

620 Graham, Stephen. WITH POOR IMMIGRANTS TO AMERICA. 1914.
Reprint. New York: Arno Press, 1974. 306 p. Illustrations.

The story of Russian immigrants who came to America in the
second decade of the twentieth century by way of Great Britain. The author describes the trip across the Atlantic, the
arrival of the immigrants in New York, and their subsequent
migration over the Alleghenies westward to Chicago. Contains many comparisons between pre-Revolutionary Russia and
the United States. First published in HARPER'S MAGAZINE
before appearing in book form.

621 Greene, Victor R. "For God and Country: The Origins of Slavic Catholic Self Consciousness in America." CHURCH HISTORY 35 (1966): 446-
60.

Examines the origins of Polish-American nationalism in the
last century, focusing on parish life in Chicago. Concludes
that ethnic self-consciousness derived not from resentment
against control of the church by non-Slavs, but from conflict
between two groups of Poles, one preaching unquestioned
loyalty to priest and hierarchy; and the other, secular nationalism. The clash resulted in the creation of the Polish National Catholic church.

622 _____. THE SLAVIC COMMUNITY ON STRIKE: IMMIGRANT LABOR
IN PENNSYLVANIA ANTHRACITE. Notre Dame, Ind.: University of
Notre Dame Press, 1968. 216 p. Notes, index.

Argues that Slavic coal miners supported the activities of the
United Mine Workers at least as enthusiastically as did older
Americans, explores the reasons for their behavior and its im-
pact upon industrial relations at the turn of the century.

623 _____. "A Study in Slavs, Strikes and Unions: The Anthracite Strike
of 1897." PENNSYLVANIA HISTORY 31 (1964): 199-215.

Describes a strike in the Pennsylvania coal fields which "shows
the attitude of immigrants toward their jobs, their employers,
labor organization and job discrimination." Immigrant Slavs
willingly joined unions to better their working conditions.

624 Gross, Leonard, ed. "The Coming of the Russian Mennonite to America:
An Analysis by Johann Epp, Mennonite Minister in Russia, 1895." MEN-
NONITE QUARTERLY REVIEW 48 (1974): 460-75.

An edited account of Epp's arguments against Mennonite immigration to America, based mostly upon his belief that the experience has caused too many immigrants to fall away from their religion.

625 Halich, Wasyl. UKRAINIANS IN THE UNITED STATES. Chicago: University of Chicago Press, 1937. 149 p. Appendices, bibliography, index.

Examines the cause for Ukrainian immigration, its contributions to industry, agriculture, business and the professions, and the immigrants' fraternal organizations, religious life, newspapers, and cultural activities.

626 Hudson, Estelle, and Maresh, Henry R. CZECH PIONEERS OF THE SOUTHWEST. Dallas: Southwest Press, 1934. 418 p. Appendix, index.

Deals with one hundred years of Czech migration to Texas, focusing on outstanding individuals and families, educators, artists, professionals, and military participants.

627 Krajsa, Joseph John. "Slovaks." SLOVAKIA 21 (1971): 145-63.

Surveys Slovak emigration to America, including the role of churches, schools, foreign language newspapers, fraternal organizations, and societies.

628 Kristofik, Joseph R. "The Slovak Image." SLOVAKIA 16 (1966): 76-79.

Discussed the inability of Slovak Americans to wield any political influence in the United States on behalf of the self-determination of their homeland. Calls upon young, educated Slovak Americans to take the lead.

629 Kutak, Robert Ingersoll. THE STORY OF A BOHEMIAN-AMERICAN VILLAGE: A STUDY OF SOCIAL PERSISTENCE AND CHANGE. 1933. Reprint. New York: Arno Press, 1970. 156 p. Footnotes.

A sociologist's dissertation on Milligan, Nebraska, undertaken "to discover which modes of behavior had persisted in the new world and which had changed and...the causes of these persistences and changes." Also sought to determine whether "the adjustment of a group of Czech immigrants to a country environment in the new world differed from that made to a city environment in America."

630 Lovrich, Frank M. "Croatians in Louisiana." JOURNAL OF CROATIAN STUDIES 7/8 (1966-67): 31-163.

Uses theoretical framework developed by sociologists to examine Croatian-American life-styles, community organization, and national associations in Louisiana. Concludes that they have maintained an ethnic identity, despite increasing pressures from within and without to Americanize.

631 _____. "The Dalmatian Yugoslavs in Louisiana." LOUISIANA HISTORY 8 (1967): 149-64.

Describes the activities of Dalmation immigrants to Louisiana since 1820. Finds that they tend to dominate the oyster and other related sea industries and that they have almost entirely resisted assimilation, maintaining much of their Old World ethnic identity and life-style.

632 Magocsi, Paul R. "Immigrants from Eastern Europe: The Carpatho-Rusyn Community of Proctor, Vermont." VERMONT HISTORY 42 (1974): 48-52.

Emphasizes immigrants' devotion to the Independent Christian church and their growingly Americanized language.

633 Miljeview, J.N. "Yugoslav People in Michigan." MICHIGAN HISTORY 25 (1941): 358-64.

Discusses the settlements of Serbians, Croatians, and Slovenians in various Michigan towns and cities; their occupations; customs; and fraternal, political, and cultural institutions. Mostly descriptive in nature.

634 Miller, Kenneth D. CZECHO-SLOVAKS IN AMERICA. New York: George H. Doran Co., 1922. 192 p. Index.

A survey of the social, economic, and religious background of the Czechoslovaks before coming to America and their experience in the United States. Emphasizes the role of religion as a force for assimilation and national unification. Part of a series sponsored by the Inter-Church World Movement.

635 Pauco, Joseph. "American Slovaks and the Beginnings of Czecho-Slovakia." SLOVAKIA 16 (1966): 63-75.

Details the unsuccessful efforts of American Slovaks and particularly Catholics to effect guarantees from the government of Czechoslovakia for the language, religion, and customs of the Slovakian people in the newly emerging state. Also deals with the impact of events in Europe on Czechs and Slovaks in America.

636 Prisland, Marie. "The Slovenians, Most Recent American Immigrants." WISCONSIN MAGAZINE OF HISTORY 13 (1950): 265-80.

A brief survey of Slovenians in Wisconsin, their organizations and churches, their culture, language, and impressions of America.

637   Procko, Bohdan P. "The Establishment of the Ruthenian Church in the United States, 1884-1907." PENNSYLVANIA HISTORY 42 (1975): 137-54.

Concerned primarily with Ruthenian (Ukrainian) immigration to the Pennsylvania coal mine region and the religious divisions among the immigrants which ultimately led to a split along Roman Catholic Uniate and Russian Orthodox lines.

638   Prpic, George J. THE CROATIAN IMMIGRANTS IN AMERICA. New York: Philosophical Library, 1971. 519 p. Maps, illustrations, tables, appendices, notes, bibliography, index.

A revised dissertation covering the entire range of Croatian immigrant activity, whether important or insignificant. Of special importance is a bibliography of Croatian writing about American dating from the 1890s.

639   Roucek, Joseph S. "Image of the Slav in United States History and in Immigration Policy." AMERICAN JOURNAL OF ECONOMICS 28 (1969): 29-48.

Examines the origins of anti-Slavic discrimination in the United States, attributing it to the efforts of organized labor, industrialists, farmers, nationalists, racists, and intellectuals. Their attitudes paved the way for the low quotas Slavs received in the immigration restriction legislation.

640   _____. "Passing of American Czechoslovaks." AMERICAN JOURNAL OF SOCIOLOGY 39 (1954): 611-25.

Concludes that with the passing of the older generation of Czechs and Slovaks in the United States, the group's language and social institutions will ultimately fade away.

641   Rovnianek, Peter V. "The Slovaks in America." SLOVAKIA 17 (1967): 173-77.

Reprint of first English article ever dealing with the Slovaks in America, first printed in CHARITIES in 1904 by editor of the Pittsburgh SLOVAK DAILY. Describes the early life, publications, and fraternal societies of the immigrants and demonstrates how their religious beliefs aided adjustment to American life.

642   Warne, Frank Julian. THE SLAV INVASION AND THE MINE WORKERS. Philadelphia: J.B. Lippincott Co., 1904. 211 p.

Discusses the impact of large numbers of Slavic anthracite coal miners upon native-born American workers and the union movement. Blames Slavs for labor unrest and violence and advocates immigration restriction.

643   Zatko, James J.   "Slovaks in the U.S.A."   SLOVAKIA 16 (1966):   41-61.

Discusses the formation of the Slovak League of America, the National Slovak Sokol, the Slovak Catholic Sokol, the Slovak Catholic Federation, and similar groups and describes their educational, economic, and political activities. Also deals with efforts to relocate Slovaks on U.S. farms and the Slovaks' role in labor unrest.

EASTERN EUROPEAN AND OTHER "NEW" IMMIGRANTS (ARABIC, ARMENIAN, GREEK, HUNGARIAN, LITHUANIAN, LATVIAN, RUMANIAN)

644   THE ARMENIAN COMMUNITY IN AMERICA: AN ANNOTATED AND CLASSIFIED BIBLIOGRAPHICAL GUIDE.   Burt Franklin Ethnic Bibliographical Guides.   Edited by Francesco Cordasco and William W. Brickman.   In preparation.

645   Aswad, Barbara C., ed.   ARABIC SPEAKING COMMUNITIES IN AMERICAN CITIES.   New York: Center for Migration Studies, 1974.   215 p. Illustrations, bibliography, index.

On the basis of field research among Americans of Lebanese, Druze, Iraqi, Yemeni, and Palestinian origin, various authors discuss similarities and differences in their migration and adaptation to life in the urban United States. Focuses on such areas as religion, economy, and community resistance to urban renewal.

646   Barton, Josef J.   PEASANTS AND STRANGERS: ITALIANS, RUMANIANS AND SLOVAKS IN AN AMERICAN CITY, 1890-1950.   Cambridge, Mass.: Harvard University Press, 1975.   217 p.   Bibliographical references, index.

Barton makes extensive use of manuscript and archival collections at the Immigrant History Research Center in his study of the development of Cleveland's ethnic communities. Finds that self-conscious ethnic communities resulted mainly from immigrant efforts to adapt their village culture to the large urban areas.

647   Burgess, Thomas.   GREEKS IN AMERICA: AN ACCOUNT OF THEIR COMING, PROGRESS, CUSTOMS, LIVING AND ASPIRATIONS.   1913. Reprint.   New York: Arno Press, 1970.   256 p.   Illustrations, appendix,

bibliography, index.

Greek immigration from the 1880s to 1913, covering their customs, religion, employment, and geographic settlement, with a chapter on "Famous American Greeks."

648 Cutsumbis, Michael. A BIBLIOGRAPHIC GUIDE TO MATERIALS ON GREEKS IN THE UNITED STATES, 1890-1968. New York: Center for Migration Studies, 1970. 100 p. Index.

A compendium of works, both published and unpublished, on Greek-American life. Also lists fraternal publications, serials, parish and archdiocesan materials, manuscript collections, and research in progress.

649 Fairchild, Henry Pratt. GREEK IMMIGRATION TO THE UNITED STATES. New Haven, Conn.: Yale University Press, 1911. 278 p. Tables, bibliography.

Effort of American anthropologist, prominent in the movement to restrict immigration, to analyze the causes of Greek migration to the United States. Discusses the immigrants' socioeconomic status here and the effects of their coming upon themselves, Greece, and the United States.

650 Galitzi, Christine A. A STUDY OF ASSIMILATION AMONG THE ROUMANIANS IN THE UNITED STATES. New York: Columbia University Press, 1929. 282 p. Appendix, bibliography, index.

Surveys the reasons for Rumanian migration, geographic and occupational distribution, living standards, and social and cultural institutions. Concludes that the immigrants' subculture and subsocieties have slowed their assimilation and maintained the primacy of ethnic contacts.

651 THE GREEK COMMUNITY IN AMERICA: AN ANNOTATED AND CLASSIFIED BIBLIOGRAPHICAL GUIDE. Burt Franklin Ethnic Bibliographical Guides. Edited by Francesco Cordasco and William W. Brickman. In preparation.

652 Hitti, Philip K. THE SYRIANS IN AMERICA. New York: George H. Doran Co., 1924. 189 p. Illustrations, appendices, index.

Surveys Syria's history; discusses the causes and character of emigration; settlement in America; and the social, educational, and religious conditions of immigrants in America.

653 THE HUNGARIAN COMMUNITY IN AMERICA: AN ANNOTATED AND CLASSIFIED BIBLIOGRAPHICAL GUIDE. Burt Franklin Ethnic Bibliographical Guides. Edited by Francesco Cordasco and William W. Brickman. In preparation.

654   Kaupas, A. "Lithuanians in America." CHARITIES 13 (1904-5): 223-35.

Deals with the European background, occupations, religion, factions, society, and educational and social characteristics of Lithuanians in the United States. Also discusses briefly their attitude toward alcoholic beverages and Poles.

655   Kayal, Philip M. "Religion and Assimilation: Catholic 'Syrians' in America." INTERNATIONAL MIGRATION REVIEW 7 (1973): 409-25.

Argues that religion played a major role in allowing Lebanese Christians of the Catholic Eastern Rite and the Syrian Orthodox Rite to develop a hyphenated culture and society in the United States. Feels that the Church needed an ethnic community to sustain it and the community required the Church to transmit culture.

656   Kernaklian, Paul. "The Armenian-American Personality and Its Relationship to Various States of Ethnicity." Ph.D. dissertation, Syracuse University, 1967. 405 p.

Contends that there has been an overemphasis on studying the assimilative process and a corresponding lack of knowledge of cultural pluralism. Based upon a two year study of Armenian Americans, concludes that there is a relationship between variations in personality and variations in ethnicity with respect to ideology, structure, and prescribed behavior.

657   Konnyu, Leslie. HUNGARIANS IN THE UNITED STATES: AN IMMIGRATION STUDY. St. Louis: American Hungarian Review, 1967. 84 p. Maps, illustrations, tables, footnotes, bibliography, index.

A brief survey of immigration, especially from 1870 to 1960, including chapters on the Americanization of Hungarians and Hungarian contributions to American life.

658   Lengyel, Emil. AMERICANS FROM HUNGARY. Peoples of America Series, edited by Louis Adamic. Philadelphia and New York: J.B. Lippincott Co., 1948. 319 p. Notes, index.

A chronological history of Hungarian immigration followed by topical chapters on immigrant contributions to American life and culture.

659   PACIFIC SYRIAN-AMERICAN GUIDE. San Francisco: Pacific Syrian-American Guide Publishing Co., 1934. 192 p. Illustrations.

Primarily a listing of prominent Syrian Americans in business and the professions in Arizona, California, Nevada, Oregon, Texas, and Washington.

660   Panagopoulos, E.P.   NEW SMYRNA: AN EIGHTEENTH CENTURY GREEK
      ODYSSEY.   Gainesville: University of Florida Press, 1966.   207 p.   Il-
      lustrations, notes, bibliography, index.

      The story of the unsuccessful colonization of the Floridas in
      the 1760s by Doctor Andrew Turnbull.   Although more than
      1,400 Greeks, Italians, and Minorcans sailed for the new set-
      tlement south of Saint Augustine, the venture failed within
      ten years when the survivors moved to Saint Augustine.

661   Paponikolas, Helen Zeese.   "Toil and Rage in a New Land: The Greek
      Immigrants in Utah."   UTAH HISTORICAL QUARTERLY 38 (1970):   100-
      203.

      Chronicles the causes of Greek migration to Utah, immigrants'
      employment in the mines and attendant labor troubles, their
      experiences during war and the depression, and their contri-
      butions to the state.

662   Ravage, Marcus E.   AN AMERICAN IN THE MAKING.   1917.   Reprint.
      New York: Dover Publishing, 1971.   325 p.

      A first person account of the immigrant experience by a Ruma-
      nian who came to America in 1900 at the age of sixteen and
      lived in New York's lower East Side.   Also a spirited defense
      of the New Immigration at a time when the movement for
      restriction was gathering momentum.

663   Roucek, Joseph S.   AMERICAN LITHUANIANS.   New York: Lithuanian
      Alliance of America, 1940.   53 p.   Bibliography.

      Very brief survey of Lithuanian migration to America, focusing
      on occupations; religious and social divisions; organizations;
      naturalization and literacy; the press; and outstanding Lithuan-
      ian Americans in music, arts, theater, literature, politics, and
      athletics.

664   _____.   "Lithuanian Immigrants in America."   AMERICAN JOURNAL OF
      SOCIOLOGY 41 (1935-36):   447-53.

      Discusses number, residency, occupations, and institutions of
      Lithuanian Americans.   Notes difficulty in separating them
      from Polish or Russian immigrants and their general slowness
      to assimilate.

665   Saloutos, Theodore.   "Causes and Patterns of Greek Emigration to the
      United States."   In DISLOCATION AND EMIGRATION: THE SOCIAL
      BACKGROUND OF AMERICAN IMMIGRATION, edited by Donald Flem-
      ing and Bernard Bailyn, pp. 381-437.   Perspectives in American History
      Series, vol. 7.   Cambridge, Mass.:   Charles Warren Center for Studies
      in American History, 1974.

Reports that Greek emigration to the United States was greatest in the period from 1900 to 1914, immediately following World War I, and since 1965. Immigrants coming before World War II were of peasant origin with little education or occupational skills. After the war, most were professionals or skilled workers with more education.

666 _____. "The Greek Orthodox Church in the United States and Assimilation." INTERNATIONAL MIGRATION REVIEW 7 (1973): 395-407.

Traces the efforts of the Church to first preserve Greek national identity, then to acknowledge the transition to Greek-American status, and finally to realize that the Church itself had become Americanized. Attributes the change to the irresistable pull of the American environment, lack of resources, and differences within the Church itself.

667 _____. THE GREEKS IN AMERICA: A STUDENTS' GUIDE TO LOCALIZED HISTORY. New York: Teachers College Press of Columbia University, 1967. 36 p. Suggested readings.

Traces origins of Greek migration to the United States, settlement patterns, institutions, and community life. Discusses immigrants' continuing concern for developments in their original homeland.

668 _____. THE GREEKS IN THE UNITED STATES. Cambridge, Mass.: Harvard University Press, 1964. 388 p. Bibliography, notes, index.

Focuses upon Greek-American institutions and culture as well as reactions to revolutionary events in the old country. Stresses divided views on both politics and religion within the community.

669 _____. THEY REMEMBER AMERICA; THE STORY OF THE REPATRIATED GREEK-AMERICANS. Berkeley and Los Angeles: University of California Press, 1956. 132 p. Tables, appendix, notes, bibliography, index.

Analyzes the motives, attitudes, status, readjustment problems, economic standing, and impact on Greece of repatriated Greek Americans.

670 Souders, D.A. THE MAGYARS IN AMERICA. New York: George H. Doran Co., 1922. 149 p. Appendices, bibliography, index.

Deals extensively with the religious adjustment of Hungarian immigrants and the opportunity for proselytizing among them. Also deals briefly with their history and conditions in Hungary and their social and economic status in the United States. Written by the superintendent of immigration of the Reformed church in the United States.

671   Szy, Tibor, ed. HUNGARIANS IN AMERICA: A BIOGRAPHICAL DI-
      RECTORY OF PROFESSIONALS OF HUNGARIAN ORIGIN IN THE
      AMERICAS. New York: Kossuth Foundation, 1966. 488 p.

      Composed of an alphabetical list of approximately 3,000 Hun-
      garian biographical sketches. They include the names of re-
      fugees who left during World War II and those who came to
      America after the Hungarian Revolution of 1956.

672   Taft, Donald R. TWO PORTUGUESE COMMUNITIES IN NEW ENGLAND.
      1923. Reprint. New York: Arno Press, 1969. 359 p. Tables, bibliog-
      raphy.

      Basically a study of the Portuguese of Portsmouth, Rhode Is-
      land, and Fall River, Massachusetts. Also discusses the racial
      composition of the Portuguese nationality and their immigra-
      tion and distribution in the United States.

673   Veidemanis, Juris. "A Twentieth Century Pioneer Settlement: Latvians
      in Lincoln County, Wisconsin." MIDCONTINENT AMERICAN STUDIES
      JOURNAL 4 (1963): 13-26.

      Discusses the difference between Latvian refugees to Wisconsin
      following World War II and the earlier Latvian immigrants.
      The later immigrants were much more urbanized and better edu-
      cated and found little in common with the descendents of the
      earlier arrivals, who had been largely peasants.

674   Xenides, J.P. THE GREEKS IN AMERICA. New York: George H.
      Doran Co., 1922. 152 p. Appendices, index.

      Survey of the European background of Greek immigrants, their
      institutions and culture in America, their special problems and
      recommendations for solution. Written by a Greek-American
      clergyman and secretary of the Greek Relief Society.

675   Yeretzian, Aram S. A HISTORY OF ARMENIAN IMMIGRATION TO
      AMERICA WITH SPECIAL REFERENCE TO CONDITIONS IN LOS ANGE-
      LES. San Francisco: R and E Research Associates, 1974. 78 p. Ap-
      pendix, notes, bibliography.

      Reprint of a 1923 thesis from the University of Southern Cali-
      fornia. Discusses Armenian migration to the United States,
      and especially to southern California, and draws a demographic,
      political, socioeconomic, and cultural profile of the Armenian-
      American community in Los Angeles.

676   Younis, Adele Linda. "The Coming of the Arabic-Speaking People to the
      United States." Ph.D. dissertation, Boston University, 1961. 377 p.

      Covers immigration from the colonial period to World War II, but emphasizes the period of greatest immigration from 1900 to 1915 and the subsequent period of restriction which nearly halted Arabic migration.

Chapter 4

ORIENTALS

CHINESE

677 Barth, Gunther. BITTER STRENGTH: A HISTORY OF THE CHINESE IN
THE UNITED STATES, 1850-1870. Cambridge, Mass.: Harvard University Press, 1964. 305 p. Notes, glossary, sources, index.

Tells of Chinese indentured emigrants who came to the United
States primarily as sojourners who hoped to return to China
after accumulating their wealth. Most, however, altered
that dream and remained in America. Drawn mainly from
newspaper accounts.

678 _____. "Chinese Sojourners in the West: The Coming." SOUTHERN
CALIFORNIA QUARTERLY 46 (1964): 55-67.

Discusses the Chinese migrants who came to the United States
as temporary laborers in the 1850s and 1860s through the
credit ticket system. Argues that they remained apart from
permanent immigrants, largely because American businessmen
copied Chinese merchants who had used district companies
and kinship organizations as means of extra-legal control.

679 Black, Isabella. "American Labour and Chinese Immigration." PAST
AND PRESENT 25 (1963): 59-76.

Surveys the attitude of American labor, especially in California, toward Chinese immigration in the early twentieth century. Finds that the Chinese were occasionally defended by
employers, Methodists, Socialists, and Mexican labor leaders,
but that their arguments were overwhelmed by references to
racism, patriotism, and economics.

680 California Chinese Exclusion Convention. PROCEEDINGS AND LIST OF
DELEGATES. San Francisco: San Francisco Star Press, 1901. 118 p.

Contains proceedings, in the form of addresses, communications, memorials, and reports, of the conference to promote

Chinese restriction. Concludes with a memorial to the president and Congress.

681   Chen, Pei-Ngor. "The Chinese Community in Los Angeles." SOCIAL CASEWORK 51 (1970): 591-98.

Indicates that a large number of elderly Chinese who had hoped to return to their native land could no longer do so because of the changed political circumstances in China. They thus remained in America, not fully assimilated and not able to rely on the traditional Chinese deference to parents for their welfare in the United States.

682   Chiu, Ping. CHINESE LABOR IN CALIFORNIA, 1850-1880: AN ECONOMIC STUDY. Madison: State Historical Society of Wisconsin, 1963. 180 p. Tables, appendices, footnotes, selected bibliography, index.

Explains that Chinese labor in mining, agriculture, woolen textiles, shoe, cigar, and clothing manufacturing did not strongly compete with white labor, but it nevertheless provided the rationale for the failure of the American dream for native whites who did not enjoy the upward economic mobility they expected.

683   Choy, Philip P. "Golden Mountain of Lead: The Chinese Experience in California." CALIFORNIA HISTORICAL QUARTERLY 50 (1971): 267-76.

A brief survey of the role of the Chinese in California history by a past president of the Chinese Historical Society of America. Based on secondary sources.

684   Choy, Wilbur W.Y. "The Chinese in California." PACIFIC HISTORIAN 11 (1967): 16-22.

Describes the reasons for the migration of Cantonese to San Francisco, Stockton, and Sacramento in the last half of the nineteenth century. Discusses their efforts to preserve an ethnic community by maintaining their rural extended kinship system and surveys Chinese-American contributions in a variety of fields.

685   Chu, George. "Chinatowns in the Delta: The Chinese in the Sacramento-San Joaquin Delta, 1870-1960." CALIFORNIA HISTORICAL SOCIETY QUARTERLY 49 (1970): 21-37.

Emphasizes that the existence of small Chinatowns in the Sacramento-San Joaquin Delta depended largely on the rise of asparagus as a major money-making crop during the period 1900-1920. With depletion of the soil, this area rapidly declined and the Chinese migrated to the larger cities.

686 Chu, Samuel, and Chu, Daniel. PASSAGE TO THE GOLDEN GATE: A HISTORY OF THE CHINESE IN AMERICA TO 1910. Garden City, N.Y.: Doubleday and Co., 1967. 117 p. Index.

Short, readable account of Chinese migration to California, impelled first by the gold rush and then by the building of the railroads. Ends with the destruction of Chinatown in the great earthquake of 1906, but looks toward the rebirth of San Francisco's Chinese community in future years.

687 Conwell, Russell Herman. WHY AND HOW. WHY THE CHINESE EMIGRATE AND THE MEANS THEY ADOPT FOR THE PURPOSE OF REACHING AMERICA. Boston and New York: Lee, Shepard & Dillingham, 1871. 283 p. Illustrations.

Describes the reasons for Chinese migration to America and the conditions encountered during the journey and concludes with five sketches of "amusing incidents" which occured during the voyage. Written by the famous "Gospel of Wealth" minister.

688 Coolidge, Mary Roberts. CHINESE IMMIGRATION. New York: Holt, 1909. 496 p. Appendix, bibliography, index.

Traces the development of anti-Chinese feeling in the United States to competition with native labor and Chinese inability to assimilate. Outlines the passage of restrictive legislation.

689 Cowan, Robert Ernest, and Dunlap, Boutwell. BIBLIOGRAPHY OF THE CHINESE QUESTION IN THE UNITED STATES. San Francisco: A.M. Robertson, 1909. 68 p.

A briefly annotated list of books and pamphlets (exclusive of government publications) relating to Chinese immigration. Over 500 entries arranged in alphabetical order.

690 Fong, Stanley L.M. "Assimilation of Chinese in America: Changes in Orientation and Social Perception." AMERICAN JOURNAL OF SOCIOLOGY 71 (1965): 265-73.

Studies the assimilation, orientation, and social perceptions of Chinese college students, using indices of progressive removal to evaluate differences between generations.

691 Gardner, John Berdan. "The Image of the Chinese in the United States, 1885-1915." Ph.D. dissertation, University of Pennsylvania, 1961. 233 p.

Explores three important, but mythical, conceptions Americans had about Chinese: (1) that they were heathens to be converted to Christianity; (2) that they were a potentially rich market for American trade; and (3) that they were a "yellow peril" which needed to be excluded from open immigration.

692 Gibson, Rev. Otis. THE CHINESE IN AMERICA. Cincinnati: Hitch-cock & Walden, 1877. 400 p.

Discusses the economic and cultural impact of Chinese immigra-tion and traces the development of the movement for restriction, concluding with an analysis of the congressional committee con-sidering the matter. Written by a Protestant minister who had done missionary work.

693 Healy, Patrick Joseph, and Chew, Ng Poon. A STATEMENT FOR NON-EXCLUSION. San Francisco, 1905. 225 p. Illustrations.

Attempts to combat the "yellow peril" propaganda of the era by discussing the positive contributions made by Oriental immigrants. The coauthor was the editor of a Chinese daily paper.

694 Hsu, Francis L.K. THE CHALLENGE OF THE AMERICAN DREAM: THE CHI-NESE IN THE UNITED STATES. Belmont, Calif.: Wadsworth, 1971. 136 p. Illustrations, tables, appendix, notes, suggestions for further reading, index.

Deals topically with the efforts of language, family, religion, friendship, adolescence, and prejudice on Chinese Americans. Concludes with a discussion of Chinese identity in American society.

695 Kraus, George. "Chinese Laborers and the Construction of the Central Pacific." UTAH HISTORICAL QUARTERLY 37 (1969): 41-57.

Describes the working and living patterns of Chinese railroad workers, their management of finances, and the attitude of Central Pacific officials toward them. Asserts that even those officials who initially opposed hiring Chinese came to appre-ciate their cleanliness and reliability.

696 Kung, S.W. CHINESE IN AMERICAN LIFE: SOME ASPECTS OF THEIR HISTORY, STATUS, PROBLEMS AND CONTRIBUTIONS. Seattle: Uni-versity of Washington Press, 1962. 352 p. Tables, appendix, notes, bibliography, index.

A twin study of both Chinese immigrants and Americans of Chinese ancestry, with an emphasis on the post-World War II period. Discusses official immigration policy, the problems of second generation Chinese and their contributions and achievements. Also information on the Chinese in Southwest Asia, Canada, and Latin America.

697 Lee, Rose Hum. THE CHINESE IN THE UNITED STATES OF AMERICA. Hong Kong: Hong Kong University Press, 1960. 465 p. Maps, tables, appendices, footnotes, bibliography, index.

Portrays "the social, economic, occupational, institutional and associational life of the Chinese in the United States" in an attempt to understand "how the process of acculturation, assimilation and integration operates when persons with distinguishable physical characteristics, bearing a different culture, come into contact with people of European origin."

698 Li, Gien Lu. CONGRESSIONAL POLICY OF CHINESE IMMIGRATION: OR LEGISLATION RELATING TO CHINESE IMMIGRATION TO THE UNITED STATES. Nashville, Tenn.: Publishing House of the Methodist Episcopal Church, South, 1916. 132 p.

Surveys the development of the restriction of Chinese immigration from 1868 to 1904. Argues that Chinese would make valuable contributions to the United States if allowed to testify in court, import wives, educate children, and vote.

699 Light, Ivan H. "From Vice District to Tourist Attraction: The Moral Career of American Chinatowns, 1880-1940." PACIFIC HISTORICAL REVIEW 63 (1974): 367-94.

Argues that early Chinatowns were indeed often filthy and violence-ridden, but not because of innate Chinese corruption so much as because organized crime controlled the area. Finally, however, as merchants sought to cultivate the tourist business, the Chinatowns were cleaned up.

700 Loewen, James W. THE MISSISSIPPI CHINESE: BETWEEN BLACK AND WHITE. Cambridge, Mass.: Harvard University Press, 1971. 433 p. Maps, charts, tables, appendices, notes, bibliography, index.

A sociologist's study of the small number of Chinese living in the Mississippi Delta and how they have accommodated themselves to changing conditions, from discrimination to eventual acceptance by native whites. Over half the book is concerned with the period from the 1940s to the present.

701 Lyman, Stanford M. CHINESE AMERICANS. New York: Random House, 1974. 213 p. Bibliography, index.

Describes the Chinese diaspora, "the background of communal organizations and their transplantation in the New World; the Anti-Chinese Movement...internal social problems and particular ways of coping with them; and the alienation, rebellion, new consciousness and transvaluation of the words 'yellow peril' in recent years."

702 _____. "Marriage and the Family Among Chinese Immigrants to America, 1850-1960." PHYLON 29 (1968): 321-30.

Argues that the social behavior of Chinese immigrants can best be understood in light of the fact that many more men than women immigrated to America and thus the Chinese, without a traditional family structure, often turned to vice and prostitution.

703 Mears, Eliot Grinnell. RESIDENT ORIENTALS ON THE AMERICAN
PACIFIC COAST: THEIR LEGAL AND ECONOMIC STATUS. Chicago:
University of Chicago Press, 1928. 545 p. Tables, footnotes, index.

A study of the situation in the 1920s of the Japanese and
Chinese in California, Oregon, and Washington. Mears compares and contrasts the rights of three groups (1) citizens, (2)
aliens ineligible for citizenship, and (3) aliens eligible for
citizenship.

704 Melendy, H. Brett. THE ORIENTAL AMERICANS. The Immigrant Heritage of America Series. New York: Twayne, 1972. 235 p. Tables,
appendix, notes, references, bibliography, index.

A historical survey of Japanese and Chinese immigration, with
particular attention to Orientals in the labor force and the
succession of restrictive laws designed to curtail their numbers
and impact in the United States.

705 Miller, Stuart Creighton. "An East Coast Perspective to Chinese Exclusion, 1852-1882." HISTORIAN 33 (1971): 183-201.

Takes issue with Mary Coolidge's CHINESE IMMIGRATION
(1909) by examining newspaper editorials of northeastern papers
in the period prior to the Chinese Exclusion Act of 1882.
Concludes that Chinese exclusion should be seen from "the
perspective of national cultural, racial, and public health
fears rather than in terms of a narrow, California-based prejudice."

706 _____. THE UNWELCOME IMMIGRANT: THE AMERICAN IMAGE OF THE
CHINESE, 1785-1882. 1969. Reprint. Berkeley and Los Angeles: University of California Press, 1974. 259 p. Notes, bibliographical notes, index.

Questions the standard impression that anti-Chinese hostility
was a product of the post-Civil War reaction in certain western
states. In particular, Miller studies the attitudes of early
traders, missionaries, and diplomats toward the Chinese.

707 Nee, Victor G., and deBary, Brett. LONGTIME CALIFORN': A DOCU-
MENTARY STUDY OF AN AMERICAN CHINATOWN. New York: Pan-
theon Books, 1973. 410 p. Appendices, maps.

Investigates San Francisco's Chinatown in its historical evolution and present state. Divides its development into five
stages: the bachelor society, the refugees, the family society,
the emergence of a new working class, and the radicals with
a new vision.

708 Riggs, Frederick W. PRESSURES ON CONGRESS: A STUDY OF THE
REPEAL OF CHINESE EXCLUSION. New York: King's Crown Press,

Columbia University, 1950. 260 p. Tables, appendices, notes, bibliography, index.

A political science dissertation which describes the background, passage, and repeal of the Chinese exclusion laws, with particular attention to the popular, administrative, and congressional pressures which made repeal possible.

709 Sandmeyer, Elmer C. THE ANTI-CHINESE MOVEMENT IN CALIFORNIA. Supplementary bibliography by Roger Daniels. Urbana: University of Illinois Press, 1973. 131 p. Footnotes, bibliography, index.

A dissertation first published in 1939 which analyzes the conditions which encouraged the movement, the source of leadership, the motives, and the methods of the exclusionists from the arrival of the Chinese to 1904.

710 Saxton, Alexander. THE INDISPENSABLE ENEMY: LABOR AND THE ANTI-CHINESE MOVEMENT IN CALIFORNIA. Berkeley and Los Angeles: University of California Press, 1971. 293 p. Illustrations, notes, bibliographical notes, index.

An analysis of California politics and labor, especially the revitalization of the Democratic party after the Civil War. That regeneration resulted, in part, from the anti-Chinese sentiments the Democrats exploited.

711 Seward, George F. CHINESE IMMIGRATION: ITS SOCIAL AND ECONOMICAL ASPECTS. 1881. Reprint. New York: Arno Press, 1970. 421 p. Footnotes, index.

Argues against the need for restriction of Chinese immigration by studying the actual number of Chinese immigrants, their contributions to the California labor force, the common objections to Chinese immigration, and the exaggerated fears of excessive immigration.

712 Starr, M.B. THE COMING STRUGGLE: OR WHAT THE PEOPLE ON THE PACIFIC COAST THINK OF THE COOLIE INVASION. 1873. Reprint. San Francisco: R and E Research Associates, 1972. 122 p.

A slim volume, polemical in tone, composed of several selections from West Coast newspapers advocating opposition to continued Chinese immigration.

713 Sung, Betty Lee. MOUNTAIN OF GOLD: THE STORY OF THE CHINESE IN AMERICA. 1967. Reprint. New York: Macmillan Co., 1972. 120 p. Charts, tables, appendix, notes, bibliography, index.

Deals with the immigrants who settled in America after being forced to leave China following the Communist accession to power. Provides biographical sketches of prominent Chinese in the United States and their attempt to balance their own ethnic identity with the opportunities in a new and different country.

714 Whitney, James Amaziah. THE CHINESE AND THE CHINESE QUESTION. 2d ed. New York: Gibbals Book Co., 1888. 198 p.

Examines the work, character, institutions, and history of Chinese people, their relations with the rest of the world, and their immigration and settlement in the United States. Last section advocates repeal of the Burlingame treaty and adoption of restrictive laws against Chinese immigration.

715 Zo, Kil Young. "Chinese Emigration into the United States, 1850-1880." Ph.D. dissertation, Columbia University, 1971. 231 p.

Relies on Chinese and Japanese language sources to trace the origin and reasons for the emigration from the remote area of Sze-yap to California from 1849 to 1882, the free immigration period.

JAPANESE

716 Bailey, Thomas A. "California, Japan and the Alien Land Legislation of 1913." PACIFIC HISTORICAL REVIEW 1 (1932): 36-59.

Details the background and effects of the Alien Land Legislation of 1913 on California, the United States, and the Japanese.

717 Blakeslee, George H., ed. JAPAN AND JAPANESE AMERICAN RELATIONS. New York: G.E. Stechert and Co., 1912. 348 p.

Contains twenty-two essays which were previously published in the JOURNAL OF RACE DEVELOPMENT. Relevant chapters include: "The Japanese in America," "The Future of the Japanese in Hawaii," and "Japanese-American Relations as Affecting the Control of the Pacific." Published as part of the Clark University addresses.

718 Bosworth, Allen R. AMERICA'S CONCENTRATION CAMPS. New York: W.W. Norton, 1967. 282 p. Illustrations, notes, index.

An account of the Japanese evacuation from the West Coast and relocation during World War II.

719 Broom, Leonard, and Kitsuse, John I. THE MANAGED CASUALTY: THE JAPANESE-AMERICAN FAMILY IN WORLD WAR II. Berkeley and Los Angeles: University of California Press, 1956. 226 p. Maps, charts, tables, notes, glossary.

After first sketching the social and cultural background of the
Japanese Americans, the administrative context of evacuation
and relocation, and the family as a social unit, presents ten
different case studies designed "to include families that repre-
sent the chief categories of religion, occupation, education,
urbanization, degree of acculturation and age and generation
composition."

720 Broom, Leonard, and Riemer, Ruth. REMOVAL AND RETURN: THE
SOCIOECONOMIC EFFECTS OF THE WAR ON JAPANESE AMERICANS.
Berkeley and Los Angeles: University of California Press, 1973. 259 p.
Maps, charts, tables, appendices, notes, bibliography.

A detailed analysis of occupational data which describes "not
only the occupational adjustments of a population, but the
distinctive part the population has played in the economy of
a region."

721 Buell, Raymond Leslie. "The Development of the Anti-Japanese Agitation in the United States." POLITICAL SCIENCE QUARTERLY Part 1,
37 (1922): 605-38; Part 2, 38 (1923): 57-81.

Discusses the conditions that fostered Japanese immigration and
the hostile reception many Japanese received in the first decade of the twentieth century, largely in the urban areas and
at the hands of labor unions. Part 2 deals with the subsequent migration of Japanese from the cities to the rural areas,
where they met an equally hostile bloc of farmers who feared
their competition.

722 _____. JAPANESE IMMIGRATION. Boston: World Peace Foundation,
1924. 99 p. Appendices.

Surveys the restriction of Japanese immigration to the United
States from the Gentlemen's Agreement to the 1924 Exclusion
Act and compares American treatment of Japanese to that of
British dominions. Concludes that British accomplished similar
results through mutual consultation with Japan, thus avoiding
insult.

723 _____. "Some Legal Aspects of the Japanese Question." AMERICAN
JOURNAL OF INTERNATIONAL LAW 17 (1923): 29-49.

Discusses the meaning of naturalization and dual citizenship
as applied to Japanese immigration and explores the legality
of the California Alien Land Law and other anti-Japanese
enactments.

724 Caudill, William. JAPANESE-AMERICAN PERSONALITY AND ACCUL-
TURATION. Provincetown, Mass.: Journal Press, 1952. 102 p. Footnotes, references.

Concludes that the "high degree of compatibility between the values and adaptive mechanisms of the Japanese Americans and the American middle class" can be seen "by their remarkable occupational distribution, the highly favorable evaluation of them by their white employers and fellow employees, their educational level averaging beyond high school graduation and their general socioeconomic orientation toward the lower middle class."

725   Coletta, Paolo E. "Bryan and the California Alien Land Legislation." PACIFIC HISTORICAL REVIEW 36 (1967): 163-87.

Describes the unsuccessful efforts of Secretary of State Bryan to persuade California to modify its discriminatory alien land law and to placate Japanese opinion. President Wilson's preoccupation with other matters prevented his success and helped poison American-Japanese relations.

726   Connor, John W. "Acculturation and Family Continuities in Three Generations of Japanese Americans." JOURNAL OF MARRIAGE AND THE FAMILY 36 (1974): 159-65.

Concludes after nearly 300 interviews that "while considerable acculturation has taken place, even the third generation of Japanese Americans still retains certain characteristics of the more traditional Japanese family system."

727   Conrat, Maisie, and Conrat, Richard. EXECUTIVE ORDER 9066: THE INTERNMENT OF 110,000 JAPANESE AMERICANS. Los Angeles: California Historical Society, 1972. 120 p. Illustrations, notes.

Almost exclusively a series of black and white photographs with little text, selected from over 25,000 photographs. Criteria for selection were both historical significance and the realism of the photographer's image. The book includes a brief introduction by Edison Uno, epilogue by former Supreme Court Justice Thomas C. Clark, and some background material on the Japanese in California.

728   Daniels, Roger. CONCENTRATION CAMPS USA: JAPANESE AMERICANS AND WORLD WAR II. Berkshire Studies in Minority History Series. New York: Holt, Rinehart and Winston, 1971. 188 p. Map, illustrations, tables, notes, note on sources, index.

Summarizes much of the work of other scholars, yet pays attention to those Japanese Americans who, while still remaining loyal to their adopted country, resisted the injustice of relocation.

729   _____. THE POLITICS OF PREJUDICE: THE ANTI-JAPANESE MOVE-

MENT IN CALIFORNIA AND THE STRUGGLE FOR JAPANESE EXCLU-
SION. University of California Publications in History Series, vol. 71.
Berkeley and Los Angeles: University of California Press, 1962. 165 p.
Appendices, notes, select bibliography, index.

Argues that Frederick Jackson Turner's frontier thesis does not
apply to California and that conservatives were generally less
repressive than the typical groups associated with liberalism,
for example, labor unions and progressives.

730   Fenwick, C.G. "The Japanese Problem." AMERICAN JOURNAL OF
INTERNATIONAL LAW 18 (1924): 518-23.

Discusses the statutory exclusion of Japanese immigrants in the
1924 National Origins Quota Act and compares it to the
Gentlemen's Agreement of 1908. Argues that exclusion is an
unreasonable blow to Japanese pride and self-esteem which
should be reversed if any hope of international friendship and
cooperation between the two nations is to be realized.

731   Girdner, Audrie, and Loftis, Anne. THE GREAT BETRAYAL: THE EVAC-
UATION OF THE JAPANESE-AMERICANS DURING WORLD WAR II.
New York: Macmillan Co., 1969. 562 p. Illustrations, appendices,
notes, bibliography, index.

Story of the evacuation of Japanese from the West Coast during
World War II. Concluding chapters bring the aftermath of
evacuation down to the mid-1960s. Title reveals the authors'
point of view.

732   Grodzins, Morton. AMERICANS BETRAYED: POLITICS AND THE JAP-
ANESE EVACUATION. Chicago: University of Chicago Press, 1949.
445 p. Appendices, bibliographical note, index.

Based on research conducted while Grodzins was a member of
the Evacuation and Resettlement Study of the University of
California. The resulting monograph is a study of the decision-
making process that led to resettlement, including regional
pressures as well as the administrative, legislative, and judicial
decisions which developed, implemented, and sanctioned the
policy.

733   Gulick, S.L. THE AMERICAN-JAPANESE PROBLEM. New York: C.
Scribner's Sons, 1914. 310 p. Appendices, index.

Seeks to create better understanding between Japanese immigrants and Americans by correcting stereotypes and misconceptions and to prove that Japanese Americans are capable of assimilation and acculturation.

734   Hata, Donald Teruo. "'Undesirables': Unsavory Elements Among the

Japanese in America Prior to 1893 and Their Influence on the First Anti-Japanese Movement in California." Ph.D. dissertation, University of Southern California, 1970. 173 p.

Argues that many Japanese immigrants before 1893 were "stranded mariners, itinerant wrestlers and entertainers, prostitutes, pimps and gamblers, student activists and lower class laborers." They thus contributed to the negative image of Orientals and paved the way for future discrimination.

735 Hosokawa, Bill. NISEI: THE QUIET AMERICANS. New York: Morrow, 1969. 497 p. Index.

Examines the early struggles of Japanese immigrants (Issei) and focuses on the difficulties of their children (Nisei), especially their treatment during World War II and their ultimate vindication.

736 Ichihashi, Yamato. JAPANESE IN THE UNITED STATES: A CRITICAL STUDY OF THE PROBLEMS OF THE JAPANESE IMMIGRANTS AND THEIR CHILDREN. Stanford, Calif.: Stanford University Press, 1932. 426 p. Appendix, bibliography.

Both a historical and sociological account of Japanese immigrants, including chapters dealing with diplomatic relations concerning immigration (the Gentlemen's Agreement and the Exclusion Law of 1924). It discusses the political nature of alien land laws and other discriminatory laws of California relating to the Japanese.

737 Ichioka, Yuji, et al. A BURIED PAST: AN ANNOTATED BIBLIOGRAPHY OF THE JAPANESE AMERICAN RESEARCH PROJECT COLLECTION. Berkeley and Los Angeles: University of California Press, 1974. 227 p. Index.

Nearly 1,500 entries of Japanese language source materials of the Japanese American Research Project Collection at UCLA. Alphabetically arranged under eighteen different categories.

738 Inui, Kiyo. THE UNSOLVED PROBLEM OF THE PACIFIC. Tokyo: Japan Times, 1925. 619 p. Appendices.

The lengthy subtitle describes the contents: "A Survey of International Contacts, Especially in Frontier Communities, with Special Emphasis upon California and an Analytic Study of the Johnson Report to the House of Representatives."

739 Iyenaga, T., and Sato, K. JAPAN AND THE CALIFORNIA PROBLEM. New York and London: G.P. Putnam's Sons, 1921. 197 p. Appendices, bibliography, index.

Discusses the origins of California's hostility toward Japanese immigration and suggests a program whereby both sides could come to a better understanding. Insists that Japanese will assimilate and acculturate rapidly if permitted.

740   Jones, Helen D., comp. "Japanese in the United States: Selected List of References." Washington, D.C.: Library of Congress, 1946. 36 p. Mimeographed.

An annotated bibliography of 268 items published or made available between 1940 and 1946 in five categories: (1) bibliographies, (2) books and pamphlets, (3) articles in periodicals, (4) periodicals, and (5) unpublished material.

741   Kawakami, Kiyoshi Karl. ASIA AT THE DOOR: A STUDY OF THE JAPANESE QUESTION IN CONTINENTAL UNITED STATES, HAWAII AND CANADA. New York and Chicago: Fleming H. Revell Co., 1914. 269 p.

Attempts to correct nativist views regarding the racial origins, the economic situation, and the desire for assimilation and acculturation of Japanese immigrants. Written during the height of the "yellow peril" hysteria in California.

742   Kitagawa, Daisuke. ISSEI AND NISEI: THE INTERNMENT YEARS. New York: Seabury Press, 1967. 174 p.

The author's "personal experience within the context of the corporate experience of Japanese Americans as a whole in their forced internment years: 1942–44." See his story as a collective autobiography in which he was only one among 110,000 people.

743   Kitano, Harry H.L. JAPANESE AMERICANS: THE EVOLUTION OF A SUBCULTURE. Englewood Cliffs, N.J.: Prentice-Hall, 1969. 186 p. Appendices, footnotes, bibliography, index.

First half of the book a historical treatment of the Japanese in the United States, with emphasis on the World War II period. Second half looks at the family, community, culture, and social deviance of Japanese Americans.

744   Lanman, Charles, ed. THE JAPANESE IN AMERICA. New York: University Publishing Co., 1872. 352 p. Illustrations.

Deals with the history of the Japanese embassy in the United States, some observations of American and Japanese life by Japanese students, and a survey of Japanese life and resources in the United States.

745   McWilliams, Carey. PREJUDICE; JAPANESE-AMERICANS: SYMBOL OF RACIAL INTOLERANCE. Boston: Little and Brown, 1944. 337 p. Notes, index.

A treatment of Japanese Americans on the West Coast in the twentieth century, emphasizing the plight of the Japanese during World War II and the accompanying race prejudice.

746 Millis, Harry Alvin. THE JAPANESE PROBLEM IN THE UNITED STATES: AN INVESTIGATION FOR THE COMMISSION ON RELATIONS WITH JAPAN APPOINTED BY THE FEDERAL COUNCIL OF THE CHURCHES OF CHRIST IN AMERICA. New York: Macmillan Co., 1915. 334 p. Illustrations, appendices.

Seeks to deal, in a balanced fashion, with the issues of Japanese immigration and the treatment of Japanese Americans, especially in California. Focuses upon their economic situation and the possibilities of assimilation.

747 Miyamoto, S. Frank. "Japanese Minority in Pacific Northwest." PACIFIC NORTHWEST QUARTERLY 54 (1963): 143-49.

Describes Japanese immigration to the Pacific Northwest between 1900 and 1924. Finds that most immigrants were unmarried males who would work in gangs in mills and on railroads. They later became workers in salmon canneries, truck farmers, and small businessmen, with their descendants making a mark in the arts and sciences of the region.

748 Modell, John. "The Japanese of Los Angeles: A Study in Growth and Accomodation, 1900-1946." Ph.D. dissertation, Columbia University, 1969. 463 p.

Declares that Los Angeles County was more hospitable to the Japanese than other areas of Japanese settlement on the West Coast. This changed with World War II, when the general population supported relocation even of second generation Japanese-American citizens.

749 _____. "Tradition and Opportunity: The Japanese Immigrant in America." PACIFIC HISTORICAL REVIEW 40 (1971): 163-82.

From interviews of Issei living in the United States in the 1960s, concludes that those who made the most complete and immediate adjustment to America were those who came from relatively deprived Japanese backgrounds and who were thus more willing to accept America and Americanization as a means of upward mobility.

750 _____, ed. THE KIKUCHI DIARY. Urbana: University of Illinois Press, 1973. 258 p. Illustrations, bibliography.

The edited diary of Charles Kikuchi, a 26-year-old Japanese American from Berkeley, California, who spent four months in the Tanforan Assembly Center, one of the "relocation" camps created by the government during the Second World War. A moving and perceptive first person account by a victim of wartime hysteria and racial prejudice.

751 Myer, Dillon S. UPROOTED AMERICANS: THE JAPANESE AMERICANS AND THE WAR RELOCATION AUTHORITY DURING WORLD WAR II. Tucson: University of Arizona Press, 1971. 360 p. Maps, illustrations, appendix, notes, bibliography, index.

A personal account of the former director of the War Relocation Authority, an agency created in 1942. Tells the story of the resettlement of over 100,000 Japanese Americans at the ten relocation centers from 1942 to 1946.

752 Nishi, Setsuko M. THE JAPANESE AMERICAN. Belmont, Calif.: Wadsworth. In preparation.

753 Nishimoto, Richard S., and Thomas, Dorothy S. THE SPOILAGE. Berkeley and Los Angeles: University of California, 1946. 388 p. Illustrations, footnotes, appendix, index.

Analyzes the experiences of Japanese Americans' evacuation and resettlement. The volume examines "the stigmatization as 'disloyal' [of]...one out of every six evacuees; the concentration and confinement of this group in the Tule Lake Center; the repressive measures undertaken by government agencies [and]...the successive protest movements of the group against these repressions, culminating in mass withdrawal from American citizenship."

754 Petersen, William [J.]. JAPANESE AMERICANS: OPPRESSION AND SUCCESS. Ethnic Groups in Comparative Perspective. New York: Random House, 1971. 268 p. Notes, bibliography, index.

A historical and sociological analysis presented in a topical framework.

755 Pursinger, Marvin G. "Japanese Settle in Oregon, 1880-1920." JOURNAL OF THE WEST 5 (1966): 251-62.

Sees the forty years prior to passage of anti-alien land laws as a period of relative calm in which Japanese immigrants worked diligently to win acceptance into the socioeconomic complex of the region.

756 _____. "Oregon's Japanese in World War II, A History of Compulsory Relocation." Ph.D. dissertation, University of Southern California, 1961. 496 p.

Concludes that "the uprisings in early 1942 to effect an evacuation and again in early 1945 to prevent the Japanese from

returning to their former residences cannot be explained as
simple outbursts of spontaneous wartime emotion." Sees a link
with earlier elements of white supremacy, the Grange, and
the American Legion.

757 Rademaker, John A. THESE ARE AMERICANS. Palo Alto, Calif.: Pacific Books, 1951. 278 p. Maps, illustrations.

Uses the Japanese Americans in Hawaii to illustrate the thesis
that minority groups in every type of society tend to develop
loyalty and allegiance to the host society.

758 Rostow, Eugene V. "The Japanese American Cases--A Disaster." THE
YALE LAW REVIEW 54 (1945): 489-533.

Severely criticizes the U.S. court system for violating the
basic principles of justice by accepting the concept of group
guilt by association in the case of Japanese Americans during
World War II.

759 Smith, Bradford. AMERICANS FROM JAPAN. Peoples of America
Series, edited by Louis Adamic. New York and Philadelphia: J.B. Lippincott Co., 1948. 409 p. Illustrations, notes, appendices, index.

Divided into two parallel parts, each following the sequence
of meeting, blending, conflict, crisis, and redemption. The
first covers the eastward migration of Japanese across the
Pacific and the second concentrates on the Japanese in America, particularly during the twentieth century.

760 Spicer, Edward H., et al. IMPOUNDED PEOPLE: JAPANESE-
AMERICANS IN THE RELOCATION CENTERS. Rev. ed. Tucson:
University of Arizona Press, 1969. 342 p. Appendices, index.

A report covering 1942-46 by four anthropologists who were
involved as community analysts for the War Relocation Authority. The 1969 edition has a lengthy introduction by Spicer.

761 Stemen, John Roger. "The Diplomacy of the Immigration Issue: A Study
in Japanese-American Relations, 1894-1941." Ph.D. dissertation, Indiana University, 1960. 355 p.

Chiefly "an account of actions taken by the Japanese Government on behalf of Japanese subjects who were deprived of or
denied real or potential rights and privileges by state or local
governments, agencies of the federal government, or by Congress and the Supreme Court of the United States."

762 Strong, Edward K., Jr. THE SECOND-GENERATION JAPANESE PROB-
LEM, 1934. Reprint. New York: Arno Press, 1970. 292 p. Tables,
footnotes, index.

Summarizes the findings of three monographs concerning the occupational and educational opportunities of Japanese Americans in these areas: vocational aptitudes of second generation Japanese in the United States; Japanese in California; and public school education of the second generation Japanese in California. In addition, provides a historical setting and discusses the nature of race prejudice in relation to the study.

763   Ten Broek, Jacobus, et al. PREJUDICE, WAR AND THE CONSTITUTION. Berkeley and Los Angeles: University of California Press, 1954. 408 p.

A report on a study (by faculty members in the social sciences at Berkeley) on the Japanese-American evacuation and resettlement, begun in 1942 and completed in 1948. Although Ten Broek was not involved in the original project he authored this study, which concentrates on the evacuation "in terms of its historical origins, its political characteristics, the responsibility for it and the legal implications arising from it."

764   Thomas, Dorothy S. THE SALVAGE: JAPANESE-AMERICAN EVACUATION AND RESETTLEMENT. Berkeley and Los Angeles: University of California Press, 1952. 637 p.

Analyzes the experiences of 36,000 Japanese Americans (one-third of all evacuees) who were later classified as "loyal" and who participated in the war effort or settled in the East or Middle West.

ORIENTAL—GENERAL AND MISCELLANEOUS

765   Alba, Jose C. "Filipinos in California." PACIFIC HISTORIAN 11 (1967): 39-41.

Describes Filipino immigration which was unrestricted from 1898 to 1934 and then subjected to a quota of 100 per year. Notes that the immigrants settled mostly in California coastal cities and entered a wide variety of occupations ranging from fruit pickers to skilled technicians.

766   Boyd, Monica. "The Changing Nature of Central and Southeast Asian Immigration to the United States: 1961-72." INTERNATIONAL MIGRATION REVIEW 8 (1974): 507-19.

Argues that the 1965 Immigration Act has significantly increased immigration to the United States from East Asia and has altered its composition because of the law's emphasis on manpower, rather than national origins, and on the reuniting of families.

767 _____. "Oriental Immigration: The Experience of the Chinese, Japanese and Filipino Populations in the United States." INTERNATIONAL MIGRATION REVIEW 5 (1971): 48-61.

A demographic analysis of immigration patterns indicates that anti-Oriental laws kept many women and children in a numerical minority among Oriental immigrants. This pattern began to alter after World War II.

768 Daniels, Roger. "The Asian American Experience." In THE REINTERPRETATION OF AMERICAN HISTORY AND CULTURE, edited by William H. Cartwright and Richard L. Watson, Jr., pp. 139-48. Washington, D.C.: National Council for the Social Studies, 1973.

A brief historiographical survey of the Chinese, Japanese, and Filipino experience in America.

769 _____. "Westerners From the East: Oriental Immigrants Reappraised." PACIFIC HISTORICAL REVIEW 35 (1966): 373-83.

Attempts to "assay an interpretation of the major features of Asian immigrant life in western society to the present day." The author concludes that despite convincing progress, Japanese and Chinese are still second-class citizens.

770 Hess, Gary R. "The 'Hindu' in America: Immigration and Naturalization Policies and India, 1917-1946." PACIFIC HISTORICAL REVIEW 38 (1969): 59-79.

Discusses the efforts of Mubarak Ali Khan, the Welfare League, J.J. Singh and Anup Singh, and events in the United States which led to the gradual abandonment of exclusion and denial of citizenship to Indians, which had been the practice since the 1920s.

771 Lasker, Bruno. FILIPINO IMMIGRATION TO CONTINENTAL UNITED STATES AND TO HAWAII. Chicago: University of Chicago Press, 1931. 445 p. Illustrations, appendices, footnotes, index.

A study commissioned by the American Council of the Institute of Pacific Relations for use at a conference of the Institute on Migration and Race Problems. Discusses Filipino immigration to the United States and Hawaii, causes for immigration, and existing policies and programs relating to restriction.

772 Mears, Eliot G. RESIDENT ORIENTALS ON THE AMERICAN PACIFIC COAST: THEIR LEGAL AND ECONOMIC STATUS. Chicago: University of Chicago Press, 1928. 548 p. Appendix, bibliography, index.

Examines the position of Japanese and Chinese Americans on the West Coast, focusing on their treaty and constitutional rights, naturalization regulations, exclusion laws, personal relations, property rights, occupational distribution, segregation, and contacts with the larger American community. Also contains important tables and documents. Argues for greater understanding and liberalization of attitudes and laws toward Orientals.

773 Munoz, Alfred N. THE FILIPINOS IN AMERICA. Los Angeles: Mountain View Publishers, 1971. 209 p. Illustrations, appendices, index.

An informal narrative about Filipinos in contemporary America, emphasizing first their place in the mainstream and then describing their activity on the farms, in the cities, in the military, and the professions.

774 Narayanan, R. "Indian Immigration and the India League of America." INDIAN JOURNAL OF AMERICAN STUDIES 2 (1972): 1-29.

Examines "the circumstances leading to the passing of the Indian Immigration and Naturalization Act of 1946 and the role played by the Indian community in working towards this legislation." Concentrates on the role of the India League of America as an important vehicle for influencing American public opinion.

775 Odo, Franklin, et al., eds. ROOTS, AN ASIAN AMERICAN READER. Los Angeles: University of California at Los Angeles Asian American Studies Center, 1971. 345 p. Illustrations.

Includes over fifty selections, mostly by Chinese and Japanese Americans, organized around the general topics of identity, history, and community. Contains a strong condemnation of anti-Oriental racism.

776 Palmer, Albert W. ORIENTALS IN AMERICAN LIFE. New York: Friendship Press, 1934. 212 p. Tables, annotated book list.

A historical survey of Chinese, Japanese, and Filipino immigration to the United States. Includes a discussion of the psychological, economic, and social problems encountered by these immigrants and their children.

777 Saniel, J.M., ed. THE FILIPINO EXCLUSION MOVEMENT, 1927-1935. Quezon City: Institute of Asian Studies, University of Philippines, 1967. 51 p.

Contains papers on California's discrimination against Filipinos and efforts to obtain exclusion by the Hawaiian Sugar Planters Association and the American Federation of Labor.

Chapter 5

RECENT ETHNICS: POST 1920S

MEXICAN AMERICAN

778 Acuna, Rodolfo. "Freedom in a Cage: The Subjugation of the Chicano in the United States." In THE REINTERPRETATION OF AMERICAN HISTORY AND CULTURE, edited by William H. Cartwright and Richard L. Watson, Jr., pp. 113-37. Washington, D.C.: National Council for the Social Studies, 1973.

A brief overview of "the Mexican American's quest for self-determination and cultural pluralism in America." Concludes with a bibliographical listing of nearly one hundred sources, mainly from the past twenty years.

779 _____. OCCUPIED AMERICA: THE CHICANO'S STRUGGLE TOWARD LIBERATION. San Francisco: Canfield Press, 1972. 282 p. Notes, index.

Author believes that "the experience of Chicanos in the United States parallels that of other Third World peoples who have suffered under the colonialism of technologically superior nations." Divided into two sections, dealing first with the U.S. conquest of the Southwest in the nineteenth century and then with the Chicano experiences in the twentieth century.

780 Almaguer, Thomas. "Class, Race, and Chicano Oppression." SOCIALIST REVOLUTION 25 (1975): 1091.

Develops a Marxist analysis of Chicano history in order to interpret the history of American minorities. Also seeks to show how class consciousness can break down racial prejudice against minorities by nonwhite working-class people.

781 Alvarez, Jose Hernandez. "A Demographic Profile of the Mexican Immigration to the United States, 1910-1950." JOURNAL OF INTER-AMERICAN STUDIES 8 (1966): 471-96.

Shows that most Mexican immigrants moved first to the Southwest, with some later moving to the Northwest. Many became
urbanized, intermarried, and improved their education.

782　Alvarez, Rodolfo. "The Psycho-Historical and Socioeconomic Development of the Chicano Community in the United States." SOCIAL SCIENCE
QUARTERLY 53 (1973): 920-42.

Identifies and describes four historical periods, each with its
own set of distinct characteristics: (1) the creation generation
of the second half of the nineteenth century, (2) the migrant
generation from 1900 to World War II, (3) the Mexican-American
generation from the 1940s to the Vietnam War, and (4) the
Chicano generation, beginning in the late 1960s.

783　Betten, Neil, and Mohl, Raymond A. "From Discrimination to Repatriation: Mexican Life in Gary, Indiana, During the Great Depression."
PACIFIC HISTORICAL REVIEW 42 (1973): 370-88.

Shows that although eagerly sought by northern industrial
cities, especially Gary, during World War I and as strike-
breakers in the 1920s, Mexicans experienced increasing hostility in the 1930s when the tensions generated by economic
collapse brought a renewal of nativism and xenophobia.

784　Bogardus, Emory S. THE MEXICAN IMMIGRANT: AN ANNOTATED
BIBLIOGRAPHY. Los Angeles: The Council on International Relations,
1929. 21 p.

An annotated bibliography on Mexican Americans between 1900
and 1928. Includes books and articles dealing with cultural
backgrounds, community life in the United States, and inter-
racial adjustment.

785　_____. "Mexican Immigrants." SOCIOLOGY AND SOCIAL RESEARCH
11 (1927): 470-88.

Analyzes the condition of Mexican immigrants with respect to
ecological factors, cultural patterns, and psychosocial processes.

786　_____. "Mexican Immigrants and Segregation." AMERICAN JOURNAL
OF SOCIOLOGY 36 (1930): 74-80.

Examines the reasons for low rate of naturalization among
Mexican immigrants. Attributes it to a combination of existing conditions in the United States and personal factors of
the migrants themselves.

787　_____. "Second Generation Mexicans." SOCIOLOGY AND SOCIAL

RESEARCH 13 (1929): 276-83.

Argues that second generation Mexican Americans are caught between the pull of two cultures and are in serious danger of becoming socially disorganized unless sympathetic Americans are willing to aid their adjustment.

788 Chavarria, Jesus. THE SOCIETY AND CULTURE OF MEXICAN AMERI-CANS. Belmont, Calif.: Wadsworth. In preparation.

789 "Chicano Experience in the United States." SOCIAL SCIENCE QUARTERLY 53 (1973): 652-950.

Nearly twenty-five different articles covering a variety of subjects on Chicanos. Articles of particular significance are separately annotated under the author's name.

790 Copp, Nelson Gage. "'Wetbacks' and 'Braceros': Mexican Migrant Laborers and American Immigration Policy, 1930-1960." Ph.D. dissertation, Boston University, 1963. 265 p.

Indicates that although the wetback and bracero episodes had their origin in the Quota Act of 1921, only after World War II did the large number of seasonal workers, most of whom did not remain permanently in the United States, cause serious problems. Author believes that the policy of permitting temporary immigration from Mexico is contradictory to the racial preference implied in the 1952 Act.

791 Corwin, Arthur F. "Causes of Mexican Emigration to the United States: A Summary View." In DISLOCATION AND EMIGRATION: THE SOCIAL BACKGROUND OF AMERICAN IMMIGRATION, edited by Donald Fleming and Bernard Bailyn, pp. 557-635. Perspectives in American History Series, vol. 7. Cambridge, Mass.: Charles Warren Center for Studies in American History, 1974.

A survey of emigration to the United States, emphasizing the last seventy-five years. Discusses the causes of legal and illegal immigration, the problems of controlling that flow since 1964, and congressional hearings on proposals in the 1970s to increase Mexican immigration.

792 _____. "Mexican-American History: An Assessment." PACIFIC HISTORICAL REVIEW 42 (1973): 269-308.

A historiographical treatment of recent literature on Mexican Americans and a discussion of two emerging schools within that literature: the "establishment school" which seeks to integrate their study into national history and the "la Raza school" which seeks to develop an exclusive history of the Mexican-American experience.

793 _____. "Mexican Emigration History, 1900-1970: Literature and Research." LATIN AMERICAN RESEARCH REVIEW 8 (1973): 3-24.

An extensive historiographical essay covering studies by U.S. historians and social scientists, the Mexican side of emigration literature, research opportunities on the subject, and a brief list of bibliographical aids.

794 Creagan, James F. "Public Law 78: A Tangle of Domestic and International Relations." JOURNAL OF INTER-AMERICAN STUDIES 7 (1965): 541-56.

Analyzes the pro and con struggle over Public Law 78 between 1948 and 1964. The law permitted easy immigration of Mexican "stoop labor" and was sponsored by farm employers, but opposed by organized labor. Repeal brought some economic hardship to Mexico and created a farm labor shortage in parts of the United States.

795 de Kerr, Louise Ano Nuevo. "Chicano Settlements in Chicago: A Brief History." JOURNAL OF ETHNIC STUDIES 2 (1975): 22-32.

Investigates the formation of the five major Chicano settlements in Chicago and briefly discusses their environment and institutional life.

796 Derbyshire, R.L. "Adaptation of Adolescent Mexican-Americans to United States Society." AMERICAN BEHAVIORAL SCIENTIST 13 (1969): 88-103.

Studies Mexican-American adolescents in east Los Angeles and attributes their high degree of deviant behavior to the conflict between their desire to identify with their families and cultural heritage and their witnessing of the denigration of those traditions by the wider society.

797 Downs, Fane. "The History of Mexicans in Texas, 1820-1845." Ph.D. dissertation, Texas Tech University, 1970. 297 p.

A study of the Spanish and Mexican natives residing in Texas, including their culture, way of life, religion, and their participation in the major historical events of the period.

798 Dworkin, Anthony Gary. "Stereotypes and Self-Images Held by Native-Born and Foreign-Born Mexican-Americans." SOCIOLOGY AND SOCIAL RESEARCH 49 (1965): 214-24.

Concludes that foreign-born Mexican-American students held more favorable self-images than those born in the United States because the former measured their prior socioeconomic condition in Mexico as a basis of comparison while the latter used American standards for evaluation.

799 Felice, Lawrence G. "Mexican American Self-Concept and Educational Achievement: The Effects of Ethnic Isolation and Socioeconomic Deprivation." SOCIAL SCIENCE QUARTERLY 53 (1973): 716-26.

Concludes that "[r]acially and ethnically segregated school climates raise barriers to the academic achievement of Mexican Americans, while promoting dropout behavior." Urges both desegregation of the schools and "the mixing of students from differing socioeconomic backgrounds."

800 Fogel, Walter A. MEXICAN-AMERICANS IN SOUTHWEST LABOR MARKETS. Mexican-American Study Project, Advance Report no. 10. Berkeley and Los Angeles: University of California Press, 1967. 222 p.

Based upon 1960 census data, compares the economic standing of Mexican Americans with that of Anglo-Americans and nonwhites. Shows that some gains have been made by the second generation Chicanos, but that the third generation has not been able to advance much further.

801 Frisbie, Parker. "Illegal Migration from Mexico to the United States: A Longitudinal Analysis (1946-1965)." INTERNATIONAL MIGRATION REVIEW 9 (1975): 3-13.

Contends that "wetbacks" or "los mojados" outnumber legal immigrants eight to one. Concludes that such agricultural economic factors as wages and investment determine the time and scope of migration and that Mexican conditions are more important than American ones.

802 _____. "Militancy Among Mexican American High School Students." SOCIAL SCIENCE QUARTERLY 53 (1973): 865-83.

Attempts to explain the fact that Mexican-American school students have been in the vanguard of militant Chicanos by analyzing a sample of over 2,000 students at two different high schools in a southwestern city.

803 Gamio, Manuel. THE MEXICAN IMMIGRANT, HIS LIFE-STORY. Chicago: University of Chicago Press, 1931. 288 p.

Includes interviews with seventy-six immigrants, more than two-thirds of whom are men. The documents are arranged under eight chapter headings, which include "Assimilation," "The Mexican American," and "Conflict and Race-Consciousness." Published as an appendix to MEXICAN IMMIGRATION TO THE UNITED STATES.

804 _____. MEXICAN IMMIGRATION TO THE UNITED STATES: A STUDY OF HUMAN MIGRATION AND ADJUSTMENT. 1930. Reprint. New York: Arno Press, 1969. 262 p. Tables, appendices, footnotes, bibliography, index.

Contains the analysis of the autobiographical material collected as part of a project of the Social Science Research Council and published as THE MEXICAN IMMIGRANT, HIS LIFE-STORY.

805 Garcia, F. Chris. "Orientations of Mexican American and Anglo Children toward the United States Political Community." SOCIAL SCIENCE QUARTERLY 53 (1973): 814-29.

Finds that differences are not large between the orientation of Mexican-American and Anglo children with regard to their attachment to the American political community. Rural Chicanos feel less attachment as they grow older because they are not exposed to as many Americanizing agencies as their city counterparts.

806 Gilmore, N. Ray, and Gilmore, Gladys W. "The Bracero in California." PACIFIC HISTORICAL REVIEW 32 (1963): 265-82.

Analyzes the temporary Mexican agricultural worker system in California from World War I to 1963, focusing on its operation, sources of opposition and support for its continuance, and a discussion of U.S. policy toward it.

807 Gonzalez, Nancie L. THE SPANISH-AMERICANS OF NEW MEXICO. Albuquerque: University of New Mexico Press, 1969. 246 p. Maps, illustrations, tables, notes, index.

A study of the sociocultural system of Spanish Americans in the state with the highest percentage of Mexicans in its population. Primarily a synthesis of relevant contemporary sociological literature.

808 Grebler, Leo. "The Naturalization of Mexican Immigrants in the United States." INTERNATIONAL MIGRATION REVIEW 1 (1966): 17-32.

Attributes the low naturalization rate among Mexican immigrants to traditional isolation, exclusion from the host society, and low educational and social status. Sees the younger generation seeking citizenship more quickly than their predecessors.

809 _____. THE SCHOOLING GAP: SIGNS OF PROGRESS. Mexican-American Study Project, Advance Report no. 7. Berkeley and Los Angeles: University of California, 1967. 48 p. Illustrations.

Based on 1950 and 1960 census data, finds that the education gap is smaller among the younger generations of Mexican Americans and for the native born as opposed to the foreign born. Still sees great disparities requiring time, reorientation of educational philosophy, strong commitment, and financial support.

810   Grebler, Leo; Moore, Joan W.; and Guzman, Ralph C. THE MEXICAN
       AMERICAN PEOPLE: THE NATION'S SECOND LARGEST MINORITY.
       New York: Free Press, 1970. 777 p. Maps, charts, tables, appendix,
       notes, bibliography.

       A "comprehensive study of the socioeconomic position of Mexi-
       can Americans in selected urban areas of the five Southwestern
       states" undertaken by the Mexican-American Study Project at
       the University of California at Los Angeles between 1964 and
       1968.

811   Gutierrez, Armando, and Hirsch, Herbert. "The Militant Challenge to
       the American Ethos: 'Chicanos' and 'Mexican Americans.'" SOCIAL
       SCIENCE QUARTERLY 53 (1973): 830-45.

       A study of Crystal City, Texas, which reveals that students
       who identified themselves as Chicanos had higher levels of
       political awareness and political cynicism, were more willing
       to engage in collective forms of political action, and were
       more sensitive to institutional discrimination than those who
       identified themselves as Mexican Americans.

812   Hadley, Eleanor M. "A Critical Analysis of the Wetback Problem."
       LAW AND CONTEMPORARY PROBLEMS 21 (1956): 334-57.

       An economic and political study of the migration of wetbacks
       during the decade, 1944-54. Concludes that the immigration
       policy of restriction toward Europe, Asia, and elsewhere
       coupled with unlimited immigration from the Western Hemi-
       sphere was unwise and unfair.

813   Heller, Celia Stopnicka. "Class as an Explanation of Ethnic Differences
       in Mobility Aspirations: The Case of the Mexican-Americans." INTER-
       NATIONAL MIGRATION REVIEW 2 (1967): 31-37.

       Challenges the popular view that there is no substantial in-
       crease in social and economic status with changes in genera-
       tion among Mexican Americans. Based upon an attitude sur-
       vey, finds that only 2 percent of young Chicanos expected to
       become unskilled laborers, while over one-third aspired to
       semiprofessional occupations and 44 percent expected to attend
       college.

814   Hernandez, Jose; Estrada, Leo; and Alvirez, David. "Census Data and
       the Problem of Conceptually Defining the Mexican American Population."
       SOCIAL SCIENCE QUARTERLY 53 (1973): 671-88.

       Three sociologists analyze definitions used by the Bureau of
       the Census for measuring the Mexican-American population
       and use the 1970 census to illustrate related methodological
       problems. They recommend certain refinements in demographic
       concepts.

815 Hoffman, Abraham. "Chicano History: Problems and Potentialities."
JOURNAL OF ETHNIC STUDIES 1 (1973): 6-12.

Stresses the need to get beyond the rhetoric of recent polemics
and into a study of the Chicano heritage by exploring the
documents and resources available.

816 _____. UNWANTED MEXICAN AMERICANS IN THE GREAT DEPRES-
SION: REPATRIATION PRESSURES, 1929-1939. Tucson: University of
Arizona Press, 1974. 207 p. Notes, index.

Deals with the immigration of 450,000 persons of Mexican
ancestry between 1929 and 1937. Although concentrating on
southern California, the author discusses deportation as a national policy and places it in the framework of U.S.-Mexi-
can relations.

817 Hufford, Charles H. THE SOCIAL AND ECONOMIC EFFECTS OF THE
MEXICAN MIGRATION INTO TEXAS. 1929. Reprint. San Francisco:
R and E Research Associations, 1971. 70 p. Tables, appendix, notes,
bibliography.

Discusses the reasons for Mexican migration and the immigrant
relation to social life in Texas, but concentrates mostly on
economic aspects: adaptability of Mexican laborers, their efficiency, and the extent to which they displace white laborers.

818 Humphrey, N.D. "Employment Patterns of Mexicans in Detroit." MONTH-
LY LABOR REVIEW 61 (1945): 913-23.

Discusses employment opportunities available to Mexican migrants in Detroit, their techniques for obtaining and retaining
employment, their coping with unemployment through both public and self-help agencies, and the factors tending toward
their assimilation.

819 _____. "The Integration of the Detroit Mexican Colony." AMERICAN
JOURNAL OF ECONOMICS AND SOCIOLOGY 3 (1944): 155-66.

Describes the efforts of some 6,000 Mexican Americans in
Detroit to achieve community unity, chiefly through the ob-
servance of religious festivals and the formation of national
societies. Concludes that their only really cohesive force is
a shared love of Mexico.

820 Jennings, Mary J. "Exploration of the Personalistic Approach in Interviews with Mexican Entrants to the United States." CIVILISATION (Bel-
gium) 14 (1964): 289-316.

Based upon interviews with sixteen illegal entrants and sixteen
contract laborers. Attempts to analyze their reasons for migrating, opinions of people in the United States, attitudes of

both the Mexican and U.S. governments, and relations among the migrants themselves. Includes sample questionnaire.

821   Johnson, John J., et al., eds. THE MEXICAN AMERICAN: A SE-LECTED AND ANNOTATED BIBLIOGRAPHY. Palo Alto, Calif.: Stanford University Center for Latin American Studies, 1969. 139 p. Index.

Detailed annotations of 268 articles and books selected from 600 works which were consulted.

822   Kibbe, Pauline S. LATIN AMERICANS IN TEXAS. Albuquerque: University of New Mexico Press, 1946. 302 p. Illustrations, appendix, footnotes, bibliography, index.

Attempts to sketch the historical and economic background of Spanish Americans, the relationship of conditions in Texas to U.S.-Latin American affairs, and solutions to problems arising from these conditions.

823   Levenstein, Harvey A. "The AFL and Mexican Immigration in the 1920s: An Experiment in Labor Diplomacy." HISPANIC AMERICAN HISTORICAL REVIEW 48 (1968): 206-19.

Discusses the efforts of Samuel Gompers and the American Federation of Labor to gain restriction of Mexican immigration through lobbying and diplomacy. Sees their major motivation as a desire to prevent future use of Mexican laborers as strike-breakers. After the failure of voluntary restriction, the AFL tried unsuccessfully to have Mexico added to the National Origins Quota System.

824   McCleskey, Clifton, and Merrill, Bruce. "Mexican American Political Behavior in Texas." SOCIAL SCIENCE QUARTERLY 53 (1973): 785-99.

Shows a relatively high degree of political alienation and low level of political efficiency among the Chicanos, who compromise nearly 20 percent of the population in Texas.

825   McLemore, S. Dale. "The Origins of Mexican American Subordination in Texas." SOCIAL SCIENCE QUARTERLY 53 (1973): 656-70.

Tests and validates the applicability of Donald Noel's general theory of the origin of ethnic stratification to Chicanos in Texas.

826   McWilliams, Carey. NORTH FROM MEXICO: THE SPANISH-SPEAKING PEOPLE IN THE UNITED STATES. 1948. Reprint. New York: Greenwood Press, 1968. 324 p. Notes on sources, notes, index.

A history of the Spanish and Mexicans in the United States beginning with settlement of the Southwest by the Spanish and ending with the conclusion of World War II.

827 Martinez, John Ramon. "Mexican Emigration to the United States, 1910-1930." Ph.D. dissertation, University of California, Berkeley, 1957. 100 p.

Deals with the background of Mexican emigration, the impact of economic and political development in the two nations, the evolution of a policy toward the traffic in both countries, and the effects of the migration on the Mexican bracero.

828 Matthiessen, Peter. SAL SI PUEDES: CESAR CHAVEZ AND THE NEW AMERICAN REVOLUTION. New York: Random House, 1970. 373 p.

A popular account of Cesar Chavez's attempts to organize the migrant farm workers of the Southwest. Portions of the book appeared earlier in THE NEW YORKER.

829 Meier, Matt S., and Rivera, Feliciano. THE CHICANOS: A HISTORY OF MEXICAN AMERICANS. New York: Hill & Wang, 1972. 302 p. Maps, glossary, bibliographic essay, index.

A popular history of Mexican Americans from the Indo-Hispanic period to the present, with emphasis on the period since the Manifest Destiny of the 1840s.

830 Metzgar, Joseph V. "The Ethnic Sensitivity of Spanish New Mexicans: A Survey and Analysis." NEW MEXICO HISTORICAL REVIEW 49 (1974): 49-73.

Using a survey of Spanish-speaking people in Albuquerque, New Mexico, in 1972, concludes that the Spanish language and culture here survived, albeit "battered and tattered and beaten perhaps." Argues that only a unified movement of Nativos can save them from ultimate extinction.

831 Metzler, William H. "Mexican Americans and the Acquisitive Syndrome." JOURNAL OF MEXICAN AMERICAN HISTORY 3 (1973): 1-12.

Argues that Mexican-American cultural values have caused many immigrants to the United States to question the traditional values of America's acquisitive society. Feels that Mexican immigrants might help Anglo-Americans to give primary concern to the well-being of all people, rather than the acquisition of material goods.

832 Miller, Charlene. "Los Golondrinos" [Migratory farm workers]. KROEBER ANTHROPOLOGY SOCIETY PAPERS 30 (1964): 51-71.

Examines the life of the bracero or golondrino, his impact upon Mexican cultural life, agricultural methods, and economy as well as his role in the American labor market. Discusses the inequities and corruptions of the "wetback" system and the possible effects of its discontinuance on both countries.

833 Mittelbach, Frank G., and Marshall, Grace. THE BURDEN OF POVER-TY. Mexican-American Study Project, Advance Report no. 5. Berkeley and Los Angeles: University of California, 1966. 65 p. Tables, appendices, footnotes.

One of a series of preliminary reports resulting from research on the Mexican-American Study Project of the University of California at Los Angeles. Provides information on the incidence of poverty in different areas, selected characteristics of the poor, and the impact of family size on poverty.

834 Mittelbach, Frank G., and Moore, Joan W. "Ethnic Endogamy--The Case of Mexican-Americans." AMERICAN JOURNAL OF SOCIOLOGY 74 (1968): 50-62.

Argues that Mexican Americans have acculturated and assimilated much more rapidly in areas like southern California, where the environment is relatively less hostile than in the Southwest, where it is historically inhospitable. Also sees important differences in attitude among the generations of Mexican Americans.

835 Mohl, Raymond A. "The SATURDAY EVENING POST and the 'Mexican Invasion.'" JOURNAL OF MEXICAN AMERICAN HISTORY 3 (1973): 131-37.

Argues that the SATURDAY EVENING POST was the leading popular organ for anti-Mexican immigrant propaganda from 1928 to 1936, serving as an outlet for the works of such nativists as Kenneth Roberts, Garet Garrett, Roy L. Gavis, and Raymond G. Carroll. Their themes paralleled charges made against southern and eastern Europeans and urged restriction of Mexican immigration.

836 Moore, Joan W., and Cuellar, Alfredo. MEXICAN AMERICANS. Englewood Cliffs, N.J.: Prentice Hall, 1970. 172 p. Charts, tables, notes, selected bibliography, index.

Covers many of the topics previously published in THE MEXICAN-AMERICAN PEOPLE: THE NATION'S SECOND LARGEST MINORITY, based on the findings of the Mexican-American Study Project at the University of California at Los Angeles. Moore was coauthor of the earlier, more detailed volume and adds little that is new in this summary treatment.

837 Moquin, Wayne, ed., with Van Doren, Charles. A DOCUMENTARY HISTORY OF THE MEXICAN AMERICANS. New York: Praeger Pub-

lishers, 1971. 399 p. Illustrations, index.

Sixty-five selections arranged chronologically and subdivided into five historical periods: the era of Spanish rule (1536-1809); Mexico's control of the Southwest (1810-48); Anglo-American conquest (1849-1910); Mexican-American immigrants (1911-39); and the reawakening of the ethnic awareness of Mexican Americans (1940-70).

838   Navarro, Eliseo. THE CHICANO COMMUNITY: A SELECTED BIBLIOGRAPHY FOR USE IN SOCIAL WORK EDUCATION. New York: Council on Social Work Education, 1971. 57 p.

Annotated bibliography of some 200 entries concerning the historical background, acculturation, education, health, religion, discrimination, politics, economics, family life, social welfare, and literature of Chicanos. Includes books, articles, newspapers, and government documents.

839   Nostrand, Richard L. "'Mexican American' and 'Chicano': Emerging Terms for a People Coming of Age." PACIFIC HISTORICAL REVIEW 42 (1973): 389-406.

Sees the increasing acceptance of "Mexican American" and "Chicano" by the society as terms for people whom society had formerly called a variety of derogatory epithets. Concludes that this indicates the minority group has begun to see itself as Mexican and the dominant society has begun to recognize them as Mexicans.

840   Olson, James S. "The Birth of a Discipline: An Essay on Chicano Historiography." SOCIAL STUDIES 65 (1974): 300-302.

A brief historiographical essay on Chicano studies that identifies three main themes: (1) the documentation of Anglo land seizure under the rationalization of "Manifest Destiny," (2) the charge of cultural genocide levied against Anglo-Americans, and (3) the issue of economic exploitation of Mexican-American labor by American employers.

841   PACIFIC HISTORICAL REVIEW 42 (1973): 269-308.

This special issue on the Chicano contains articles by Arthur F. Corwin, Carey McWilliams, Felix Almaraz, Jr., William B. Taylor, Elliott West, Charles Wollenberg, Neil Betten, Raymond Mohl, and Richard Nostrand.

842   Penalosa, Fernando. "The Changing Mexican-American in Southern California." SOCIOLOGY AND SOCIAL RESEARCH 51 (1967): 405-17.

Contends that the popular stereotype of Mexican Americans as migratory farm workers does not square with reality in southern California, where 79 percent are native born, 84 percent urban, only 23 percent unskilled labor, and but 12 percent farm workers. Predicts increased mobility and political power for them in a pluralistic society.

843   Pitt, Leonard. THE DECLINE OF THE CALIFORNIOS: A SOCIAL HIS-TORY OF THE SPANISH SPEAKING CALIFORNIANS, 1846-1890. Berkeley and Los Angeles: University of California Press, 1966. 324 p. Illustrations, footnotes, notes, glossary, bibliography, index.

A scholarly social history of Mexicans in southern California with emphasis on the period from 1846 to 1865.

844   Reisler, Mark. "The Mexican Immigrant in the Chicago Area during the 1920s." JOURNAL OF THE ILLINOIS STATE HISTORICAL SOCIETY 66 (1973): 144-58.

Describes the reasons for Mexican migration to Chicago, immigrants' employment and settlement patterns, their religious and communal organizations, and the prejudice and discrimination against them. Concludes that life was in many respects a form of bondage that made it difficult to both earn a living and preserve native culture.

845   Robinson, Cecil. "Spring Water with a Taste of the Land." AMERICAN WEST 3 (1966): 6-15.

Argues that the persistence of Mexican culture and values is largely responsible for the American Southwest's continued resistance to urban blight. Surveys the literature of the people of the area and sees a revival of interest in things Mexican in contrast to the pressures for Anglo-conformity.

846   Rochin, Refugio I. "The Short and Turbulent Life of Chicano Studies: A Preliminary Study of Emerging Programs and Problems." SOCIAL SCIENCE QUARTERLY 53 (1973): 884-94.

An analysis of the data from questionnaires sent to nearly thirty directors of Chicano studies programs on college campuses.

847   Rosaldo, Renato; Calvert, Robert A.; and Seligman, Gustav L. CHICANO: THE EVOLUTION OF A PEOPLE. Minneapolis: Winston Press, 1973. 461 p.

A collection of fifty articles from previously published sources providing a historiography of the subject for use in college courses.

848   Samora, Julian. LOS MOJADOS: THE WETBACK STORY. Notre Dame, Ind.: University of Notre Dame Press, 1971. 205 p. Illustrations,

tables, appendices, bibliography, index.

Reviews current literature on the topic, provides a brief history of illegal Mexican immigration, then discusses the how and why of wetback immigration. The final chapter suggests possible solutions to the problem. Produced through the United States-Mexico Border Studies Project.

849 Samora, Julian, and Lamanna, Richard. MEXICAN-AMERICANS IN A MID-WEST METROPOLIS: EAST CHICAGO. Berkeley and Los Angeles: University of California Press, 1967. 164 p. Maps, tables, appendices.

Advance Report by the Mexican-American Study Project of the University of California at Los Angeles. After studying the family, church, education, employment, occupational status, and political influence of Mexican Americans in this midwestern city, the authors conclude that the pattern is not radically different from the situation in the Southwest.

850 Sanchez, George I. FORGOTTEN PEOPLE. Albuquerque, N.M.: Calvin Horn, Publisher, 1967. 98 p. Tables.

Argues that the Spanish-descended population of New Mexico is the victim of discrimination in the areas of economics, education, and public services.

851 Scott, Robin Fitzgerald. "The Mexican-American in the Los Angeles Area, 1920-1950: From Acquiescence to Activity." Ph.D. dissertation, University of Southern California, 1971. 387 p.

Examines the causes and effects of discrimination in historical perspective. Mexican Americans changed their manner and methodology to gain acceptance in Los Angeles, beginning with acquiescence and then turning to political activism, especially after World War II.

852 Scruggs, Otey M. "Texas and the Bracero Program, 1942-1947." PACIFIC HISTORICAL REVIEW 32 (1963): 251-64.

Focuses upon Mexican and American governmental attitudes toward the admission of temporary agricultural workers into Texas. Also describes the discrimination suffered by braceros and how they seek to counteract it.

853 Servin, Manuel P. "The Pre-World War II Mexican-American: An Interpretation." CALIFORNIA HISTORICAL SOCIETY QUARTERLY 45 (1966): 325-38.

A revised section of "The Postwar Mexican-American: A Non-achieving Minority" delivered before the 1965 meeting of the Western History Association. This is a study of Mexi-

can immigrants born before 1926, drawn from the works of
Paul Taylor and Emory Bogardus, personal interviews, and the
boyhood recollections of the author. Argues that Mexican
Americans were highly regarded before 1942 until attacks by
young "pochucos" on U.S. servicemen gave the entire group an
undeserved reputation for lawlessness and disloyalty.

854 _____, ed. THE MEXICAN AMERICANS: AN AWAKENING MINORI-
TY. Beverly Hills, Calif.: Glencoe Press, 1970. 235 p. Footnotes.

A chronological arrangement of sixteen articles, some published
here for the first time, concerning the Mexican Americans,
especially during the twentieth century.

855 Shockley, John Staples. CHICANO REVOLT IN A TEXAS TOWN. Notre
Dame, Ind.: University of Notre Dame Press, 1974. 302 p.

Examines the impact of a Chicano political "takeover" on the
town of Crystal City, Texas, "the spinach capital of the world."
Concludes that the conditions were unique and cannot be dupli-
cated elsewhere in the state.

856 Simmons, Ozzie G. "Mutual Images and Expectations of Anglo-Americans
and Mexican-Americans." DAEDALUS 90 (1961): 286-99.

Argues that both groups have contradictory and negative images
of each other, with Anglos retaining ideas of Mexican inferiority while forcing Americanization and the latter disliking
Anglo culture but being willing to embrace it as the price for
social mobility.

857 Simon, Daniel T. "Mexican Repatriation in East Chicago, Indiana."
JOURNAL OF ETHNIC STUDIES 2 (1974): 11-23.

The story of local efforts to solve the Depression by an American Legion program of repatriating over 1,000 Mexicans in
1932. Sees the move as a simplistic effort that succeeded
only in arousing hostile racial feelings.

858 Steiner, Stan. LA RAZA: THE MEXICAN AMERICANS. New York:
Harper & Row, 1970. 418 p. Illustrations, sources, index.

An impressionistic survey of the contemporary Mexican encounter with the dominant culture of the United States in the Southwest.

859 Stoddard, Ellwyn R. "The Adjustment of Mexican American Barrio Families to Forced Housing Relocation." SOCIAL SCIENCE QUARTERLY 53
(1973): 749-59.

From a study of residents of a Chicano section of El Paso,

finds that "rather than the extended or nuclear family being
the basic social unit to which barrio residents were oriented,
it was the mini-neighborhood, that visiting clique, which
emerges as the critical social unit in this particular Mexican-
American barrio."

860 Taylor, Paul S. MEXICAN LABOR IN THE UNITED STATES, 1930-32.
1930. Reprint. New York: Arno Press, 1970. Vol. 1, 464 p. Maps,
tables, appendix, footnotes, index. Vol. 2, 284 p. Maps, tables,
footnotes, index.

Originally published as volumes 6 and 7 of the University of
California Publications in Economics. The first volume covers
California, Colorado, and Texas and volume 2 focuses on
Bethlehem, Pennsylvania, and particularly on Chicago. Pro-
vides a statistical analysis of migration patterns and employ-
ment distribution.

861 Tebbel, John, and Ruiz, Ramon E. SOUTH BY SOUTHWEST: THE MEXI-
CAN-AMERICAN AND HIS HERITAGE. Garden City, N.Y.: Doubleday
and Co., 1969. 120 p. Index.

A short readable treatment of Mexican Americans, focusing upon their ethnic identity and the historical evolution of Mexico
from the colonial and revolutionary era to a modern state.
The last section explores the changing relationship between
Mexico and the United States.

862 Tirado, Miguel David. "Mexican American Political Organization the
Key to Chicano Power." AZTLAN 1 (1970): 53-78.

A re-evaluation of the assumption that "the Spanish surname
population [has] not formed clubs which could serve their political interests." He offers instead many examples of Mexican-
American community political organizations.

863 Trejo, Arnulfo D. BIBLIOGRAFICA CHICANA: A GUIDE TO INFOR-
MATION SOURCES. Detroit: Gale Research Co., 1975. 193 p. Index, glossary.

Contains about 500 annotated items under the categories of
general reference works, humanities, social sciences, history,
and applied sciences. Also includes a profile of Chicano
newspapers and periodicals and publishers devoted to Chicano
studies.

864 Tuck, Ruth D. NOT WITH THE FIST: MEXICAN-AMERICANS IN A
SOUTHWEST CITY. New York: Harcourt, Brace & World, 1946.
234 p. Footnotes, selected bibliography.

Uses the name "Descanso" in place of the actual small southwestern city she studies from early settlement to the end of World War II, when more militant service veterans returned home.

865 Vigil, Ralph H. "New Ethnic Literature: A Review Essay." NEW MEXICO HISTORICAL REVIEW 49 (1974): 153-70.

A review essay of FOREIGNERS IN THEIR NATIVE LAND: HISTORICAL ROOTS OF THE MEXICAN AMERICANS, an anthology of more than sixty selections dealing with the pre-twentieth century, edited by David J. Weber; CHICANO: THE EVOLUTION OF A PEOPLE, a selection of over fifty articles, edited by Renato Rosaldo, Robert A. Calvert, and Gustav L. Seligmann; CHICANOS AND NATIVE AMERICANS: THE TERRITORIAL MINORITIES, fifteen selections edited by Rudolph de la Garza et al.; and RISE OF THE UNMELTABLE ETHNICS by Michael Novak.

866 Weber, David J., ed. FOREIGNERS IN THEIR NATIVE LAND: HISTORICAL ROOTS OF THE MEXICAN AMERICANS. Albuquerque: University of New Mexico Press, 1973. 288 p. Illustrations, notes, index.

A collection of Spanish, Mexican, and American writings from the sixteenth century to the beginning of the twentieth century. The editor provides a lengthy historical introduction to each of the five chronologically-arranged units.

867 Welch, Susan; Comer, John; and Steinman, Michael. "Political Participation Among Mexican Americans: An Exploratory Examination." SOCIAL SCIENCE QUARTERLY 53 (1973): 799-813.

Studies two Nebraska Mexican-American communities "to describe the level of political participation among Mexican Americans and contrast it with other groups; second, to delineate some dimensions of participation among Mexican-Americans; and third, to explain differences in political participation among them."

868 Winn, Charles Carr. "Mexican-Americans in the Texas Labor Movement." Ph.D. dissertation, Texas Christian University, 1972. 217 p.

Analysis of Mexican-American participation in the organized labor movement which reveals that, although Anglo competition for union jobs tends to decrease Mexican-American involvement, racial discrimination does not play an important role in determining participation in organized labor.

869 Wollenberg, Charles. "MENDEZ v. WESTMINSTER: Race, Nationality and Segregation in California Schools." CALIFORNIA HISTORICAL QUARTERLY 53 (1974): 317-32.

Discusses the historical evolution of the segregation of Mexican-American school children in California down to its eventual
abolition by the Mendez decision in 1947. Deals largely with
the pro and con debate over segregation and court decisions
prior to the Mendez one.

CUBAN

870 Detter, Raymond A. "The Cuban Junta and Michigan: 1895-1898."
MICHIGAN HISTORY 48 (1964): 35-46.

Examines the role played by Cuban exiles in influencing public opinion and politicians to support Cuban independence,
eventually culminating in the Spanish-American War, using
Michigan as a test case. Based largely upon Cuban diplomatic correspondence.

871 Rogg, Eleanor Meyer. THE ASSIMILATION OF CUBAN EXILES: THE
ROLE OF COMMUNITY AND CLASS. New York: Aberdeen, 1974.
241 p. Tables, appendices, bibliography.

A study of Cuban refugees who fled Cuba in 1959 and eventually settled in West New York, New Jersey, a town of 35,000.
Composed mainly of a statistical analysis based on extensive
personal interviews conducted in Spanish.

872 Thomas, John F. "Cuban Refugees in the United States." INTERNA-
TIONAL MIGRATION REVIEW 1 (1967): 46-57.

Traces the evolution of American efforts to aid the 300,000
Cuban refugees who fled from Castro's Cuba between 1959 and
1966. Concentrates upon the Cuban Refugee Program and its
financial and resettlement assistance.

873 Walsh, Msgr. Bryan O. "Cuban Refugee Children." JOURNAL OF IN-
TERNATIONAL-AMERICAN STUDIES AND WORLD AFFAIRS 13 (1971):
378-415.

The story of the 14,000 unaccompanied child refugees from
Cuba who came to America between 1959 and 1971. Most of
these children were sent by parents who wanted to stay to
fight Castro but who were afraid that their children might be
sent to Russia for Communist indoctrination. As the volume of
refugees increased, the U.S. government took over the program originally undertaken by Catholic relief agencies.

874 Wenk, Michael. "Adjustment and Assimilation: The Cuban Refugee Experience." INTERNATIONAL MIGRATION REVIEW 3 (1968): 39-49.

Concludes that most of the 180,000 Cuban refugees have suc-

cessfully adjusted to life in America and are regaining the
status they held in Cuba before emigrating.

PUERTO RICAN

875 Cordasco, Frank M. "The Puerto Rican Child in the American School."
JOURNAL OF HUMAN RELATIONS 15 (1967): 500-509.

Discusses the serious difficulties encountered by Puerto Rican
children in the New York City schools, especially in learning
the language and in trying to maintain ethnic identity and
culture while learning American ways. These disabilities have
made them the least educated of all the city's ethnic or racial groups.

876 Fitzpatrick, Joseph P. PUERTO RICAN AMERICANS: THE MEANING
OF MIGRATION TO THE MAINLAND. Ethnic Groups in American Life
Series, edited by Milton M. Gordon. Englewood Cliffs, N.J.: Prentice-
Hall, 1971. 192 p. Tables, figures, footnotes, index.

A study of recent Puerto Rican immigration to the United
States, with special reference to New York.

877 Handlin, Oscar. THE NEWCOMERS: NEGROES AND PUERTO RICANS
IN A CHANGING METROPOLIS. Garden City, N.Y.: Doubleday and
Co., 1962. 177 p. Bibliography.

Argues that New York's Puerto Ricans and Negroes are merely
the most recent examples of the recurring pattern of newcomers
who will eventually be accepted into the city's mainstream.

878 Koss, Joan Dee. "Puerto Ricans in Philadelphia: Migration and Accomodations." Ph.D. dissertation, University of Pennsylvania, 1965. 539 p.

After extensive studying and interviewing of over one hundred
Puerto Ricans who had moved to Philadelphia or had returned
from Philadelphia to Puerto Rico, delineates the pattern of
social and cultural accomodation made by new immigrants to
the city.

879 Lewis, Oscar. LA VIDA: A PUERTO RICAN FAMILY IN THE CULTURE
OF POVERTY--SAN JUAN AND NEW YORK. New York: Random
House, 1965. 669 p.

Based largely on tape recorded interviews of 100 Puerto Rican
families in San Juan and their relatives in New York. Most
of the book is in the form of actual comments, made under
assumed names, illustrating the cultural effects of extreme
poverty in both cities.

880 Macisco, John J. "Assimilation of Puerto Ricans on the Mainland: A Socio-Demographic Approach." INTERNATIONAL MIGRATION REVIEW 2 (1968): 21-37.

Compares first and second generation Puerto Rican Americans on indices of age, educational status, occupation, percentage of out-group marriage and fertility, and concludes that the second generation is moving toward the U.S. national averages in most of these categories.

881 Mills, C. Wright; Goldsen, Rose Kohn; and Senior, Clarence. THE PUERTO RICAN JOURNEY: NEW YORK'S NEWEST MIGRANTS. New York: Russell and Russell, 1950. 238 p. Appendices, notes, sources, indices.

A sociological study begun in 1947 and completed in 1950 which makes extensive use of interviews, survey research, and statistical data to determine the experiences of Puerto Rican immigrants in New York, particularly in Spanish Harlem and the Morrisania area of the Bronx. It is divided into three main sections, beginning with the immigrants to Puerto Rico, then in transit, and finally in their new city.

882 Padilla, Elena. UP FROM PUERTO RICO. New York: Columbia University Press, 1958. 317 p. Illustrations.

Anthropological analysis based upon two-and-one-half years of field work in a Puerto Rican ghetto. Focuses upon information networks of communication through which advice on the courts, welfare officers, and medical problems are circulated.

883 Rand, Christopher. THE PUERTO RICANS. New York: Oxford University Press, 1958. 178 p.

A series of articles on New York Puerto Ricans which appeared earlier in modified form in THE NEW YORKER.

884 Rodriguez, Clara. "Puerto Ricans and the Melting Pot: A Review Essay." JOURNAL OF ETHNIC STUDIES 1 (1974): 89-98.

A critical review of Glazer and Moynihan's BEYOND THE MELTING POT (2d ed.) with special reference to the Puerto Ricans and aimed at exposing the flaws of a nonstructural approach, the authors' assimilationist bias and their lack of experience in the Puerto Rican community.

885 Senior, Clarence. THE PUERTO RICANS: STRANGERS--THEN NEIGHBORS. Chicago: Quadrangle Books, 1965. 128 p. Maps, illustrations, bibliography.

Contends that the statistical evidence on education, economics,

housing, welfare, and criminality disproves many of the popular stereotypes concerning Puerto Ricans. Also contends that
they have moved toward assimilation and integration.

886   Seplowin, Virginia M.   "Training and Employment Patterns of Puerto Ricans in Philadelphia."   Ph.D. dissertation, University of Pennsylvania,
1969. 362 p.

"Examine[s] conditions among the Puerto Ricans in Philadelphia
of persons who apply for manpower training and persons who
seek employment only and reject training." Suggests ways to
improve training and employment services for Puerto Ricans.

SPANISH-SPEAKING—GENERAL

887   Alford, Harold J.   THE PROUD PEOPLES: THE HERITAGE AND CULTURE
OF SPANISH-SPEAKING PEOPLES IN THE UNITED STATES.   New York:
David McKay Co., 1972.   325 p.   Bibliography, index.

From Spanish explorers to Cesar Chavez, this brief survey "is
designed to dramatize the chronology, the contributions, the
difficult status, the desperate needs and the dynamic potential
of the people of Spanish descent who live and work in every
part of the land...." Also includes biographical summaries
of outstanding Spanish-speaking people in the United States.

888   Burma, John H.   SPANISH-SPEAKING GROUPS IN THE UNITED STATES.
Durham, N.C.: Duke University Press, 1954.   214 p.   Maps, appendix,
footnotes, bibliography, index.

Sociological discussion of the Hispanos of New Mexico, the
Puerto Ricans of New York, and the Filipinos of the West
Coast and an analysis of Spanish and Mexican Americans in
the twentieth century.

889   Shannon, Lyle W., and Shannon, Magdaline.   MINORITY MIGRANTS IN
THE URBAN COMMUNITY: MEXICAN-AMERICAN AND NEGRO ADJUST-
MENT TO INDUSTRIAL SOCIETY.   Beverly Hills, Calif.: Sage Publica-
tions, 1973.   335 p.   Appendix, indices.

Revisits Racine, Wisconsin, ten years after previous study to
analyze progress of Afro- and Mexican Americans in socioeconomic mobility and to evaluate their efforts at perpetuating
identity and culture.

REFUGEES AND DISPLACED PERSONS

890   Adams, Walter, ed.   THE BRAIN DRAIN.   New York: Macmillan Co.,
1968.   273 p.   Footnotes, index.

A collection of papers presented in 1967 at an international conference in Switzerland. The general subject of these essays is the international migration of engineers, scientists, and professionals to the United States. The problem is considered from the perspective of different case studies and from an analytical economic framework.

891 ANNALS OF THE AMERICAN ACADEMY OF POLITICAL AND SOCIAL SCIENCES 203 (1939): 1-271.

Special issue on "Refugees," edited by Francis J. Brown. An anthology of articles by several scholars on the underlying factors behind the pre-World War II refugee problem, its composition and character, the human side of the problem, and a variety of possible solutions ranging from relocation in underdeveloped countries to revision of U.S. immigration laws.

892 Fermi, Laura. ILLUSTRIOUS IMMIGRANTS: THE INTELLECTUAL MIGRATIONS FROM EUROPE, 1930-1941. Chicago: University of Chicago Press, 1968. 398 p. Illustrations, notes, index.

Describes the flight of prominent European artists and intellectuals to the United States before World War II, their settlement here, their achievements, and an evaluation of the impact of their migration on both Europe and America.

893 Fields, Harold. THE REFUGEE IN THE UNITED STATES. New York: Oxford University Press, 1938. 229 p. Appendices, bibliography.

Discusses Russian, German, Ukrainian, Greek, Armenian, and other 1930s refugees to the United States, focusing on their naturalization, assimilation, marriage and family, and literature and the efforts of social agencies to provide financial and other types of aid.

894 Fleming, Donald, and Bailyn, Bernard, eds. THE INTELLECTUAL MIGRATION: EUROPE AND AMERICA, 1930-1960. Perspectives in American History Series, vol. 2. Cambridge, Mass.: Charles Warren Center for Studies in American History, 1969. 748 p. Illustrations, footnotes, index.

A collection of fourteen essays or memoirs of the migration of German-speaking emigrants from Hitler's Europe. After an initial essay by Peter Gay on the Weimar culture, providing a background for subsequent chapters, much of the remainder of the book examines the scientific contributions of the emigres.

895 Fortney, Judith. "International Migration of Professionals." POPULATION STUDIES 24 (1970): 217-34.

A statistical summary of immigration over recent decades showing a high number of professionals, especially since the 1965 immigration law. Many of these professionals come from less-developed countries.

896   Friedman, Saul S.   NO HAVEN FOR THE OPPRESSED: UNITED STATES POLICY TOWARD JEWISH REFUGEES, 1938-1945. Detroit: Wayne State University Press, 1973. 315 p. Notes, index.

Argues that American complicity allowed the systematic extinction of the Jews by Germans through opposition to changing restrictive immigration laws, through the efforts of organized labor to keep Jews out of the country, and through the inaction and internal division of American Jews.

897   Grubel, H.G.   "The Immigration of Scientists and Engineers to the United States, 1949-1961." JOURNAL OF POLITICAL ECONOMY 74 (1966): 368-78.

Discusses the migration of future scientists and engineers to the United States, claiming that they comprised 5 percent of the graduates of U.S. schools of higher learning. They added about a billion dollars to national income, while constituting a "brain-drain" of anywhere from 20 to 40 percent of first degree earners in several European nations.

898   Hall, Dudley S., and Herberle, Rudolph.   NEW AMERICANS: A STUDY OF DISPLACED PERSONS IN LOUISIANA AND MISSISSIPPI. Baton Rouge, La.: Displaced Persons Commission, 1951. 93 p.

A study of displaced persons from Eastern Europe who were settled in the South following World War II, their characteristics and adjustment to their relocation. Includes several photographs of DPs and their housing and charts of demographic aspects of the New Immigrant.

899   Kent, Donald P.   REFUGEE INTELLECTUAL: THE AMERICANIZATION OF THE IMMIGRANTS OF 1933-1941. New York: Columbia University Press, 1953. 317 p. Bibliography.

Based upon questionnaires and interviews with the German and Austrian intellectuals who fled from Europe to the United States between 1933 and 1941. Concerned mostly with their adjustment to the American environment.

900   Lasby, Clarence George.   PROJECT PAPERCLIP: GERMAN SCIENTISTS AND THE COLD WAR. New York: Atheneum, 1971. 338 p. Notes, bibliographic comment, index.

The story of the U.S. government's program, code named "Paperclip," which brought to the United States 642 German and Austrian scientists between May 1945 and December 1952.

Discusses their role in the cold war race for military and scientific supremacy between the United States and Russia.

901   LAW AND CONTEMPORARY PROBLEMS 21 (1956): 1-752.

Entire issue is devoted to immigration. Contains a dozen articles by historians, political scientists, sociologists, and economists, focusing mainly on contemporary aspects of immigration restriction and the McCarran-Walter Act.

902   Lorimer, M. Madeline. "America's Response to Europe's Displaced Persons, 1945-1952: A Preliminary Report." Ph.D. dissertation, St. Louis University, 1964. 361 p.

After sketching the international setting for the problem of repatriation and relocation of displaced persons, details the political fight in the United States over the Displaced Persons Act and the subsequent work of the commission created by the act.

903   Manning, John. "Canada's Most Valuable Export." MIDWEST QUARTERLY 9 (1968): 157-67.

Discussion by a Canadian scholar of the "brain drain" which brings thousands of Indian, Chinese, and African teachers, physicians, scientists, and engineers to Canadian universities and firms for training and then on to the United States. Contains account of the international conference on the brain drain held in Lausanne, Switzerland, in August 1967.

904   Markowitz, Arthur A. "Humanitarianism Versus Restrictionism: The United States and the Hungarian Refugees." INTERNATIONAL MIGRATION REVIEW 7 (1973): 46-59.

Describes the efforts of hard-line immigration restrictionists in Congress to oppose President Eisenhower's lenient proposal for the resettlement of Hungarian refugees in 1957. Eventually they forced Eisenhower to lower the quota, leaving the United States near the bottom of the list in refugees admitted, in terms of numbers and wealth.

905   Saenger, Gerhart. TODAY'S REFUGEES, TOMORROW'S CITIZENS: A STORY OF AMERICANIZATION. New York and London: Harper & Brothers, 1941. 286 p. Index.

Discusses the European refugees fleeing from Hitler in the late 1930s, their social adjustment to the United States, occupational and residential relocation, family life, contributions to America, and the outlook for the future.

906   Soskis, Philip. "The Adjustment of Hungarian Refugees in New York."

INTERNATIONAL MIGRATION REVIEW 2 (1967): 40-46.

Summarizes a survey of 200 randomly-selected Jewish refugees from the 1956 Hungarian Revolution whom the New York Association for New Americans helped relocate in New York.

907 Taeuber, Alma F., and Taeuber, Karl E. "Recent Immigration and Studies of Ethnic Assimilation." DEMOGRAPHY 4 (1967): 798-808.

Contends that because recent immigrants come from a much higher socioeconomic status than those who came before the imposition of the quota system, studies that arbitrarily combine these two groups produce confusing results. Tabulation of foreign born by year of arrival would, the authors argue, "improve the sociological utility of data for ethnic groups."

908 Weiner, Charles. "A New Site for the Seminar: The Refugees and American Physics in the Thirties." PERSPECTIVES IN AMERICAN HISTORY 2 (1968): 190-234.

Discusses the experiences of German and Austrian refugee physicists of the 1930s and their impact on the discipline. Contends that their interaction with the new American environment was shaped by the internationalization of physics, the self-improvement of American scientists, the dissolution of physics in Nazi Germany, their experience during their nomadic stage, and their reception in the United States.

909 Weinstock, S.A. "Acculturation and Occupation: A Study of the 1956 Hungarian Refugees in the United States." PUBLICATION RESEARCH GROUP FOR EUROPEAN MIGRATION PROBLEMS 15 (1969): 1-127.

Concerned mainly with the adjustment made by individual Hungarian refugees to life in the United States over a period of time. Also discusses the definition and context of acculturation and the history of Hungary from 1914 to 1956.

910 Wetzil, Charles John. "The American Rescue of Refugee Scholars and Scientists from Europe, 1933-1945." Ph.D. dissertation, University of Wisconsin, 1964. 446 p.

Investigates the role played by voluntary American organizations and philanthropic benefactors in rescuing scholars who were persecuted or barred from teaching by the Axis powers.

911 Wyman, David S. PAPER WALLS: AMERICA AND THE REFUGEE CRISIS, 1938-1941. Amherst: University of Massachusetts Press, 1968. 306 p. Appendices, sources, notes, index.

A critical appraisal of American refugee policy toward Jews fleeing Germany between 1938 and U.S. entry into World War II. Discusses the diplomatic efforts, congressional involvement, and administrative decisions and policies that failed to save a large number of Jews seeking asylum in America.

Chapter 6

ACCULTURATION, ASSIMILATION, ETHNICITY, AND RESTRICTION

GENERAL STUDIES OF ETHNICITY

912 Abbott, Grace. THE IMMIGRANT AND THE COMMUNITY. 1917. Reprint. New York: Jerome S. Ozer, 1971. 298 p. Index.

Analysis by a prominent social worker of the problems faced by immigrants in the courts, in public health, poverty, education, politics, labor unions, in finding employment, and in avoiding exploitation.

913 American Jewish Committee. GROUP LIFE IN AMERICA: A TASK FORCE REPORT. New York: 1972. 111 p.

Summary of the results and recommendations of an American Jewish Committee task force study on group life in the 1970s by consultant Seymour Martin Lipset.

914 Appel, John J. "American Negro and Immigrant Experience: Similarities and Differences." AMERICAN QUARTERLY 18 (1966): 95-103.

Argues that Negroes had a harder time progressing than immigrants because of racial and caste status. Discusses the competition between Negroes and immigrants for jobs, housing, and education and concludes that blacks have had to emulate the former's ethnic solidarity and chauvinism in order to advance.

915 Barron, Milton L. THE BLENDING AMERICAN: PATTERNS OF INTER-MARRIAGE. Chicago: Quadrangle Books, 1972. 338 p. Bibliography, index.

An anthology by a variety of authors on racial, ethnic, and religious intermarriage, the attempts of institutions to regulate it, and postmarital consequences for the parties and their children.

916 _____, ed. MINORITIES IN A CHANGING WORLD. New York: Alfred A. Knopf, 1967. 474 p. Bibliography, index.

Thirty-three selections by various scholars on ethnic minorities in the United States and other societies. About one-third deal with American Negroes.

917 Barton, Josef J. "Immigration and Social Mobility in an American City: Studies of Three Ethnic Groups in Cleveland, 1890-1950." Ph.D. dissertation, University of Michigan, 1971. 292 p.

Studies the experience of Roman Catholic Italians, Byzantine Rite and Eastern Orthodox Rumanians, and Roman Catholic Slovaks to answer three questions: (1) what was the significance of different migration patterns in the social adjustment of newcomers? (2) how did ethnic leadership emerge in the process of migration? and, (3) what relation did ethnic origins have to the process of occupational adjustment in America?

918 Bayor, Ronald Howard. "Ethnic Conflict in New York City, 1929-1941." Ph.D. dissertation, University of Pennsylvania, 1970. 287 p.

Chooses the leading Old Immigrant ethnic groups in New York from the period--Germans, Irish--and New Immigrant Jews and Italians in order to determine how these groups saw their status threatened. Social mobility, cultural differences, the effects of the Depression, and international affairs were factors affecting that status.

919 Bender, Eugene I., and Kagiwada, George. "Hansen's Law of 'Third Generation Return' and the Study of American Religio-Ethnic Groups." PHYLON 29 (1968): 360-70.

Studies Marcus Lee Hansen's analysis of the third generation immigrants who "already secure in their Americaness took pride in the past and formed historical societies to record their ethnic history." Author suggests a refinement of this thesis in light of Karl Mannheim's ideas concerning generations.

920 Berkson, Isaac B. THEORIES OF AMERICANIZATION: A CRITICAL STUDY. 1920. Reprint. New York: Arno Press, 1969. 226 p. Footnotes, selected references.

A dissertation which studies Americanization with reference to Jews. It discusses various types of ethnic relationships possible in a democracy and then suggests a plan for Americanizing Jews through an altered educational system.

921 Berry, Brewton. RACE AND ETHNIC RELATIONS. 3d ed. Boston: Houghton Mifflin Co., 1965. 435 p. Illustrations, footnotes, bibliography, index.

A textbook which describes and analyzes "the phenomena which arise when groups of people who differ racially and culturally come into contact with one another." As a sociologist, Berry is interested in relationships.

922 Betten, Neil, and Mohl, Raymond A. "Ethnic Adjustment in the Industrial City: The International Institute of Gary, 1919-1940." INTERNATIONAL MIGRATION REVIEW 6 (1972): 361-76.

A case study of the work of the International Institutes set up in more than sixty U.S. cities by the YWCA, Department of Immigration, and foreign communities after World War I. Using largely immigrant stock social workers, the institute sought to give practical economic and social aid to Gary's various nationalities while seeking to preserve their cultural heritage.

923 Bodger, John Charles. "The Immigrant Press and the Union Army." Ph.D. dissertation, Columbia University, 1951. 427 p.

Concludes that the immigrant press generally supported the union cause, but with some reservations. For example, Democratic journals which had supported Douglas in 1860 criticized Lincoln's handling of the war and the recruitment of immigrants in Europe and Canada; radical Republican German papers supported Fremont over Lincoln in 1864 and criticized Union army treatment of some Germans; and Conservative Republican journals never criticized Lincoln or the army but devoted print to the achievements of their immigrant soldiers in the war.

924 Bodnar, John E., ed. THE ETHNIC EXPERIENCE IN PENNSYLVANIA. Lewisburg, Pa.: Bucknell University Press, 1973. 330 p. Maps, tables, notes.

Collection of twelve essays on Irish, Poles, Amish, blacks, Italians, Ruthenians, Ukrainians, Croats, East European Jews, South Slavs, and occupational mobility of immigrants in Pennsylvania. Deals with first generation immigrants in particular areas of the state and shows that new arrivals often suffered as much discrimination from earlier immigrants as they did from the dominant Anglo-Saxon majority.

925 Bogardus, Emory S. ESSENTIALS OF AMERICANIZATION. 3d ed., rev. Los Angeles: University of Southern California Press, 1919. 303 p.

Investigates the concept of Americanization with respect to its industrial, racial, social, political, and educational phases. Warns that it not only entails new loyalties on the part of the foreign born, but also efforts by native Americans to understand and improve their own standards and traditions.

926   Bowers, David F., ed. FOREIGN INFLUENCES IN AMERICAN LIFE:
       ESSAYS AND CRITICAL BIBLIOGRAPHIES. Princeton, N.J.: Princeton
       University Press, 1944. 252 p. Illustrations, footnotes.

       Collection of brief essays covering the Americanization of the
       immigrant, ethnic factors in the American economic ethic,
       the immigrant in politics, and the ethnic impact from a socio-
       logical point of view. Includes a topically arranged annotated
       bibliography.

927   Bradburn, Norman M.; Sudman, Seymour; and Gockel, Galen L. RACIAL
       INTEGRATION IN AMERICAN NEIGHBORHOODS: A COMPARATIVE
       SURVEY. Chicago: National Opinion Research Center, 1970. 599 p.
       Tables, appendix.

       The results of a comprehensive national survey begun in 1967
       which seeks to determine whites' willingness to live in racially
       integrated neighborhoods. It deals "mainly with higher income
       black and white families in middle-class neighborhoods."

928   Breton, Raymond. "Institutional Completeness of Ethnic Communities and
       the Personal Relations of Immigrants." AMERICAN JOURNAL OF SO-
       CIOLOGY 70 (1964): 193-205.

       Contends that there is a direct relationship between the ability
       of receiving societies to attract immigrants into their social
       boundaries and the institutional completeness of the ethnic
       community.

929   Brooks, Charlotte, ed. THE OUTNUMBERED; STORIES, ESSAYS AND
       POEMS ABOUT MINORITY GROUPS BY AMERICA'S LEADING WRITERS.
       New York: Delacorte Press, 1969. 158 p.

       An anthology containing works by many of America's finest
       authors on the plight of Armenians, Irish, Bohemians, Jews,
       Amerindians, and Afro-Americans. Concludes with a poem
       by Langston Hughes on cultural pluralism.

930   Brown, Lawrence Guy. IMMIGRATION: CULTURAL CONFLICTS AND
       SOCIAL ADJUSTMENTS. New York: Longmans, Green & Co., 1933.
       388 p. Appendix, index.

       Argues that the acculturation of immigrants has been greatly
       complicated by the rapidly changing nature of American urban-
       industrial society. Deals separately with the old and new im-
       migration and Orientals.

931   Burma, John H. "Some Cultural Aspects of Immigration: Its Impact, Es-
       pecially on Our Arts and Sciences." LAW AND CONTEMPORARY PROB-
       LEMS 21 (1956): 284-98.

An examination by a sociologist of the underlying principle of
the McCarran-Walter Act of 1952: "that it is not desirable
for the United States to permit more than a small amount of
immigration and that such immigration should be specifically
and unequally allocated among various countries." Concludes
that the assumptions and artificial distinctions upon which the
act rests are false.

932 Campisi, Paul J. "Ethnic Family Patterns." AMERICAN JOURNAL OF
SOCIOLOGY 8 (1948): 443-49.

Contends that acculturation and adjustment to new circumstances have produced profound changes in the family structure
of Italian Americans, especially among the second generation.

933 Chudacoff, Howard P. "A New Look at Ethnic Neighborhoods: Residential Dispersion and the Concept of Visibility in a Medium-Sized City."
JOURNAL OF AMERICAN HISTORY 60 (1973): 76-93.

A case study of Omaha, Nebraska, from 1880 to 1920 reveals
fairly high mobility among urban ethnic groups rather than
concentrations in specific groups.

934 Cole, Donald B. IMMIGRANT CITY: LAWRENCE, MASSACHUSETTS,
1845-1921. Chapel Hill: University of North Carolina Press, 1963.
248 p. Maps, illustrations, footnotes, bibliography.

Covers the history of one of the nation's most heavily foreign-
stock cities (90 percent in 1910) from the Irish potato famine
to immigration restriction, focusing on the role of these ethnic groups in the Lawrence textile strike of 1912.

935 Conroy, Hillary, and Miyakawa, Scott, eds. EAST ACROSS THE PA-
CIFIC: HISTORICAL AND SOCIOLOGICAL STUDIES OF JAPANESE IM-
MIGRATION AND ASSIMILATION. Santa Barbara, Calif.: Clio Press,
1972. 322 p.

Thirteen essays, some of a sociological and others of a historical nature, which generally support the editors' contention
that the Japanese have more successfully assimilated with
American society than have many European, Christian, and
Caucasian immigrants. Not all essays deal with immigration
to the continental United States.

936 Cordasco, Francesco [M.], and Galatioto, Rocco. "Ethnic Displacement in
the Interstitial Community: The East Harlem (New York City) Experience."
PHYLON 31 (1970): 302-12.

Discusses the breakup of the Italian-American community in
east Harlem and the displacement of its population by Puerto
Ricans, Jews, and blacks.

937 Davidson, Chandler, and Gaitz, Charles M. "Ethnic Attitudes as a Basis for Minority Cooperation in a Southwestern Metropolis." SOCIAL SCI- ENCE QUARTERLY 53 (1973): 738-48.

A 1969-70 study which shows that Mexican Americans in Hous- ton were "(a) more tolerant of blacks than were Anglos, (b) more likely to perceive barriers to minority opportunities than Anglos and (c) more sympathetic to measures for achieving minority equality than Anglos."

938 Davis, Philip, and Schwartz, Bertha, eds. IMMIGRATION AND AMERI- CANIZATION. New York: Ginn, 1920. 672 p. Appendix, bibliog- raphy, index.

Anthology of works by scholars and politicians on the charac- teristics of various immigrant groups, the effects of immigration, regulatory legislation, and efforts at Americanization.

939 Degh, Linda. "Approaches to Folklore Research Among Immigrant Groups." JOURNAL OF AMERICAN FOLKLORE 79 (1966): 551-56.

Argues that New Immigrants planned to return to their native lands, but were forced to remain in the United States by eco- nomic and political pressures. Provides a research design for studying their adaptation, especially the changes in their folk- tales, the interrelation with other immigrant groups, and their absorption of elements of American culture.

940 Dinnerstein, Leonard, and Jaher, Frederic Cople, eds. THE ALIENS: A HISTORY OF ETHNIC MINORITIES IN AMERICA. New York: Appleton- Century-Crofts, 1970. 347 p. Bibliographical references.

Contains articles by twenty-three scholars on discrimination against Indians, blacks, Orientals, Mexican Americans, Puerto Ricans, and a wide variety of European immigrants. Arranged in four chronological periods: colonial, young republic, the era of industrialization, and contemporary America.

941 Doeppers, Daniel F. "The Globeville Neighborhood in Denver." GEO- GRAPHICAL REVIEW 57 (1967): 506-22.

Studies the role of religious and ethnic institutions as an aging East European neighborhood experiences an ethnic change to- ward Mexican-American dominance.

942 Drachsler, Julius. DEMOCRACY AND ASSIMILATION: THE BLENDING OF IMMIGRANT HERITAGES IN AMERICA. 1920. Reprint. Westport, Conn.: Greenwood Press, 1971. 240 p. Appendices, bibliography, index.

Documents the failure of forced Americanization campaigns and the need for a pluralistic conception of democracy.

943 Duncan, Otis Dudley, and Lieberson, Stanley. "Ethnic Segregation and Assimilation." AMERICAN JOURNAL OF SOCIOLOGY 64 (1959): 364-74.

A study of residential patterns in Chicago from 1930 to 1950 which verifies the fact that the longer the residency, the greater the assimilation, but which also found that such facts "did not disrupt a pattern of differential segregation and spatial separation of ethnic colonies."

944 Eisele, J. Christopher. "John Dewey and the Immigrants." HISTORY OF EDUCATION QUARTERLY 15 (1975): 67-86.

Argues that, contrary to the views of many revisionist writers, John Dewey favored the preservation of cultural differences and ethnic variables. Feels Dewey accepted the need for socialization through public schooling but not the destruction of ethnic identity or culture.

945 Eisenstadt, Shmuel Noah. "Analysis of Patterns of Immigration and Absorption of Immigrants." POPULATION STUDIES 7 (1953): 167-80.

Contends that most studies of assimilation err in neglecting the interaction and modification of the structures of both immigrant and the host societies. Argues that in an industrialized, democratic state immigrants are pressured to assimilate, unlike in colonial countries where they are allowed to establish sectors on their own.

946 Esslinger, Dean R. IMMIGRANTS AND THE CITY: ETHNICITY AND MOBILITY IN A NINETEENTH-CENTURY MIDWESTERN COMMUNITY. Port Washington, N.Y.: Kennikat, 1975. 155 p. Appendices, notes, bibliography, index.

A highly quantified study of immigrant geographic and social mobility in South Bend, Indiana, between 1850 and 1880. Finds a reasonably high degree of mobility in the 10,000 cases considered.

947 Feinstein, Otto. CULTURE, INSTITUTIONS, POWER AND ETHNIC GROUPS IN THE CITY. Lexington, Mass.: Heath Lexington Books, 1971. 382 p. Footnotes.

Edition of papers presented in connection with the 1970 Conference on Ethnic Communities of Greater Detroit, sponsored by thirty-nine ethnic organizations and twenty-three institutions. Nearly thirty-five authors discuss ethnicity on the national level and in Detroit, focusing on ethnic voting power for ethnic groups.

948 Fishman, Joshua A., et al. LANGUAGE LOYALTY IN THE UNITED
STATES: THE MAINTENANCE AND PERPETUATION OF NON-ENGLISH
MOTHER TONGUES BY AMERICAN ETHNIC AND RELIGIOUS GROUPS.
Janua Linguarum, Series Maior, no. 21. The Hague: Mouton, 1966.
478 p. Appendices, footnotes, index.

An exploration of "self-maintenance efforts, rationales and
accomplishments of non-English speaking immigrants...." Published in an earlier mimeographed form as a three volume report to the Language Research Section of the U.S. Office of
Education and titled "Language Loyalty in the United States."

949 Gallaway, Lowell E., and Vedder, Richard K. "The Increasing Urbanization Thesis--Did 'New Immigrants' to the United States have a Particular Fondness for Urban Life?" EXPLORATIONS IN ECONOMIC HISTORY
8 (1971): 305-19.

Concludes, after a number of statistical tests, that contrary
to popular belief, the New Immigrants did not have a greater
propensity than their predecessors to settle in urban areas.

950 Gelfand, Donald E., and Lee, Russell D., eds. ETHNIC CONFLICTS
AND POWER: A CROSS-NATIONAL PERSPECTIVE. New York: Wiley,
1973. 354 p. Footnotes, references.

Composed of thirty-four readings for a course on minorities,
based on the theoretical framework of conflict theory. Most
were originally published in the 1960s.

951 Giordano, Joseph. ETHNICITY AND MENTAL HEALTH. New York:
National Project on Ethnic America of the American Jewish Committee,
1973. 50 p. Charts, notes, references.

Attempts to answer the question, "How important to mental
health practice in the 1970s are the conscious and unconscious
forces of ethnic group life in America?" In particular it deals
with underutilization of mental health resources by lower class
ethnic communities and how that can be changed.

952 Gittler, Joseph B. UNDERSTANDING MINORITY GROUPS. New York:
Wiley, 1956. 148 p.

An anthology of works by several scholars dealing with the
cultural outlook of Catholics, Amerindians, Jews, Afro-
Americans, Japanese, and Puerto Ricans. Includes an introduction and a summary essay by the editor on the philosophical and ethical dimensions of intergroup relation.

953 Glaser, Daniel. "Dynamics of Ethnic Identification." AMERICAN SO-
CIOLOGICAL REVIEW 23 (1958): 31-40.

Provides a model for studying ethnic identification and atti-

tudes toward other ethnic groups. Sets up four degrees of identification along a continuum based upon ethnic ideology,
association preferences, and feelings aroused by ethnic contacts.

954　Glasrud, Bruce A., and Smith, Alan M., eds. PROMISES TO KEEP: A
PORTRAYAL OF NON-WHITES IN THE UNITED STATES. Chicago: Rand
McNally, 1972. 398 p. Footnotes, selected bibliography, index.

A chronological arrangement of articles by two dozen recent
historians covering the experience of nonwhites: Indians,
blacks, Mexican Americans, Orientals, and Puerto Ricans.

955　Glazer, Nathan. "Blacks and White Ethnics: The Difference and the
Political Difference it Makes." SOCIAL PROBLEMS 18 (1971): 444–61.

Questions Robert Blauner's contention that black development
should be seen in terms of internal colonialism which does not
hold true for white ethnic groups. Glazer agrees that this
may apply in the South, but in northern cities residential segregation and economic and political development do not reveal
striking differences.

956　_____. "Ethnic Groups in American From National Culture to Ideology."
In FREEDOM AND CONTROL IN MODERN SOCIETY, edited by Monroe
Berger, Theodore Abel, and Charles H. Page, pp. 158–73. New York:
Van Nostrand, 1954.

Discusses the "new" and "old" immigrants in relation to the
stereotype concepts of "melting pot" and "nation of nations."
Believes that the older immigrant groups tended to maintain
their ethnic identity in ethnic settlements across the country
perhaps more than the later immigrants of the 1890s.

957　_____. "The Immigrant Groups and American Culture." YALE REVIEW
48 (1959): 382–97.

Shows that the impact of immigration on American culture was,
in part, destructive. That is, immigration, like science and
industry, has altered the uniqueness of the culture and therefore, has helped destroy it, creating a mass culture in its
place.

958　_____. "The Integration of American Immigrants." LAW AND CON-
TEMPORARY PROBLEMS 21 (1956): 256–69.

Sees "integration" as a more expressive term than "assimilation"
or "Americanization" and discusses relations between immigrants
and the host society in the areas of social problems, political
behavior, and cultural interaction. Argues that the social
problems generally cleared up with economic progress, that the
immigrants then quickly embraced the political system, and

that they have both altered and adjusted to American culture.

959 _____. "Slums and Ethnicity." In SOCIAL WELFARE AND URBAN PROBLEMS, edited by Thomas D. Sherrard, pp. 84-112. New York: Columbia University Press, 1971.

Argues that ethnicity can be used as a resource against urban blight because it provides a living and valuable culture to humanize slum life and because there are differences in the way various groups respond to such problems. Compares the Afro-American approach to slum living to that of earlier European immigrants.

960 _____. "When the Melting Pot Doesn't Melt." NEW YORK TIMES MAGAZINE, 2 January 1972, pp. 12-31.

Discusses the resistance of Jews in Forest Hills, New York, to an integrated public housing project, and attributes their hostility to efforts to protect hard-won middle class status and security rather than to outright racism.

961 Glazer, Nathan, and Moynihan, Daniel Patrick. BEYOND THE MELT-ING POT: THE NEGROES, PUERTO RICANS, JEWS, ITALIANS AND IRISH OF NEW YORK CITY. Rev. ed. Cambridge, Mass.: M.I.T. Press, 1963. 360 p. Maps, tables, notes, index.

Deals with the culture and institutions of New York's five largest ethnic groups. The original chapters argued ethnicity was fading but the revised introduction explores the resurgence of ethnic consciousness in the previous decade.

962 _____, eds. ETHNICITY: THEORY AND EXPERIENCE. Cambridge, Mass.: Harvard University Press, 1975. 531 p. Bibliographies, index.

Contains a wide range of essays discussing the nature and saliency of ethnic identification in a variety of settings from the United States to Guyora, Pakistan, China, and North Africa.

963 Gleason, Philip. "The Melting Pot: Symbol of Fusion or Confusion?" AMERICAN QUARTERLY 16 (1964): 20-26.

Argues that the melting pot concept, for all its ambiguities, is still very valuable, not as a theoretical model of acculturation and assimilation, but as a symbol of ethnic interaction.

964 Gobetz, Giles Edward. "The Ethnic Ethics of Assimilation: Slovenian View." PHYLON 27 (1966): 268-73.

Discusses the views of Slovenian-American intellectuals toward assimilation. Since they viewed total assimilation as disloyal

to their heritage and complete separation as ungrateful to their
new homeland, they sought the golden mean by avoiding mixed
marriages and preserving their language, while assimilating in
other ways.

965   Goering, John M. "The Emergence of Ethnic Interests: A Case of Seren-
dipity." SOCIAL FORCES 49 (1971): 379-84.

Concludes from a sample of 100 Irish and Italians that third
generation ethnic consciousness emerges not because of organizational activity but rather in response to disillusionment with
the "American Dream."

966   Gomez, Rudolph, ed. THE SOCIAL REALITY OF ETHNIC AMERICA.
Lexington, Mass.: D.C. Heath & Co., 1974. 412 p. Notes.

A text from previously published sources consisting of nearly
thirty different readings about blacks, Indians, Japanese, and
Mexican Americans arranged to present an overview of their
number, attitudes, grievances, activities, and leadership.

967   Gordon, Milton [M.]. ASSIMILATION IN AMERICAN LIFE: THE ROLE OF
RACE, RELIGION AND NATIONAL ORIGINS. New York: Oxford University Press, 1964. 266 p. Index.

A concise, readable sociological treatise on assimilation and
ethnicity which compares the models of Anglo-conformity,
melting pot, and cultural pluralism, assessing their implications for intergroup relations.

968   Greeley, Andrew M. THE DENOMINATIONAL SOCIETY. Glenview,
Ill.: Scott, Foresman, 1972. 266 p. Bibliography.

Discusses the nature, origins, and functions of religion, its
organizational and ethnic implications, the myth of seculari-
zation, civil religion, and conflict. Concludes that America
is a nation of denominational pluralism.

969   _____. ETHNICITY IN THE UNITED STATES: A PRELIMINARY RECON-
NAISSANCE. New York: Wiley, 1974. 324 p. Bibliography, index.

An attempt to test empirically many of the current conceptions
about ethnicity through a survey conducted by the author and
his staff at the National Opinion Research Center.

970   _____. "Making it in America: Ethnic Groups and Social Status."
SOCIAL POLICY 4 (1973): 21-29.

Contends that, contrary to current prevailing views, most white
ethnic groups are making significant gains in education, occupation, unions, and intergenerational mobility. Also argues

that they continue to remain primarily Democratic in their political behavior despite the tendency of liberal Democrats to write them off and Republicans to count them.

971 _____. WHY CAN'T THEY BE LIKE US? New York: E.P. Dutton and Co., 1971. 192 p. Appendix, bibliography, index.

Views white ethnic groups as "totemic clans" whose cultural diversity is vital to the continuation of a pluralistic society based upon equality of opportunity.

972 Greeley, Andrew M., and Sheatsley, Paul B. "Attitudes Toward Deseg-regation." SCIENTIFIC AMERICAN 225 (1971): 13-19.

Surveys attitudes toward integration according to many vari-ables, including religion and ethnicity. Concludes that favor-able attitudes have increased significantly among ethnic Catho-lics over the past decade while Jews have expressed growing reservations.

973 Griffen, Clyde. "Making It in America: Social Mobility in Mid-Nineteenth Century Poughkeepsie." NEW YORK HISTORY 51 (1970): 479-99.

Concludes that upward social mobility was easier in smaller than in larger cities. German Protestants and Jews had spe-cific skills and thus enjoyed greater mobility than did the un-skilled German Catholics, Irish, and blacks.

974 Handlin, Oscar. "Historical Perspectives on the American Ethnic Group." DAEDALUS 90 (1961): 220-32.

Discusses the role which ethnic affiliation has played in locat-ing the individual within the large society and speculates that ethnicities may either serve as barriers to depersonalization or reinforcements of it.

975 Higham, John. SEND THESE TO ME: JEWS AND OTHER IMMIGRANTS IN URBAN AMERICA. New York: Atheneum, 1975. 259 p. Notes, index.

A collection of nine essays on the general theme of the inter-action between the American creed of an open society and ethnic self-consciousness, with special reference to the Jewish experience. Discusses the tensions among assimilation, plu-ralism, and racism.

976 Hollinger, David A. "Ethnic Diversity, Cosmopolitanism and the Emer-gence of the American Liberal Intelligentsia." AMERICAN QUARTERLY 27 (1975): 133-51.

Documents the growth of a "cosmopolitan nationalism" among

many intellectuals in the twentieth century which rejects both
a forced assimilation or acculturation and an alienated paro-
chialism, but aims at preserving subgroups and subcultures as
"repositories for insights and experiences that can be drawn
upon in the interests of a more comprehensive outlook on the
world."

977   Jaworski, Irene D.   BECOMING AMERICAN: THE PROBLEMS OF IMMI-
      GRANTS AND THEIR CHILDREN.   New York: Harper & Row, 1950.
      113 p.

      Studies the varying problems experienced by different immi-
      grant groups as a guide to understanding the attitudes and
      intergroup relations of the current American population.

978   Jones, Frank E.   "A Sociological Perspective on Immigrant Adjustment."
      SOCIAL FORCES 35 (1956):   39-47.

      Contends that earlier theories of immigrant adjustment are in-
      adequate because they were based upon an individual, rather
      than a group, frame of reference.   Proposes a functional group
      analysis that studies the interaction between native and immi-
      grant in a role system as well as the host society's methods
      of dealing with new members.

979   Jones, Howard Mumford.   O STRANGE NEW WORLD.   New York: Vik-
      ing Press, 1964.   396 p.   Illustrations, reference notes, index.

      Analyzes the formation of the dominant Anglo-American culture
      to which later groups are asked to acculturate.   Focuses on
      the colonial period of U.S. history.

980   Kallen, Horace M.   CULTURAL PLURALISM AND THE AMERICAN IDEA.
      Philadelphia: University of Pennsylvania Press, 1956.   208 p.   Biblio-
      graphical footnotes.

      An elaboration of the concept of cultural pluralism by its
      foremost spokesman.   Also contains critiques of the idea by
      nine other scholars and a rejoinder by Kallen.

981   Kirk, Gordon William, Jr.   "The Promise of American Life: Social Mo-
      bility in a Nineteenth Century Immigrant Community, Holland, Michigan,
      1847-1894."   Ph.D. dissertation, Michigan State University, 1970.   299
      p.

      Study of a small community as a typical representative of "an
      ethnically homogeneous community experiencing rapid economic
      and population growth."   There was substantial economic and
      occupational mobility during the early period, but this de-
      clined as industrialization increased.

982 Knoke, David, and Felson, Richard B. "Ethnic Stratification and Political Cleavage in the United States, 1952-68." AMERICAN JOURNAL OF SOCIOLOGY 80 (1974): 630-43.

Based upon five national survey samples, concludes that ethnic politics follows a "cultural lag model" in which the effects of ethnicity on politics persist via an intergenerational socialization of traditional ethnic group loyalties.

983 Kolm, Richard. "The Change of Cultural Identity: An Analysis of Factors Conditioning the Cultural Integration of Immigrants." Ph.D. dissertation, Wayne State University, 1966. 265 p.

Finds that problems of migration and immigration are best understood within the framework of the interrelationship of culture, society, and personality as derived from the symbolic interaction theory. These lead to an understanding of the problems involved in value adjustment, changes in attitude and behavior, and the redefinition of identity and self-concept on the part of migrants.

984 Kramer, Judith R. THE AMERICAN MINORITY COMMUNITY. New York: Thomas Y. Crowell, 1970. 293 p. Footnotes, bibliography, index.

Examines the common position of national, racial, and religious minorities in the United States. Discusses the nature and function of ethnic communities through three generations, the consequences of deculturation, and the variables of color, class, culture, and religion.

985 LaGumina, Salvatore J., and Cavaioli, Frank J. THE ETHNIC DIMENSION IN AMERICAN SOCIETY. Boston: Holbrook Press, 1974. 364 p. Appendix, bibliography.

An effort to demonstrate the common experience of European, African, Oriental, and Latin American immigrants throughout the span of American history.

986 Laumann, Edward O. "The Social Structure of Religious and Ethno-Religious Groups in the Metropolitan Community." AMERICAN SOCIOLOGICAL REVIEW 34 (1969): 182-97.

An analysis of the formation of friendships among fifteen religious and twenty-seven ethno-religious groups in Detroit. Confirms the belief that the social structure breaks down into Protestant, Catholic, and Jew and further that the selection of friends within each group usually follows socioeconomic lines.

987 Lieberson, Stanley. ETHNIC PATTERNS IN AMERICAN CITIES. Glencoe, Ill.: Free Press, 1963. 230 p. Tables, appendices, selected bib-

liography, index.

A sociological dissertation which makes a ten-city comparative study of residential and occupational segregation and assimilation in the twentieth century.

988 _____. "A Societal Theory of Race and Ethnic Relations." AMERICAN SOCIOLOGICAL REVIEW 26 (1961): 902-10.

Argues that the cycle of race relations in a society dominated by a migrant population differs markedly from that in a society controlled by an indigenous population. Feels that this is one of the main reasons for the wide variations in race relations among societies.

989 _____. "Suburbs and Ethnic Residential Patterns." AMERICAN JOURNAL OF SOCIOLOGY 67 (1962): 673-81.

Analyzes the residential pattern of first and second generation immigrants over a twenty-year period in several metropolitan areas. Discovers that there is a parallel between the patterns of segregation of certain nationalities in the center city and in the suburbs of that same city.

990 Light, Ivan H. ETHNIC ENTERPRISE IN AMERICA: BUSINESS AND WELFARE AMONG CHINESE, JAPANESE AND BLACKS. Berkeley and Los Angeles: University of California Press, 1972. 209 p. Illustrations, tables, appendix, footnotes, bibliography, index.

Studies a variety of Oriental and black organizations, such as credit associations, urban and business leagues, church associations, mutual aid societies and voluntary associations.

991 McDonagh, Edward C., and Richards, Eugene S. ETHNIC RELATIONS IN THE UNITED STATES. New York: Appleton-Century-Crofts, 1953. 408 p. Tables, selected readings, index.

A selection of readings and articles which seeks to examine the nature of ethnic groups; to study blacks, Jews, Mexicans, Indians, Japanese, Chinese, and European immigrants in reference to four aspects of status: social, educational, legal, and economic; and to provide some suggestions for improving ethnic relations.

992 MacDonald, J. Frederick. "The Foreigner in Juvenile Series Fiction, 1900-1945." JOURNAL OF POPULAR CULTURE 8 (1974): 534-48.

Finds that the foreigner in juvenile series fiction of the era was "portrayed in general as an ignorant, unwashed, thieving and sinister character who is alien to American values, and was contrasted sharply to the Anglo-Saxon hero of the piece."

993   McKenna, Marian C. "The Melting Pot: Comparative Observations in
      the United States and Canada." SOCIOLOGY AND SOCIAL RESEARCH
      53 (1969): 443-47.

      Explores the historical reasons for and implications of the dif-
      ference between the melting pot idea of the United States and
      the mosaic idea of Canada, which encourages cultural plural-
      ism.

994   Marden, Charles F., and Meyer, Gladys. MINORITIES IN AMERICAN
      SOCIETY. 3d ed. New York: Van Nostrand, 1968. 497 p. Tables,
      index.

      A sociological study of different ethnic minorities considered
      against the dominant culture of English-speaking white Chris-
      tians. Discusses the concept of race and devotes a chapter
      each to Mexican Americans, Puerto Ricans, Chinese, Japa-
      nese, Indians, and natives of Hawaii. Also explores Catholic-
      Protestant and Jewish-gentile relations.

995   Matthews, Fred H. "The Revolt Against Americanism: Cultural Pluralism
      and Cultural Relativism as an Ideology of Liberation." CANADIAN RE-
      VIEW OF AMERICAN STUDIES 1 (1970): 4-31.

      Discusses the opposition of immigrant intellectuals and Ameri-
      can radicals to forced Americanization in the World War I
      period. Prominent in this movement were Horace Kallen,
      Randolph Bourne, John Collier, Ruth Fulton Benedict, and
      Margaret Mead.

996   Meister, Richard J. RACE AND ETHNICITY IN MODERN AMERICA.
      Boston: D.C. Heath & Co., 1974. 198 p. Footnotes.

      Five sections, each containing four previously published works,
      relate to (1) the process of assimilation, (2) the questioning
      of assimilation, (3) the post-World War II period, (4) the per-
      sistence of race and ethnicity, and (5) critics of the new race
      and ethnic consciousness.

997   Miller, Douglas T. "Immigration and Social Stratification in Pre-Civil
      War New York." NEW YORK HISTORY 49 (1968): 157-68.

      Argues that the massive immigration to New York City in the
      1840s and 1850s depressed wage scales, widened the gap be-
      tween the middle and laboring classes, and hardened social
      lines. Sees this as a major cause for the nativism of the era.

998   Nahirny, Vladimir C., and Fishman, Joshua A. "American Immigrant
      Groups: Ethnic Identification and the Problem of Generation." SOCIO-
      LOGICAL REVIEW 13 (1965): 311-26.

      Argues that ethnic awareness disappears over three generations,

with the sons and daughters of immigrants remaining acutely
conscious of their ethnicity despite acculturation and the stress
of gradual disengagement. Insists that the third generation
generally has few ethnic bonds.

999   Nam, Charles B. "Nationality Groups and Social Stratification in Ameri-
       ca." SOCIAL FORCES 37 (1959): 328-33.

       Presents statistical evidence regarding the status levels of Irish,
       Germans, Russians, and Italians, their relative changes in
       status level, and the pattern of that variance in different
       areas of the country. Argues that national differences in sta-
       tus are narrowing and will tend to even out eventually.

1000   Newman, Katherine D. THE AMERICAN EQUATION: LITERATURE IN
       A MULTI-ETHNIC CULTURE. Boston: Allyn and Bacon, 1970. 380 p.
       Index.

       An anthology that contains works by a wide variety of authors
       writing about dozens of different ethnocultural groups. Or-
       ganized around the general themes of self-definition, the at-
       tractive alternative, the complimentary self, and the American
       metaphor.

1001   Newman, William M. AMERICAN PLURALISM: A STUDY OF MINORITY
       GROUPS AND SOCIAL THEORY. New York: Harper & Row, 1973.
       307 p. Index.

       Analyzes basic concepts and frameworks, social processes of
       pluralism, the theory of social conflict, and the consequences
       of intergroup conflicts. Concludes with a discussion of the
       social uses of science in buttressing racism and the problem of
       "multiple realities."

1002   Olneck, Michael R., and Lazerson, Marvin. "The School Achievement
       of Immigrant Children: 1900-1930." HISTORY OF EDUCATION QUAR-
       TERLY 14 (1974): 435-82.

       Deals primarily with first and second generation Jewish and
       Italian Americans in the nation's twelve largest cities. Argues
       that they acted on group values and preferences in responding
       to the public schools and that these helped determine the
       choices and cultural trade-offs they made and the levels of
       their disaffection.

1003   Park, Robert E. IMMIGRANT PRESS AND ITS CONTROL. Westport,
       Conn.: Greenwood, 1922. 468 p. Index.

       Discusses the reasons for the existence of the immigrant press,
       its contents, its evolution and decline, and efforts to control
       it by political managers and foreign governments.

1004 Park, Robert E., and Miller, Herbert A. OLD WORLD TRAITS TRANS-
PLANTED. 1921. Reprint. New York: Arno Press and New York Times,
1969. 306 p. Maps.

Argues that assimilation is inevitable, but that immigrant institutions and culture form a healthy bridge between old and new
and that forced Americanization is counterproductive.

1005 Passi, Michael Matthew. "Mandarins and Immigrants: The Irony of Ethnic Studies in America Since Turner." Ph.D. dissertation, University of
Minnesota, 1972. 248 p.

Argues that ethnic studies have ignored ethnic consciousness
and cultural pluralism and have mistakenly stressed the assimilationist ideas of a homogeneous American culture. Traces
this theme from the late nineteenth century to 1960, which
the author sees as marking the beginning of rejection by social
scientists of the assimilationists' perspective.

1006 Pavlak, Thomas J. "Social Class, Ethnicity and Racial Prejudice." PUB-
LIC OPINION QUARTERLY 37 (1973): 225-31.

Based upon a survey of white ethnic lower middle class manual
workers in Chicago. Suggests that racial hostility may largely
reflect socioeconomic competition rather than inherent racial
prejudice, since the degree of racial prejudice among ethnic
Americans lessens with increasing social status.

1007 Plax, Martin. "On Studying Ethnicity." PUBLIC OPINION QUARTERLY
36 (1972): 99-104.

Contends that current theories concerning the influence of
identity on voter behavior do not delve deeply enough into
the subject. Based upon a sample in Buffalo, New York,
argues that focusing upon ethnic consciousness and saliency
at various stages of acculturation will improve understanding
of this phenomenon.

1008 Rose, Arnold, and Rose, Caroline. AMERICA DIVIDED: MINORITY
GROUP RELATIONS IN THE UNITED STATES. New York: Alfred A.
Knopf, 1949. 342 p. Notes, bibliography, index.

A topical treatment covering the position of minorities in the
economic, legal, political, and social spheres, with later
chapters on ethnicity, differences among races, and the psychology of prejudice.

1009 Rose, Peter [I.]. THEY AND WE: RACIAL AND ETHNIC RELATIONS
IN THE UNITED STATES. New York: Random House, 1968. 149 p.
Appendix, selected readings, index.

Discusses race, ethnicity and social status, the various ethnic components of American society, theories of assimilation and acculturation, the nature of prejudice, the practice of discrimination, and various reactions to discrimination.

1010 _____, ed. NATION OF NATIONS: THE ETHNIC EXPERIENCE AND THE RACIAL CRISIS. New York: Random House, 1972. 351 p.

A collection of thirty previously published essays or articles by novelists, journalists, sociologists, and historians on the melting pot thesis, the experience of white and colored immigrants, and competition among minorities.

1011 Rosenthal, Eric. "Acculturation Without Assimilation? The Jewish Community of Chicago, Illinois." AMERICAN JOURNAL OF SOCIOLOGY 66 (1960): 275-88.

Accounts for the large Jewish community in the northern part of the city and suburbs as a result of both the housing market generally and the desire for voluntary segregation, which have thus prevented large-scale assimilation.

1012 Rubin, Israel. "Ethnicity and Cultural Pluralism." PHYLON 36 (1975): 140-49.

Discusses the dimensions of the current reawakening of interest in ethnicity and takes a middle-of-the-road position, rejecting total assimilation as a "fanciful illusion" while doubting that there is sufficient "commitment to distinct important values and concomitant readiness to invest resources and effort on behalf of their preservation."

1013 Schermerhorn, Richard A. COMPARATIVE ETHNIC RELATIONS: A FRAMEWORK FOR THEORY AND RESEARCH. New York: Random House, 1969. 282 p. Appendices, bibliography, index.

Criticizes the theory of ethnics as "victims" and attempts to view relations between majority and minority groups in the wider context of societal relations.

1014 Schlesinger, Arthur M. "The Role of the Immigrant." In PATHS TO THE PRESENT, edited by Arthur M. Schlesinger, pp. 51-76. New York: Macmillan Co., 1949. Bibliography, index.

Paints immigrants as diverse people, all of whom chose America. Calls for a recognition of cultural pluralism as America's answer to European segregation based on nationality.

1015 Segal, Bernard E., ed. RACIAL AND ETHNIC RELATIONS. New York: Thomas Y. Crowell Co., 1966. 492 p.

Contains selections by a wide variety of authorities organized

around the following general topics: theoretical perspectives,
examples of ethnic and racial subcultural variation, the scope
and quality of racial and ethnic attitudes, the differences between southern and northern patterns of separation and subordination, desegregation, integration and attitude change, the
search for Negro identity, and prospects for the future in racial and ethnic relations.

1016 Shannon, Lyle W. "The Economic Absorption and Cultural Integration of
Immigrant Workers." AMERICAN BEHAVIORAL SCIENTIST 13 (1969):
36-56.

Contends that the individual characteristics and group identities
of migrant workers greatly influence the opportunities and prob-
abilities for upward social mobility.

1017 Shibutani, Tamotsu, and Kwan, Kian M. ETHNIC STRATIFICATION: A
COMPARATIVE APPROACH. New York: Macmillan Co., 1965. 626 p.
Footnotes, selected readings, index.

A sociology text in which the authors develop a theory of
interethnic contacts and a set of generalizations that permit
them to examine "diverse and seemingly unrelated episodes
as manifestations of the same recurrent processes."

1018 Shumsky, Neil Larry. "Zangwill's THE MELTING POT: Ethnic Tensions
on Stage." AMERICAN QUARTERLY 27 (1975): 29-41.

Discusses the apparent contradictions in the play with regard
to the nature of assimilation and attributes them largely to
Zangwill's distinction between the Jewish religion and the
Jewish race, feeling the former to be consistent with American
identity and the latter, incompatible.

1019 Simirenko, Alex. PILGRIMS, COLONISTS AND FRONTIERSMEN: AN
ETHNIC COMMUNITY IN TRANSITION. New York: Free Press of
Glencoe, 1964. 232 p. Tables, appendix, notes, bibliography, index.

Revised version of a sociology dissertation which "examines
the dynamics of social and cultural change that accompanied
the formation and transformation of the Minneapolis Russian
community." It studies the first and second generation immigrants in terms of class, status, and power.

1020 Simpson, George Eaton, and Yinger, Milton J. RACIAL AND CULTURAL
MINORITIES: AN ANALYSIS OF PREJUDICE AND DISCRIMINATION.
3d ed. New York: Harper & Row, 1965. 582 p. Footnotes, bibliography, index.

A sociological synthesis of recent scholarship on prejudice and
discrimination with emphasis on Jews and blacks.

1021 Smith, William C. AMERICANS IN THE MAKING: THE NATURAL HIS-
TORY OF THE ASSIMILATION OF IMMIGRANTS. New York: D. Appleton and Co., 1939. 454 p. Footnotes, bibliography, index.

A sociologist's study of the process of assimilation among first
and second generation immigrants and appraisal of their contributions to America.

1022 Thernstrom, Stephan. "Immigrants and WASPs: Ethnic Differences in Oc-
cupational Mobility in Boston, 1890-1940." In NINETEENTH CENTURY
CITIES: ESSAYS IN THE NEW URBAN HISTORY, edited by Stephan
Thernstrom and Richard Sennett, pp. 125-64. New Haven, Conn.: Yale
University Press, 1969.

One of a collection of papers prepared for the Yale Conference
on the Nineteenth-Century Industrial City, held in November
1968. Concludes that "there were dramatic differences in the
occupational opportunities open to immigrants, the children of
immigrants, and Americans of native stock, with the second
generation in a particularly critical and uncertain position vis-
a-vis both their parents and their more established WASP rivals."

1023 Vander Zanden, James W. AMERICAN MINORITY RELATIONS: THE
SOCIOLOGY OF RACE AND ETHNIC GROUPS. New York: Ronald
Press, 1963. 470 p. Tables, footnotes, bibliography, index.

A theoretical and descriptive analysis of "the sociological
foundations of race and minority relations," with sections on
the sources of prejudice and discrimination, intergroup relations, and minority reactions to dominance and social change.

1024 Vecoli, Rudolph J. "Ethnicity: A Neglected Dimension of American
History." In THE STATE OF AMERICAN HISTORY, edited by Herbert
J. Bass, pp. 70-88. Chicago: Quadrangle Books, 1970.

Links the neglect of ethnicity to the assimilationist assumptions
of historians and sociologists, reinforced by the acculturation
of even ethnic historians into the Anglo-American intellectual
milieu.

1025 Veidmanis, Juris. "Neglected Areas in the Sociology of Immigrants and
Ethnic Groups in North America." SOCIOLOGICAL QUARTERLY 4 (1963):
325-33.

Based upon twelve years of research on 45,000 post-World
War II Latvian immigrants, questions the applicability of
Lloyd W. Warner and Leo Srole's timetables and Robert E.
Park's "race relations cycle." Favors Milton Gordon's model
of different paces for acculturation and assimilation.

1026 Ward, David. CITIES AND IMMIGRANTS: A GEOGRAPHY OF CHANGE

IN NINETEENTH CENTURY AMERICA. New York: Oxford University
Press, 1973. 164 p. Photographs, charts, tables, notes, bibliography,
index.

A geographer investigates "the spatial effects of selective urban growth and international differentiation...." The first
part of the book explores the effects of regional economic
growth and migration on urbanization and the second part
considers the internal differentiation of urban settlements.

1027 Warner, W. Lloyd, and Srole, Leo. SOCIAL SYSTEMS OF AMERICAN
ETHNIC GROUPS. New Haven, Conn.: Yale University Press, 1945.
296 p. Charts, tables, appendix, index.

Examines the interplay of class ethnicity among the various
elements of Yankee City in residence patterns, occupations,
family, religion, education, and associational life.

1028 Wenk, Michael; Tomasi, Silvano M.; and Baroni, Gino; eds. PIECES OF
A DREAM: THE ETHNIC WORKER'S CRISIS WITH AMERICA. Staten Island, N.Y.: Center for Migration Studies, 1972. 212 p.

A collection of fifteen articles and speeches by scholars, political figures, and ethnic community leaders who deal with a
panoply of interaction among ethnics and public policy, the
media, community development, neighborhoods, ethnic studies,
tax reform, politics, social reform, and organized labor.

1029 Wheeler, Thomas C., ed. THE IMMIGRANT EXPERIENCE: THE AN-
GUISH OF BECOMING AMERICAN. New York: Dial Press, 1972.
210 p.

An anthology of first person accounts by writers of Irish, Italian, Norwegian, Puerto Rican, Chinese, African, Jewish, English, and Polish extraction. Wheeler contributes a perceptive
introduction on the destruction of ethnic culture.

1030 Williams, Robin M. STRANGERS NEXT DOOR: ETHNIC RELATIONS
IN AMERICAN COMMUNITIES. Englewood Cliffs, N.J.: Prentice-Hall,
1964. 434 p. Appendices, index.

Based on sociological research for the Cornell Studies in Intergroup Relations, provides general discussions of ethnocentrism
and prejudice as well as a variety of data on which the generalizations are based.

1031 Woods, Frances Jerome. CULTURAL VALUES OF AMERICAN ETHNIC
GROUPS. New York: Harper & Brothers, 1956. 402 p. Illustrations,
bibliography.

Contrasts Negro, Oriental, Mexican, Jewish, and European
cultures and values with that of the host society with respect

to family, religion, government, economics, education, and recreation. Based upon case records, documents, personal experiences, and interviews.

1032 Woods, Robert A., ed. THE CITY WILDERNESS: A SETTLEMENT STUDY. Boston: Houghton, Mifflin & Co., 1898. 319 p. Illustrations, index.

A series of articles by the residents and associates of the South End House in Boston. Deals with the ethnic composition of the neighborhood, historical development, the incidence of crime, and the roles of the church and education.

1033 Yetman, Norman R., and Steele, C. Hoy. MAJORITY AND MINORITY: THE DYNAMICS OF RACIAL AND ETHNIC RELATIONS. Boston: Allyn and Bacon, 1971. 621 p. Footnotes.

An anthology of nearly forty articles dealing with the contemporary United States which attempts "to portray and to analyze the dynamics of racial and ethnic relations within the context of a general theoretical understanding of the broader field of majority-minority relations."

PREJUDICE, DISCRIMINATION, AND RESTRICTION

1034 Alexander, Robert C. "A Defense of the McCarran-Walter Act." LAW AND CONTEMPORARY PROBLEMS 21 (1956): 382-400.

Examines the quota system in some detail to show that the system attempts to steer a middle course between those who favor total exclusion and those who want no restrictions.

1035 Baker, Donald G. "Identity, Power and Psychocultural Needs: White Responses to Non-Whites." JOURNAL OF ETHNIC·STUDIES 1 (1974): 16-44.

Focuses on the three factors which he thinks are of considerable importance in explaining white hostility to nonwhites and the former's need to find in the latter a convenient scapegoat.

1036 Barry, Colman J. "Some Roots of American Nativism." CATHOLIC HISTORICAL REVIEW 44 (1958): 137-46.

Calls for an interpretative study of the roots of American nativism rather than a historical examination of the organized movements which have received attention.

1037 Benkart, Paula K. "Changing Attitudes of Presbyterians Toward Southern and Eastern European Immigrants, 1880-1914." JOURNAL OF PRESBYTERIAN HISTORY 49 (1971): 222-45.

Argues that the attitude of leading Presbyterians toward the

New Immigrants went through three distinct phases: (1) up to 1895 they were hostile and fearful of a Catholic conspiracy; (2) from then until 1904 they grew gradually more sympathetic; and (3) after 1904 Presbyterians worked hard to promote the physical and social welfare of the immigrants, with an eye toward winning them over to American Protestantism.

1038 Bennett, Marion T. AMERICAN IMMIGRATION POLICIES, A HISTORY. Washington, D.C.: Public Affairs Press, 1963. 362 p. Appendices, references, bibliography, index.

A chronological account of the evolution of immigration restriction policy with emphasis on the period from 1950 to 1962. Describes the ways policy changes have affected the composition of U.S. population.

1039 Bernard, William S., ed. AMERICAN IMMIGRATION POLICY: A RE-APPRAISAL. New York: Harper & Row, 1950. 278 p. Charts, appendices, bibliography, index.

Summarizes the findings of the National Committee on Immigration Policy. Discusses background of the quota system and its effect on immigration and speculates upon the economic and international effects of a more open immigration system.

1040 Berthoff, Rowland T. "Southern Attitudes toward Immigration, 1865-1914." JOURNAL OF SOUTHERN HISTORY 17 (1951): 328-60.

Contends that although harbingers of the "New South" tried to encourage immigration to their area, a countercurrent of underlying hostility by many Southerners, who saw immigrants as a convenient scapegoat for their problems, vitiated the efforts of the former.

1041 Billington, Ray A. PROTESTANT CRUSADE, 1800-60: A STUDY OF THE ORIGINS OF AMERICAN NATIVISM. New York: Macmillan Co., 1938. 436 p. Maps, appendix, bibliography, index.

The classic study of pre-Civil War nativism which focuses primarily on its intellectual roots and stresses its anti-Catholicism.

1042 Birnbaum, Mariana D. "On the Language of Prejudice." WESTERN FOLKLORE 30 (1971): 247-68.

Studies the attitude of the United States towards its immigrants and the evolution of slang phrases and derogatory remarks often used to describe different ethnic groups.

1043 Blum, John M. "Nativism, Anti-Radicalism, and the Foreign Scare, 1917-20." MIDWEST JOURNAL 3 (1950-51): 46-53.

Deals with the devastating impact of the Red Scare and related governmental curtailments of civil liberties for immigrant groups. Also discusses briefly the relationship between nativism and antiradicalism.

1044 Bogardus, Emory S. IMMIGRATION AND RACE ATTITUDES. 1928. Reprint. New York: Jerome S. Ozer, 1971. 268 p. Bibliographies.

Studies varying racial attitudes in eastern, southern, and western sections of the United States, based upon case histories, surveys, and social distance studies.

1045 Bruce, John Campbell. THE GOLDEN DOOR: THE IRONY OF OUR IMMIGRATION POLICY. New York: Random House, 1954. 244 p.

Reporter for the SAN FRANCISCO CHRONICLE recounts the stories of several individuals who have suffered as a result of the immigration law. His intention is to draw attention to the defects of the 1952 law, thereby promoting a revised immigration law.

1046 Carlson, Lewis H., and Colburn, George H., eds. IN THEIR PLACE: WHITE AMERICA DEFINES HER MINORITIES, 1850-1950. New York: Wiley, 1973. 351 p. Bibliography.

A collection of original source material presenting scholarly, popular, and governmental rationales for discrimination against Amerindians, Afro-Americans, Chicanos, Orientals, Jews, and southern and eastern European immigrants.

1047 Carman, Harry J., and Luthin, Reinhard H. "Some Aspects of the Know-Nothing Movement Reconsidered." SOUTH ATLANTIC QUARTERLY 39 (1940): 213-34.

A discussion of the movement in certain key states and in politics generally during the 1840s and 1850s.

1048 Clark, Jane Perry. DEPORTATION OF ALIENS FROM THE UNITED STATES TO EUROPE. 1931. Reprint. New York: Arno Press, 1969. 524 p. Appendices, footnotes, bibliography, index.

Based on statutes, legal decisions, and immigrant case files, describes the adoption, interpretation, and administration of U.S. deportation laws.

1049 Coben, Stanley. "A Study in Nativism: The American Red Scare of 1919-20." POLITICAL SCIENCE QUARTERLY 79 (1964): 52-75.

Shows that while the Red Scare was a revitalization movement, it did not succeed in helping the society adapt to new conditions. Rather it succeeded only in fostering a spirit of conformity, a satisfaction with the status quo, and an assumption that reform ideologies were foreign enemies.

1050 Curran, Thomas J. "Assimilation and Nativism." INTERNATIONAL MIGRATION DIGEST 3 (1966): 15-25.

Concludes that the virulent nativism of the 1840s and 1850s actually fostered Irish-American nationalism by causing the immigrants to forget Old World differences and band together against a common enemy.

1051 _____. XENOPHOBIA AND IMMIGRATION, 1820-1930. New York: Twayne, 1975. 214 p. Notes, bibliography, index.

Focuses on the Oriental exclusion movement of the 1880s and the National Origins Quota Act of the 1920s to examine the meaning of xenophobia and the forces behind it.

1052 Daniels, Roger, and Kitano, Harry H.L. AMERICAN RACISM: EXPLORATION OF THE NATURE OF PREJUDICE. Englewood Cliffs, N.J.: Prentice Hall, 1970. 155 p. Appendix, bibliography, index.

Deals with discrimination against nonwhites, the maintenance of a two category system, the practice of racism from 1769 to the present, and the notion of boundary maintenance. Concludes with a discussion of the ethnic crisis of our time.

1053 Daniels, Roger, and Olin, Spencer C., Jr., eds. RACISM IN CALIFORNIA: A READER IN THE HISTORY OF OPPRESSION. New York: Macmillan Co., 1972. 345 p. Suggestions for further reading.

Contains contributions from nearly twenty-five different authors or sources. Its first four sections deal respectively with Indians, Asians, Chicanos, and blacks, while the last section, which is also the briefest, discusses "The Ethnic Crisis of Our Time." Similar in format to the Dryden or D.C. Heath series.

1054 Davis, Lawrence B. IMMIGRANTS, BAPTISTS AND THE PROTESTANT MIND IN AMERICA. Urbana: University of Illinois Press, 1973. 230 p. Footnotes, bibliography, index.

Published dissertation which analyzes religious nativism from the 1880s to the 1920s from the perspective of northern Baptists in particular, and Protestants in general. Because Baptist opposition was based less on ethnic origin than on religious persuasion, Baptists were more tolerant of many immigrants whom they saw as possible converts.

1055 Dinnerstein, Leonard, ed. ANTISEMITISM IN THE UNITED STATES. New York: Holt, Rinehart and Winston, 1971. 140 p. Suggestions for further reading.

Essays covering four general topics: (1) the roots of anti-Semitism; (2) anti-Semitism in modern American history; (3) its various manifestations; and (4) the issue of black anti-Semitism. Contributors include historians as well as contemporary writers who offer differing reasons for the existence of anti-Semitism in the United States.

1056 Divine, Robert. AMERICAN IMMIGRATION POLICY, 1924-1952. New Haven, Conn.: Yale University Press, 1957. 191 p. Appendix, bibliographical essay, index.

Discusses the evolution of immigration restriction from the nineteenth century through the National Origins Quota Act, displaced persons legislation, and the McCarran-Walter Act.

1057 Eckerson, Helen F. "Immigration and National Origins." THE ANNALS OF THE AMERICAN ACADEMY OF POLITICAL AND SOCIAL SCIENCE 367 (1966): 4-14.

Concludes that the National Origins Quota System reduced the total volume of immigration but failed to reorient it toward northern and western Europeans because only half the quotas assigned to those people were actually used and such nonquota people as Western Hemisphere emigrants, refugees, and relatives of former immigrants skewed the curve.

1058 Fong, Hiram. "Immigration and Naturalization Laws: Today's Need for Naturalization Law Reform." INTERNATIONAL MIGRATION REVIEW 5 (1971): 406-18.

The U.S. senator from Hawaii reviews the history of immigration and naturalization laws and suggests sweeping reforms to eliminate discrimination.

1059 Franklin, Frank G. LEGISLATIVE HISTORY OF NATURALIZATION IN THE UNITED STATES. 1906. Reprint. New York: Arno Press, 1969. 308 p. Footnotes, bibliography, index.

A chronological treatment from the American Revolution to the Civil War with chapters on the acts passed in 1790, 1795, 1798, 1802, 1813, and 1824. The final chapters trace the development of nativism and the Know-Nothings.

1060 Friedman, Norman L. "Nativism." PHYLON 28 (1967): 408-15.

Sees Philadelphia as a microcosm of colonial America in its growing antipathy toward German Americans in the 1750s. Notes that the city's leadership regarded the Germans as stupid and ignorant, largely because of their reluctance to learn English.

1061 Glidden, William Barnes. "Casualties of Caution: Alien Enemies in America, 1917-1919." Ph.D. dissertation, University of Illinois at Urbana-Champaign, 1970. 431 p.

Describes the plight of four million resident aliens from Germany or Austria-Hungary who suffered government sanctioned discrimination during World War I. Tells also of the 2,300 who were sent to the three internment camps administered by the army.

1062 Greeley, Andrew M. "Ethnicity and Racial Attitudes: The Case of the Jews and the Poles." AMERICAN JOURNAL OF SOCIOLOGY 80 (1975): 909-33.

Based upon a survey of members of ten ethnic groups in fifteen American cities that have experienced racial unrest. Although Jews were the most sympathetic to black progress and Poles the least, none of the data justifies branding any of the ten as "racist."

1063 Handlin, Oscar. RACE AND NATIONALITY IN AMERICAN LIFE. Boston: Little and Brown, 1957. 218 p. Notes.

Discusses the common historical roots of racism and nativism as "rational justification, scientific theory and emotional reaction." Contains a detailed critique of the Dillingham Commission Report.

1064 Hartley, William G. "United States Immigration Policy: The Case of the Western Hemisphere." WORLD AFFAIRS 135 (1972): 54-70.

Notes that at about the same time that the 1965 Immigration Act eliminated the national origins provision and restricted the unlimited immigration which the Western Hemisphere had enjoyed, European immigration declined and that from the Caribbean nations increased. Thus European quotas have gone unfilled while those from the Caribbean countries are filled each year.

1065 Hartmann, Edward G. THE MOVEMENT TO AMERICANIZE THE IMMIGRANT. New York: Columbia University Press, 1948. 276 p. Appendices, bibliography, index.

Details the build-up of the Americanization movement by social agencies, industry, and state and federal government agencies; its intensification during World War I and its postwar culmination.

1066 Heald, Morrell. "Business Attitudes toward European Immigration, 1880-1900." JOURNAL OF ECONOMIC HISTORY 13 (1953): 291-304.

Finds that business attitudes on this issue were shaped largely by reliance on secondary sources and popular accounts. Thus "[b]y failing to consider the immigration problem clearly on its economic merits, business contributed to the atmosphere of fear, confusion and distrust that surrounded the national debate over immigration policy."

1067 Heizer, Robert F., and Almquist, Alan J. THE OTHER CALIFORNIANS: PREJUDICE AND DISCRIMINATION UNDER SPAIN, MEXICO AND THE UNITED STATES TO 1920. Berkeley and Los Angeles: University of California Press, 1971. 278 p. Illustrations, tables, footnotes, bibliography, index.

Provides "a social history of non-Anglo ethnic groups in California's past as illustrated by attitudes of prejudice and acts of discrimination directed against these groups." Second half of the book deals with Mexicans, Chinese, and Japanese.

1068 Higham, John. "American Immigration Policy in Historical Prospective." LAW AND CONTEMPORARY PROBLEMS 21 (1956): 213-35.

A chronology of immigration restriction from the 1870s to the mid 1950s, weaving federal legislation into the general pattern of immigration.

1069 _____. "Another Look at Nativism." CATHOLIC HISTORICAL REVIEW 44 (1958): 147-58.

Finds that the source of nativism lies less in the newness of the society than in the sense of economic and social competitiveness, which creates tensions between Americans and newly arriving immigrants.

1070 _____. "Anti-Semitism in the Gilded Age: A Reinterpretation." MISSISSIPPI VALLEY HISTORICAL REVIEW 43 (1957): 559-78.

From the social and economic turmoil of the Gilded Age emerged three groups whose anti-Semitism exceeded mere social discrimination: agrarian radical Populists, patrician intellectuals of the East, and many of the poorer classes in the urban areas. Because of their differences on other issues, the three never cooperated in their opposition to the Jews.

1071 _____. STRANGERS IN THE LAND: PATTERNS OF AMERICAN NATIVISM, 1860-1925. 1955. Reprint. New York: Atheneum, 1968. 330 p. Bibliography, index.

The definitive study of the intellectual and political roots of the post-Civil War resurgence of nativism, which culminated in the restrictionist legislation of the 1920s.

1072 Jaffe, Louis L. "The Philosophy of Our Immigration Law." LAW AND

CONTEMPORARY PROBLEMS 21 (1956): 358-75.

A study of the philosophy behind immigration policy prior to restrictive legislation in the 1920s, the implications of the McCarran-Walter Act and prospects and suggestions for a new policy.

1073 Kane, Michael B. MINORITIES IN TEXTBOOKS: A STUDY OF THEIR TREATMENT IN SOCIAL STUDIES TEXTS. Chicago: Quadrangle Books, 1970. 147 p. Appendices, footnotes.

A chapter each on textbook treatment of Jews, Afro-Americans, and the minorities persecuted under Nazism and a brief summary of "other minorities in America."

1074 Kansas, Sidney. U.S. IMMIGRATION; EXCLUSION AND DEPORTATION, AND CITIZENSHIP OF THE UNITED STATES OF AMERICA. 3d ed. New York: Matthew Bender Co., 1948. 460 p. Appendices, index.

Part 1 gives a history of immigration legislation, the provisions of the Immigration Acts of 1917 and 1924 and various executive orders or statutes applying to immigration or deportation. Part 2 covers the Nationality Act of 1940 and relevant nationality regulations.

1075 Kantrowitz, Nathan. "Ethnic and Racial Segregation in the New York Metropolis, 1960." AMERICAN JOURNAL OF SOCIOLOGY 74 (1969): 685-95.

Concludes that interethnic segregation (e.g., Poles from Italians) has experienced only a minimal decline from 1930 to 1960 and has persisted into the second generation.

1076 Kingsley, J. Donald. "Immigration and Our Foreign Policy Objectives." LAW AND CONTEMPORARY PROBLEMS 21 (1956): 299-310.

Argues that discriminatory immigration policies based on racist assumptions affect the image of the United States in the eyes of most foreigners much more than do propaganda efforts and, therefore, there is a need for a more liberal immigration policy.

1077 Kinzer, Donald L. AN EPISODE IN ANTI-CATHOLICISM: THE AMERICAN PROTECTIVE ASSOCIATION. Seattle: University of Washington Press, 1964. 342 p. Notes, bibliography, index.

Core of the book analyzes the APA from 1893 to 1896, concluding with a chapter on the decline of the association during the twentieth century, even though anti-Catholic hostility was high.

1078 Kolodny, Ralph L. "Ethnic Cleavages in the United States: An Historical Reminder to Social Workers." SOCIAL WORK 14 (1969): 13-23.

Stresses that in addition to class differences, ethnic differences should also be important to social workers. A brief examination of intergroup relations illustrates "the pervasiveness of ethnic tensions and suggests the degree to which ethnicity must be taken into account in social planning and treatment.

1079 Leonard, Henry B. "Louis Marshall and Immigration Restriction, 1906-1924." AMERICAN JEWISH ARCHIVES 24 (1972): 6-26.

Reports that as founder and president of the American Jewish Committee, Marshall led opposition to immigration restriction, especially of East European Jews. He nevertheless wanted rapid assimilation of the New Immigrants.

1080 _____. "The Open Gates: The Protest Against the Movement to Restrict European Immigration, 1896-1924." Ph.D. dissertation, Northwestern University, 1967. 306 p.

Contends that Jews, immigrants, businessmen, and some social workers felt for different reasons that a policy of immigration restriction violated either their interests or ideals. They thus opposed literacy tests or head taxes in the early 1900s, but the nationalism of the war brought a renewed call for restriction and the old coalition collapsed.

1081 Lieberman, Jethro K. ARE AMERICANS EXTINCT? New York: Walker, 1968. 204 p. Appendix, notes, bibliography, index.

An emotional critique of the National Origins Quota System from its roots to repeal, emphasizing its political, legal, and administrative vagaries.

1082 Linnemann, William R. "Immigrant Stereotypes: 1880-1900." STUDIES IN AMERICAN HUMOR 1 (1974): 28-39.

Discusses, with examples, the formation of stereotypes of Irish, Jewish, Chinese, Italian, and German immigrants in the mass media and the theater in the nineteenth century. Concludes that they constitute a record of prejudice rather than a source of amusement.

1083 Lorence, James J. "Business and Reform: The American Asiatic Association and the Exclusion Laws, 1905-1907." PACIFIC HISTORICAL REVIEW 39 (1970): 421-38.

The story of the American Asiatic Association, a group of American business interests involved in Far Eastern trade, and their attempts to modify restrictionist policies in response to Chinese boycotts of American goods.

1084 McGann, Sr. Agnes Geraldine. NATIVISM IN KENTUCKY TO 1860.
Washington, D.C.: Catholic University of America Press, 1944. 172 p.
Footnotes, bibliography, index.

A dissertation which studies "the rise, progress, and decline
of Nativism as an anti-foreign, anti-Catholic social and political movement in Kentucky prior to the Civil War." Pays
particular attention to Louisville and the role of the LOUIS-
VILLE COURIER-JOURNAL.

1085 McWilliams, Carey. BROTHERS UNDER THE SKIN. Boston: Little and
Brown, 1944. 326 p.

Analyzes roots of prejudice against variety of nonwhite peoples
in the United States including Amerindians, Chinese, Mexicans, Japanese, Hawaiians, Puerto Ricans, and Afro-Americans.

1086 _____. A MASK FOR PRIVILEGE: ANTI-SEMITISM IN AMERICA.
Boston: Little and Brown, 1948. 299 p. Notes, index.

A discussion of anti-Semitism from the 1870s to the 1940s, its
origin, persistence, and role in American history.

1087 Mann, Arthur. "Attitudes and Policies on Immigration; An Opportunity
for Revision." AMERICAN JEWISH HISTORICAL SOCIETY 46 (1957):
289-305.

Compares the racist and nativist climate which produced immigration restriction with the more pluralistic atmosphere of the
1950s and argues for sweeping revision of the laws.

1088 _____. "Gompers and the Irony of Racism." ANTIOCH REVIEW 13
(1953): 203-14.

Discusses the irony of Jewish immigrant and labor leader Samuel
Gompers, who was loud in his call for restrictionism and for
maintaining the Anglo-Saxon dominance in America's ethnic
composition.

1089 Morris, Terry. BETTER THAN YOU: SOCIAL DISCRIMINATION AGAINST
MINORITIES. New York: Institute of Human Relations Press, 1971.
64 p.

A free-lance magazine writer looks at how social snobbery
and discrimination has handicapped ethnic groups, particularly
Jews, in America.

1090 Murphy, Paul L. "Intolerance in the 1920s." JOURNAL OF AMERICAN
HISTORY 51 (1964): 60-76.

Attributes the decade's intolerance to a complex of political,

economic, and demographic causes and cautions historians
against relying solely on borrowed social science models in
explaining its origins.

1091 Murray, Robert K. RED SCARE: A STUDY IN NATIONAL HYSTERIA,
1919-1920. Minneapolis: University of Minnesota Press, 1955. 337 p.
Notes, bibliographic essay, index.

Intensive look at the origins, course, and decline of the anti-
radical, anti-foreign hysteria following World War I.

1092 Overdyke, W. Darrell. THE KNOW-NOTHING PARTY IN THE SOUTH.
Baton Rouge: Louisiana State University Press, 1950. 321 p. Illustrations, appendix, footnotes, bibliographical note, index.

Includes a general discussion of southern nativism during the
first half of the nineteenth century and then explores in detail
the rise and decline of nativism between 1850 and 1860.

1093 Risch, Erna. "Encouragement of Immigration as Revealed in Colonial
Legislation." VIRGINIA MAGAZINE OF HISTORY AND BIOGRAPHY 65
(1937): 2-10.

Argues that colonial Virginia encouraged immigration by mora-
toriums on debt, exemption from taxes, bounties, easy land
acquisition, naturalization, voting rights, and other induce-
ments.

1094 Robbins, Richard. "The Refugee Status: Challenge and Response." LAW
AND CONTEMPORARY PROBLEMS 21 (1956): 311-33.

Calls for a revision of the national origins quota system which
would allow for increases in total quotas and the transfer of
quotas from western European countries, where quotas go unfilled, to countries which have small quotas. Also calls for
closer coordination between immigration and refugee policy
development and implementation.

1095 Roche, John P. "The Expatriation Decisions: A Study in Constitutional
Improvisation and the Uses of History." AMERICAN POLITICAL SCIENCE
REVIEW 58 (1964): 72-80.

Traces the history of expatriation decisions and analyzes the
reasoning and the logic behind them. Contends that the existing statutes are confusing and that they fail to distinguish
between "transfers of loyalty" and "betrayals of allegiance."

1096 Rosenfield, Harry N. "The Prospects for Immigration Amendments." LAW
AND CONTEMPORARY PROBLEMS 21 (1956): 401-26.

Defines and assesses factors for or against revision of immigration laws by examining three types of issues: general policy issues, specific policy issues, and technical issues.

1097 Ruetten, Richard T., and McCoy, Donald R. QUEST AND RESPONSE: MINORITY RIGHTS AND THE TRUMAN ADMINISTRATION. Lawrence: University of Kansas Press, 1973. 427 p. Notes, bibliography, index.

Includes a study of blacks, Indians, Mexicans, Puerto Ricans, Japanese, Chinese, and Jews in the post-World War II period based on exhaustive research. Concludes that the Truman presidency marked a watershed in civil rights history and showed an increasing tolerance of ethnic minorities.

1098 Sellin, Henry, ed. PROCEEDINGS OF THE NEW YORK UNIVERSITY CONFERENCE ON PRACTICE AND PROCEDURE UNDER THE IMMIGRATION AND NATIONALITY ACT. New York: Oceana Publications, 1954. 145 p. Footnotes, appendix.

Proceedings of a conference in June 1953 which dealt with technical aspects of procedural provisions of the McCarran-Walter Act of 1952. The seven speakers were either immigration officials or attorneys.

1099 Selznick, Gertrude J., and Steinberg, Stephen. TENACITY OF PREJUDICE: ANTI-SEMITISM IN CONTEMPORARY AMERICA. Patterns of American Prejudice Series. New York: Harper & Row, 1969. 248 p. Tables, appendices, footnotes, index.

Part of a University of California five-year study on anti-Semitism. Attempts to determine the extent, location, and explanation of contemporary anti-Semitism.

1100 Sewrey, Charles Louis. "The Alleged 'Un-Americanism' of the Church as a Factor in Anti-Catholicism in the United States, 1860-1914." Ph.D. dissertation, University of Minnesota, 1955. 412 p.

After investigating the relationship between anti-Catholicism and the belief that the Church was a threat to American institutions, concludes that "anti-Catholicism was based partly upon genuine ideological differences between the traditional Catholic position and the typical American viewpoint."

1101 Shalloo, J.P. "United States Immigration Policy, 1882-1948." In ESSAYS IN HISTORY AND INTERNATIONAL RELATIONS IN HONOR OF GEORGE HUBBARD BLAKESLEE, edited by Dwight E. Lee and George E. McReynolds, pp. 126-52. Worcester, Mass.: Clark University Press, 1949.

A chronological summary of successive immigration laws by a sociologist. Sees the period from 1882 to 1924 as an attempt to develop a selective policy to satisfy the demands of labor and patriotic groups pushing for restriction. From 1924 to 1948 the author sees a refinement of the policy which admitted immigrants after careful screening.

1102 Solomon, Barbara Miller. ANCESTORS AND IMMIGRANTS: A CHANGING NEW ENGLAND TRADITION, 1956. Reprint. Chicago: University of Chicago Press, 1972. 210 p. Notes, sources, index.

Discusses the impact of mass immigration upon New England democratic thought and the conversion of all but a small minority to the nativism of the Immigration Restriction League.

1103 Spengler, Joseph J. "Issues and Interests in American Immigration Policy." ANNALS OF THE AMERICAN ACADEMY OF POLITICAL AND SOCIAL SCIENCE 316 (1958): 43-51.

Contends that a majority of Americans favored the restrictionist immigration policies still in effect in 1958. Attributes this attitude to noneconomic sentiments, doubting that business interests had much effect on immigration policy.

1104 Steinfield, Melvin. CRACKS IN THE MELTING POT: READINGS IN RACISM AND DISCRIMINATION IN AMERICAN HISTORY. Beverly Hills, Calif.: Glencoe Press, 1973. 365 p. Bibliography, Index.

An anthology of essays detailing patterns of discrimination directed at the whole spectrum of ethnic, racial, and religious minorities in the United States.

1105 Tomasi, Lydio F. THE ETHNIC FACTOR IN THE FUTURE OF INEQUALITY. Staten Island, N.Y.: Center for Migration Studies, 1972. 28 p. Notes.

Posits the basis for a theory of ethnicity based upon the human needs for belongingness, self-esteem, and mutual understanding.

1106 Wang, Peter Heywood. "Legislating 'Normalcy': The Immigration Act of 1924." Ph.D. dissertation, University of California-Riverside, 1971. 235 p.

Discusses support for and opposition to the Johnson bill of 1924. Wang sees the act as indicative of the intense nationalism of the 1920s, typified by a desire to return to simpler times through isolationism, prohibition, the Red Scare, and the Klan.

1107 Wasserman, Jack. "Some Defects in the Administration of Our Immigration Laws." LAW AND CONTEMPORARY PROBLEMS 21 (1956): 376-81.

After briefly examining the conduct of immigration and con-

sular officers and analyzing the extent of their encroachment
on the rights of immigrants, concludes that changes in immigration laws must improve the administrators and administrative
machinery which implement the law.

1108 Weber, Francis J. "Irish-born Champion [John J. Cantwell] of the Mexican-Americans." CALIFORNIA HISTORICAL SOCIETY QUARTERLY 49
(1970): 233-49.

A study of the work of Los Angeles Archbishop John Joseph
Cantwell and the Catholic church in behalf of thousands of
Mexicans who fled their country because of the anti-religious
campaign of the Mexican government.

1109 Zeisel, Hans. "The Race Question in American Immigration." SOCIAL
RESEARCH 16 (1949): 222-29.

Analyzes the evolution of the Immigration and Naturalization
Service's checklist of races and peoples, an effort to record
the race and religion of each immigrant. Notes the fuzzi-
ness of its categories and the fact that Mexicans and Hebrew,
about one-fourth the total, have not appeared in these statistics since 1943.

THE DEBATE OVER RESTRICTION

Between 1900 and the passage of the National Origins Quota Act there
was a national debate over the merits of immigration restriction, resulting in various books and articles, many of a polemical nature. The following are a representative cross section of that debate. The preponder-
ance are in favor of restriction, but that was a fair reflection of the
mood of the country. No annotation is provided because many of the
titles are self-explanatory and the items are largely proselytizing in nature.

Pro Restriction

1110 Bocock, J.P. "Irish Conquest of Our Cities." FORUM 17 (1894): 186-
95.

1111 Brown, Gilbert L. "Intelligence as Related to Nationality." JOURNAL
OF EDUCATION RESEARCH 3 (1922): 324-27.

1112 Burr, Clinton S. AMERICA'S RACE HERITAGE; AN ACCOUNT OF THE
DIFFUSION OF ANCESTRAL STOCKS IN THE UNITED STATES DURING
THREE CENTURIES OF NATIONAL EXPANSION AND A DISCUSSION
OF ITS SIGNIFICANCE. New York: National Historical Society, 1922.
337 p. Bibliography.

1113 Collins, James H. "Who Will Do Our Dirty Work Now?" SATURDAY EVENING POST 6 (1924): 122-30.

1114 Conklin, Edward Grant. "Some Biological Aspects of Immigration." SCRIBNER'S MAGAZINE 69 (1921): 352-59.

1115 Creel, George. "Close the Gates!" COLLIER'S 72 (1922): 9-18.

1116 _____. "Melting Pot or Dumping Ground." COLLIER'S 67 (1921): 9-26.

1117 Curran, Henry H. "Fewer and Better." SATURDAY EVENING POST 197 (1924): 59-62.

1118 _____. "Fewer and Better, or None." SATURDAY EVENING POST 196 (1924): 153-57.

1119 Davis, James. "How the Immigration Laws Are Now Working." AMERICAN REVIEW OF REVIEWS 58 (1922): 509-16.

1120 _____. "Immigration and Naturalization." OUTLOOK 131 (1922): 256-60.

1121 _____. SELECTED IMMIGRATION. St. Paul, Minn.: Scott-Mitchell Publishing Co., 1925. 227 p. Appendices.

1122 Fairchild, Henry Pratt. IMMIGRATION. New York: Macmillan Co., 1913. 500 p. Bibliography, index.

1123 _____. IMMIGRATION, A WORLD MOVEMENT AND ITS AMERICAN SIGNIFICANCE. Rev. ed. New York: Macmillan Co., 1925. 520 p. Bibliography, index.

1124 _____. "The Immigration Law of 1924." QUARTERLY JOURNAL OF ECONOMICS 38 (1924): 653-65.

1125 _____. THE MELTING POT MISTAKE. Boston: Little and Brown, 1926. 226 p.

1126 Garis, Roy L. IMMIGRATION RESTRICTION: A STUDY OF THE OPPOSITION TO AND REGULATION OF IMMIGRATION INTO THE UNITED STATES. New York: Macmillan Co., 1927. 354 p. Illustrations, bibliography, index.

1127 ____. "The Necessity of Excluding Inferior Stock." CURRENT HIS-TORY 24 (1926): 666-71.

1128 ____. "Our Immigration Policy." NORTH AMERICAN REVIEW 220 (1924): 63-77.

1129 Garrett, Garet. "As Citizens Thereof." SATURDAY EVENING POST 197 (1924): 6-7.

1130 Grant, Madison. THE CONQUEST OF A CONTINENT. New York: C. Scribner's Sons, 1934. 395 p. Bibliography.

1131 ____. THE PASSING OF THE GREAT RACE. New York: C. Scribner's Sons, 1918. 264 p. Maps, charts, appendix, bibliography, index.

1132 Grant, Madison, and Davidson, Charles S. THE FOUNDERS OF THE RE-PUBLIC ON IMMIGRATION, NATURALIZATION AND ALIENS. New York: C. Scribner's Sons, 1928. 92 p.

1133 Grose, Howard B. ALIENS OR AMERICANS? New York and Toronto: Young People's Missionary Movement, 1906. 337 p. Illustrations, appendices, bibliography.

1134 Hall, P.F. IMMIGRATION. New York: H. Holt and Co., 1906. 338 p. Appendices, bibliography, index.

1135 Sweeney, Arthur. "Mental Tests for Immigrants." NORTH AMERICAN REVIEW 215 (1922): 600-612.

1136 Ward, Robert. "Higher Mental and Physical Standards for Immigrants." SCIENTIFIC MONTHLY 19 (1924): 533-47.

1137 Warne, Frank Julian. IMMIGRANT INVASION. New York: Dodd, Mead & Co., 1913. 316 p. Illustrations, bibliography, index.

1138 ____. THE TIDE OF IMMIGRATION. New York: D. Appleton and Co., 1916. 364 p. Charts, index.

1139 Whelpley, James Davenport. THE PROBLEM OF THE IMMIGRANT. London: Chapman and Hall, 1905. 295 p.

Anti Restriction

1140 Antin, Mary. THEY WHO KNOCK AT OUR GATES. Boston and New

York: Houghton Mifflin Co., 1914. 142 p. Illustrations.

1141 Boas, Franz. "Fallacies of Racial Inferiority." CURRENT HISTORY 25 (1927): 676-83.

1142 Bremer, Edith T., and Fisher, Galen M. "Immigration, A Look Ahead." SURVEY 52 (1924): 207-12.

1143 Calverton, V.F. "The Myth of Nordic Superiority." CURRENT HISTORY 24 (1926): 671-77.

1144 Dickinson, E.D. "The Meaning of Nationality in the Recent Immigration Acts." AMERICAN JOURNAL OF INTERNATIONAL LAW 19 (1925): 344-47.

1145 Douglas, Paul H. "Is the New Immigration More Unskilled than the Old?" PUBLICATIONS OF THE AMERICAN STATISTICAL ASSOCIATION 16 (1918-19): 393-403.

1146 Edgerton, John E. "Immigration and Industry." FORUM 70 (1923): 1866-70.

1147 Frank, G. "Sensible Immigration Policy." CENTURY MAGAZINE 108 (1924): 135-39.

1148 Gillman, Joseph M. "Statistics and the Immigration Problem." AMERICAN JOURNAL OF SOCIOLOGY 20 (1924): 29-48.

1149 Phelps, Edith M. RESTRICTION OF IMMIGRATION. New York: H.W. Wilson Co., 1924. 118 p. Bibliography.

1150 Speek, Peter A. "The Meaning of Nationality and Americanization." AMERICAN JOURNAL OF SOCIOLOGY 32 (1926): 237-49.

THE NEW ETHNICITY

1151 Bernard, William S. "New Directions in Integration and Ethnicity." INTERNATIONAL MIGRATION REVIEW 5 (1971): 464-73.

Summarizes the proceedings of the Tenth Annual Seminar on the Integration of Immigrants, held in 1970, at which Nathan Glazer, Philip Soskis, Epifania Resposo, and Reverend Joseph Fitzpatrick were speakers.

1152 _____, ed. IMMIGRANTS AND ETHNICITY: TEN YEARS OF CHANG-
ING THOUGHT. New York: American Immigration and Citizenship Conference and National Project on Ethnic America, 1972. 73 p.

Contains excerpts of papers read by seventeen sociologists and
historians organized around the general themes of the meaning
of integration, ethnic groups in a pluralistic society, and in-
terrelationships between immigrants and Negroes.

1153 Feldstein, Stanley, and Costello, Lawrence, eds. THE ORDEAL OF AS-
SIMILATION: A DOCUMENTARY HISTORY OF THE WHITE WORKING
CLASS, 1830S TO THE 1970S. Garden City, N.Y.: Anchor Press,
1974. 500 p. Index.

Compilation of source and original materials which ties together immigration and labor history around the cultural and
economic struggles of the white ethnic working class.

1154 Greeley, Andrew M. "American Sociology and the Study of Ethnic Immigrant Groups." INTERNATIONAL MIGRATION DIGEST 1 (1964):
107-13.

Faults sociologists for failing to appreciate the continued importance of primary relationships, such as ethnic groups, because of their concern for studying secondary relationships.
Sees ethnic collectivity as a bridge between the two sets of
relationships providing social location and self-identification
and even performing some of the functions of an interest
group.

1155 _____. "The Rediscovery of Diversity." ANTIOCH REVIEW 31 (1971):
343-66.

Argues that there has been a dramatic increase of interest in
America's cultural heterogeneity in recent years, even among
respectable academics. This has led, in turn, to a rediscovery of "middle America," a growing militancy among white
ethnic groups, and a new appreciation for diversity.

1156 Greer, Colin, ed. DIVIDED SOCIETY: THE ETHNIC EXPERIENCE IN
AMERICA. New York: Basic Books, 1974. 405 p. Appendices, footnotes, bibliography, index.

An anthology of previously published scholarly works dating
mainly from the 1960s and 1970s and organized thematically
into three sections: (1) the nature and extent of assimilation
and mobility; (2) characteristics of ethnic groups which have
determined their experience in America; and (3) "interaction
of class and ethnic issues." A revisionist reaction to the
"Handlin School" of ethnic studies.

1157 Kamphoefner, Walter D. "St. Louis Germans and the Republican Party, 1848-1860." MID-AMERICA 57 (1975): 68-88.

Concludes that the GOP attracted a large portion of the German immigrant vote in St. Louis because the Republican leaders avoided nativism and temperance crusades and emphasized the Free-Soil position on slavery.

1158 Krickus, Richard J. "The White Ethnics: Who Are They and Where Are They Going?" CITY 5 (1971): 23-33.

Discusses the efforts of working-class white ethnics who are organizing in industrial areas of the Northeast on environmental and economic issues and what that portends for future racial harmony.

1159 Levine, Irving M., and Herman, Judith. "The Life of White Ethnics." DISSENT 19 (1972): 286-94.

Stresses interethnic cooperation rather than separatism as a means of solving economic problems to the satisfaction of the individual and society generally. It is a suggestion for effectively organizing the white ethnics who comprise the working class.

1160 Magner, Thomas F. "The Rise and Fall of the Ethnics." JOURNAL OF GENERAL EDUCATION 25 (1974): 253-64.

Notes the dramatic rise in ethnic consciousness of the past decade, but still argues that it is really the death spasm of ethnicity, generated largely by "professional ethnics." Attributes this death to the loss of language, migration to the suburbs, the end of immigration, and intermarriage.

1161 Makielski, Stanislaw J., Jr. BELEAGUERED MINORITIES. San Francisco: W.H. Freeman and Co., 1973. 227 p. Bibliographies, index.

An examination of how minority groups use politics to achieve various goals and an analysis of the conditions which determine success or failure.

1162 Novak, Michael. THE RISE OF THE UNMELTABLE ETHNICS: POLITICS AND CULTURE IN THE SEVENTIES. New York: Macmillan Co., 1971. 292 p. Notes, bibliography, index.

The most complete and articulate statement of the "new ethnicity" of the 1970s by a prominent ethical philosopher of Slovak ancestry. Deals especially with the relationship between white ethnics and the liberal-intellectual community.

1163 Ryan, Joseph W., ed. WHITE ETHNICS: LIFE IN WORKING CLASS

AMERICA. Englewood Cliffs, N.J.: Prentice Hall, 1973. 177 p. Resources, bibliography.

Contains sixteen articles defining white ethnicity; its private life in family, religion, and neighborhood; its public life in school, at work, and in politics; and discusses its recent resurgence.

1164 Ward, David. "The Emergence of Central Immigrant Ghettoes in American Cities: 1840-1920." ANNALS OF THE ASSOCIATION OF AMERICAN GEOGRAPHERS 58 (1968): 343-59.

Uses the experience of Boston to emphasize that the "timing and dimensions of the expansion of the different specialized functional areas of the central business district affected not only the location and longevity of immigrant ghettoes, but also the disposition of the distinctive residential quarters which developed beyond the expanding fringe of the central business district."

IMMIGRANTS AND U.S. INSTITUTIONS

1165 Abramson, Harold J. "Ethnic Diversity within Catholicism: A Comparative Analysis of Contemporary and Historical Religion." JOURNAL OF SOCIAL HISTORY 4 (1971): 359-88.

Concludes from a study of six American Catholic ethnic groups that those with "a long native history of religious conflict and competition identify strongly with the Church, regularly participate in its activities and contribute to its prevailing views." Those without a history of religious conflict tend to act in the opposite fashion.

1166 Barbash, Jack. "Ethnic Factors in the Development of the American Labor Movement." In INTERPRETING THE LABOR MOVEMENT, pp. 70-82. Champaign, Ill.: Industrial Relations Research Association, 1952.

Discusses ethnic influences on organized labor and concludes that they have been most important in internal politics of unions rather than as a consideration in policy making. Stresses that unions have provided a constructive mechanism for moderating ethnic rivalries in the interest of common socio-economic goals.

1167 Berrol, Selma Cantor. "Immigrants at School: New York City, 1898-1914." Ph.D. dissertation, City University of New York, 1967. 438 p.

A historical study describing "the impact of the Jewish and Italian immigrants on the public school consolidation in 1898 to the end of the period of greatest immigration in 1914." Discusses compulsory education, new curricula, and increased opportunity as the outgrowth of immigrant pressure.

1168 Blumenthal, Sonia. "The Private Organizations in the Naturalization and Citizenship Process." INTERNATIONAL MIGRATION REVIEW 5 (1971): 448-62.

A summary of the history and activities of various private organizations by the executive secretary of the American Immigration and Citizenship Conference. Stresses the need for new legislation regarding naturalization.

1169 Blumenthal, Sonia, and Murphy, Ruth. "The American Community and the Immigrant." ANNALS OF THE AMERICAN ACADEMY OF POLITICAL AND SOCIAL SCIENCE 367 (1966): 115-26.

Concludes that today's immigrants have a multiplicity of services available to aid their adjustment to the United States, indicating that the native-born community has matured and became more understanding and accepting.

1170 Buroker, Robert L. "From Voluntary Association to Welfare State: The Illinois Immigrants' Protective League, 1906-1926." JOURNAL OF AMERICAN HISTORY 58 (1971): 643-60.

Examines the motives and programs of the intellectuals and social workers who founded the League and evaluates its achievements and the reasons behind its demise.

1171 Carlson, Robert A. "Americanization as An Early Twentieth-Century Adult Education Movement." HISTORY OF EDUCATION QUARTERLY 10 (1970): 440-64.

Explores the thinking of John R. Commons, Edward A. Ross, and Frances Kellor to show that many progressives wanted to use adult education to Americanize the immigrants.

1172 Cohen, David K. "Immigrants and the Schools." REVIEW OF EDUCATIONAL RESEARCH 40 (1970): 13-27.

Concludes from an analysis of data from the first three decades of the twentieth century that there was no significant difference in educational performance between first generation immigrant children and the native white population.

1173 Dolan, Jay P. THE IMMIGRANT CHURCH: NEW YORK'S IRISH AND GERMAN CATHOLICS, 1815-1865. Baltimore: Johns Hopkins Press, 1975. 221 p. Notes, bibliography, index.

Deals with the impact of the mass migration of German and Irish Catholics on the predominantly Anglo-American Catholic church in New York City before the Civil War. Also deals with the reaction of the Catholic immigrants to the social unrest of the period.

1174 Feldman, Herman. RACIAL FACTORS IN AMERICAN INDUSTRY. 1931. Reprint. New York: Jerome S. Ozer, 1971. 318 p. Footnotes, index.

Considers the condition of blacks and immigrants during the decade of the 1920s followed by a set of remedies for the problems of discrimination. Devotes chapters to Orientals, Mexicans, and Indians.

1175 Gleason, Philip. "Immigration and American Catholic Intellectual Life." REVIEW OF POLITICS 26 (1964): 147-73.

Discusses the Catholic church as an "institutional immigrant," and analyzes the intellectual life of Catholic immigrants and ethnic groups. Ends by comparing the intellectual outlook and achievement of Catholic and Jewish immigrants.

1176 Greeley, Andrew M. "Civic Religion and Ethnic Americans." WORLD VIEW 16 (1973): 21-27.

Argues that there is a civil religion existing among white ethnic groups which emphasizes such key concepts as optimism, progress, social justice, pluralism, the freedom and dignity of the individual, orderly process, and patriotic symbols, and that, if properly appealed to, it can generate ethnic support for a more open, decent society.

1177 Harkness, Georgia E. THE CHURCH AND THE IMMIGRANT. New York: George H. Doran Co., 1921. 110 p. Footnotes, bibliography, index.

A handbook for the Catholic social activist, designed "to bring the church and the immigrant into more harmonious fellowship." After presenting the immigrant in his European and American settings, Harkness spends considerable time discussing how the New Immigrant is to be Americanized.

1178 Korman, Gerd. INDUSTRIALIZATION, IMMIGRANTS AND AMERICAN-IZERS: THE VIEW FROM MILWAUKEE, 1866-1921. Madison: State Historical Society of Wisconsin, 1967. 202 p. Bibliography, index.

Focuses on the "pecking order" of various immigrant groups in Milwaukee industry and the efforts of business to Americanize the workers through a system of industrial "education."

1179 Lannie, Vincent P. "Alienation in America: The Immigrant Catholic and Public Education in Pre-Civil War America." REVIEW OF POLITICS 32 (1970): 503-21.

Discusses the encounter of Catholic immigrants with the pervasive Protestant influence in public schools, which resulted in "social dislocation, religious and ethnic turmoil, and the eventual establishment of a separate system of Catholic education in the United States."

1180 Leinenweber, Charles. "The American Socialist Party and 'New' Immigrants." SCIENCE AND SOCIETY 32 (1968): 1-25.

Blames Socialist party policies for the failure to recruit the New Immigrants at the turn of the century. After analyzing the attitude of organized labor and various socialist organizations, the author concludes that only the Industrial Workers of the World actively cultivated the New Immigrants. The Socialist party, led by a right-wing group and motivated by racism and nativism, chose not to affiliate with the immigrants.

1181 Leiserson, William M. ADJUSTING IMMIGRANT AND INDUSTRY. 1924. Reprint. New York: Arno Press, 1969. 356 p. Tables, footnotes, index.

Describes the methods of various social agencies which deal with immigrants and which attempt to Americanize them.

1182 Leonard, Henry B. "The Immigrants' Protective League of Chicago, 1908-1921." JOURNAL OF THE ILLINOIS STATE HISTORICAL SOCIETY 66 (1973): 271-301.

Details the activities of Chicago social workers to protect immigrants against exploitation and discrimination and to facilitate their adjustment to American life during the Progressive era.

1183 Linkh, Richard M. AMERICAN CATHOLICISM AND EUROPEAN IMMIGRANTS, 1900-1924. Staten Island, N.Y.: Center for Migration Studies, 1975. 200 p. Notes, selected bibliography.

Deals with the efforts of the Catholic church and its associated institutions to cope with the New Immigration and the attempts of the latter to work through Church agencies to survive and prosper. Concludes with a discussion of the Church's attitudes toward assimilation and restriction.

1184 Manning, Caroline. THE IMMIGRANT WOMAN AND HER JOB. 1930. Reprint. New York: Arno Press and New York Times, 1970. 179 p. Illustrations, appendix, tables.

This is a report on immigrant women "designed to show how and to what extent these women are fitting into American industrial life, how necessary such employment is for the women and what it means to them and to their families, and how much of their time and strength is given to American industry."

1185 Murphy, John C. AN ANALYSIS OF THE ATTITUDES OF AMERICAN CATHOLICS TOWARD THE IMMIGRANT AND THE NEGRO. Washington, D.C.: Catholic University of American Press, 1940. 158 p. Bibliography.

Contends that the Catholic church and Catholic observers have generally considered questions about immigrants and Negroes primarily with respect to their effect on the Church, rather than upon the larger society.

1186 Polard, Diane S. "Educational Achievement and Ethnic Group Membership." COMPARATIVE EDUCATION REVIEW 17 (1973): 362-74.

A sample of over 400 seventh-grade students from five ethnic groups, Dutch, German, Irish, Italian, and Polish, reveals: (1) "children from different ethnic groups show differences in the motivational dynamics thought to underlie achievement"; and (2) "the variables that correlate with and predict achievement vary according to the ethnic backgrounds of the students."

1187 Rosenblum, Gerald. IMMIGRANT WORKERS: THEIR IMPACT ON AMERICAN LABOR RADICALISM. New York: Basic Books, 1973. 180 p. Index.

Compares the conservatism of American unionism with that of Europe and traces it primarily to the social disorganization and isolation engendered by the uprooting of immigrant laborers.

1188 Smith, Timothy L. "Immigrant Social Aspirations and American Education, 1880-1930." AMERICAN QUARTERLY 21 (1969): 524-43.

Argues that immigrants' economic, communal, and civic aspirations account for their emphasis on the importance of education for their children as much as any compulsory education acts or pressures from Americanizing groups.

1189 Tangwall, Wallace Fred. "Immigrants in the Civil War: Some American Reactions." Ph.D. dissertation, University of Chicago, 1962. 74 p. Bibliography.

Discusses the changing attitudes toward immigrants engendered by the Civil War in both the North and the South. Sees the South as attributing its defeat to "foreign mercenaries" while blaming their own immigrants for deserting them. Sees the North as bestowing qualified acceptance upon their immigrants for battlefield bravery, even upon the Irish and Germans, who had earlier inspired nativist reaction.

1190 Wade, Richard C. "Historical Analogy and Public Policy: The Black and Immigrant Experience in Urban America." In ESSAYS IN URBAN AMERICA, edited by Robert F. Oaks, Bruce I. Ambacher, Richard G. Miller, and Richard C. Wade, pp. 127-47. Austin: University of Texas

Press, 1975. Tables, notes, bibliography.

Insists that the immigrant and black experiences in the city cannot be compared because the latter has been trapped in ghettos almost entirely because of racial prejudice and segregation.

1191 White, Lynn Cromwell. THREE HUNDRED THOUSAND NEW AMERICANS: THE EPIC OF A MODERN IMMIGRANT-AID SERVICE. New York: Harper & Row, 1957. 423 p. Appendices, notes, references, index.

A history of the United Service for New Americans and its predecessor organizations, from 1934 to 1954. Concerned primarily with Jewish emigrants from Hitler's Germany.

1192 White, William Bruce. "The Military and the Melting Pot: The American Army and Minority Groups, 1865-1924." Ph.D. dissertation, University of Wisconsin, 1968. 422 p.

Traces the role of the military as an employer of blacks, Indians, and immigrants. Concludes that the segregation of blacks into separate units, although done for different reasons, had the effect of giving blacks a sense of identity and pride, while attempts to integrate Indians and immigrants largely failed.

1193 Wright, Carroll D. "The Influence of Trade Unions on Immigrants." BULLETIN OF THE BUREAU OF LABOR 56 (1905): 1-8.

The text of a letter from the Labor Commissioner to President Theodore Roosevelt regarding trade union attempts to organize the immigrants in Chicago's meat packing industry.

ETHNIC POLITICS

1194 Allswang, John M. A HOUSE FOR ALL PEOPLE, 1890-1936. Lexington: University of Kentucky Press, 1971. 212 p. Appendix, bibliographic essay, index.

Examines the political behavior of Chicago's nine largest ethnic groups and the forces which brought them all together under the umbrella of the Democratic party by 1936.

1195 Bailey, Harry A., Jr., and Katz, Ellis, eds. ETHNIC GROUP POLITICS. Columbus, Ohio: Merrill Publishing Co., 1969. 331 p.

Anthology of essays by political scientists and sociologists on the political behavior of ethnic groups, their impact on urban politics, and the persistence of ethnic voting.

1196 Brownell, Blaine A., and Stickle, Warren E. BOSSES AND REFORMERS.

Boston: Houghton Mifflin Co., 1973. 244 p. Bibliographical essay.
An anthology of contributions by both historical figures and
modern day scholars, many of which deal with the interaction
between immigrant groups and the urban political machine.

1197 Buenker, John D. "Dynamics of Chicago Ethnic Politics, 1900-1930."
JOURNAL OF THE ILLINOIS STATE HISTORICAL SOCIETY 67 (1974):
175-200.

Discusses the various roles which politics played in the life of
Chicago's immigrant groups, the conditions which determined
their degree of success, and the reasons for their party affiliation.

1198 _____. URBAN LIBERALISM AND PROGRESSIVE REFORM. New York:
C. Scribner's Sons, 1973. 239 p. Notes, bibliography, index.

Details reformist activities of urban, foreign stock Democratic
legislators in New York, New Jersey, Massachusetts, Connecticut, Rhode Island, Ohio, and Illinois during the Progressive
era.

1199 Campbell, Ballard C. "Ethnicity and the 1893 Wisconsin Assembly."
JOURNAL OF AMERICAN HISTORY 67 (1975): 74-94.

Details the ethnic differences between the two major parties in
the legislature and discusses the influence of the ethnocultural
backgrounds of legislators and their constituents on their votes
on various cultural issues.

1200 Carey, John Joseph. "Progressives and the Immigrant, 1885-1915." Ph.D.
dissertation, University of Connecticut, 1968. 180 p.

Since social settlements and charitable organizations in New
York, Chicago, and Boston had the closest contact with immigrants of any reform agencies, a sample of sixty individuals
involved with social work was selected for study. Although
firsthand contact with immigrants and their problems made reformers more sympathetic, they operated outside of government
and business and were generally unable to improve the economic condition of the immigrant.

1201 Enloe, Cynthia H. ETHNIC CONFLICT AND POLITICAL DEVELOPMENT.
Boston: Little, Brown and Co., 1973. 282 p. Footnotes, index.

Challenges the narrow focus of development theory on the na-
tion-state by calling attention to the importance of ethnic
identity. Examples come from several countries and cultures
throughout the world.

1202 Feldman, Egal. "Prostitution, the Alien Woman and the Progressive Ima-
gination." AMERICAN QUARTERLY 19 (1967): 192-206.

Analyzes the efforts of Progressive era social reformers to establish a connection between commercialized prostitution and
immigration and to help its female "victims" without providing
a strong argument for immigration restriction.

1203 Fuchs, Lawrence H. "Some Political Aspects of Immigration." LAW AND
CONTEMPORARY PROBLEMS 21 (1956): 270-83.

An attempt by a political scientist "to show the extent to
which the historic American policy of welcoming immigrants
has shaped the pluralistic character of American politics and
briefly to explore contemporary developments and the implied
changes which will be wrought by the present restrictive immigration policy."

1204 _____, ed. AMERICAN ETHNIC POLITICS. New York: Harper &
Row, 1968. 304 p. Bibliography.

An anthology dealing with various aspects of the impact of
ethnicity on political behavior. Articles cover a wide variety
of national groups and historical periods.

1205 Gerson, Louis L. THE HYPHENATE IN RECENT AMERICAN POLITICS
AND DIPLOMACY. Lawrence: University of Kansas Press, 1964. 262 p.
Appendix, notes, index.

Explores the attitudes of hyphenated Americans toward U.S.
foreign policy and their influence upon it. Focuses upon
both world wars, the cold war, and possible future behavior.

1206 Gordon, Daniel N. "Immigrants and Urban Governmental Form in American Cities, 1933-1960." AMERICAN JOURNAL OF SOCIOLOGY 74
(1968): 158-71.

Study of 268 American cities during a thirty-year period reveals a high correlation between the presence of immigrants
and the mayor-council form of government.

1207 Greeley, Andrew M. BUILDING COALITIONS: AMERICAN POLITICS
IN THE 1970S. New York: New Viewpoints, 1974. 430 p. Bibliographical references.

Argues that the American political system dictates the policies
of conflict, consensus, coalition, and compromise among geographic, socioeconomic, and ethnoreligious groups. Includes
a defense of white ethnics against charges of racism and conservatism and provides a critique of liberal intellectuals for
their unwillingness to coalesce with the former.

1208 _____. "Political Attitudes Among American White Ethnics." PUBLIC OPINION QUARTERLY 36 (1972): 213-20.

Uses data generated by the National Opinion Research Center to argue that blue-collar white ethnics score significantly higher than the national average on such liberal issues as civil rights, welfare, and identification with the Democratic party. Chastises liberal intellectuals for stereotyping.

1209 _____. "Political Participation Among Ethnic Groups in the United States: A Preliminary Reconnaissance." AMERICAN JOURNAL OF SOCIOLOGY 80 (1974): 170-204.

Argues that there are significant differences in levels of political participation among ethnoreligious groups, even if one allows for class, region, age, and sex; that there are "ethnic political styles"; and that these are the result of Old World cultural heritage, experience at the time of immigration, and continuing traditions since that time.

1210 Guzman, Ralph C. "The Function of Anglo-American Racism in the Political Development of CHICANOS." CALIFORNIA HISTORICAL QUARTERLY 50 (1971): 321-37.

Argues that "American racism in the Southwest limited and attempted to destroy the political development of a people whose major crime was grinding poverty." The author examines the political implications of stereotypes about Chicanos.

1211 Hawkins, Brett W., and Lorinskas, Robert A., eds. THE ETHNIC FACTOR IN AMERICAN POLITICS. Columbus, Ohio: Merrill Publishing Co., 1970. 197 p.

Anthology of ten articles organized around the topics of the persistence of ethnicity, ethnic voting, policy attitudes, and the impact of ethnic considerations on political forms and policy outputs.

1212 Humphrey, Craig R., and Louis, Helen Brock. "Assimilation and Voting Behavior: A Study of Greek Americans [1968]." INTERNATIONAL MIGRATION REVIEW 7 (1973): 34-45.

Tests the theories of assimilation and mobilization in ethnic voting against the reaction of Greek Americans to the vice-presidential candidacy of Spiro Agnew in 1968 and concludes that ethnicity had a decided influence in weaning many Greeks from their normally Democratic moorings.

1213 Ireland, Owen S. "The Ethnic Religious Dimension of Pennsylvania Politics, 1778-1779." WILLIAM AND MARY QUARTERLY 30 (1973): 423-48.

Based upon voting patterns in the legislature and the counties,
contends that ethnoreligious divisions played a leading role in
the politics of Revolutionary Pennsylvania. Sees in the independence movement, as led by Quakers and Presbyterians,
against the Anglican-dominated College of Philadelphia, the
Test Acts and the state constitution as illustrative examples.

1214 Kleppner, Paul. THE CROSS OF CULTURE: A SOCIAL ANALYSIS OF
MIDWESTERN POLITICS, 1850-1900. New York: Free Press, 1970. 402 p.
Bibliography.

Posits conflict between Democratic "ritualists" and Republican
"pietists" as the controlling factor in partisan politics in the
Midwest until the Depression. The nomination of the pietistic
William Jennings Bryan temporarily realigned the groups.

1215 Koepplin, Leslie Wayne. "A Relationship of Reform Immigrants and Progressives in the Far West." Ph.D. dissertation, University of California,
Los Angeles, 1971. 239 p.

Concludes from his study of California, Oregon, Washington,
Idaho, Montana, and Nevada, that there was no strong antipathy between Progressives and immigrants and that not only
did the immigrant press support several Progressive measures,
but immigrants themselves were sometimes Progressives.

1216 Levy, Mark R., and Kramer, Michael S. THE ETHNIC FACTOR: HOW
AMERICA'S MINORITIES DECIDE ELECTIONS. New York: Simon and
Schuster, 1972. 252 p. Appendices, bibliography, index.

Discussion of the varying degrees of political influence exer-
cised by blacks, Chicanos, Puerto Ricans, Jews, Irish, Slavs,
and Italians, especially in presidential elections.

1217 Litt, Edgar. BEYOND PLURALISM: ETHNIC POLITICS IN AMERICA.
Glenview, Ill.: Scott, Foresman and Co., 1970. 190 p. Notes, bibliographic essay.

Discusses the social, individual, and organizational bases of
ethnic politics and various patterns ranging from accommodation
to separatism to radicalism. The last section compares the
differing ethnic political styles of Jews, Irish Catholics, and
Negroes.

1218 _____. "Ethnic Status and Political Perspectives." MIDWEST JOURNAL
OF POLITICAL SCIENCE 5 (1961): 276-83.

Finds that Jews with strong feelings of ethnic subordination
are less likely to be politically active, tolerant, or altruistic.
Feels that ethnically determined political responses are primarily based upon perceptions of outside hostility that weaken

the member's sense of control over his environment and his participation.

1219 Luebke, Frederick C. ETHNIC VOTERS AND THE ELECTION OF LIN-COLN. Lincoln: University of Nebraska Press, 1971. 226 p. Bibliographical references.

Essays by eleven scholars dealing with the role played by ethnic group voters in 1860, especially in the Midwest.

1220 Miller, Sally M. THE RADICAL IMMIGRANT. New York: Twayne, 1974. 212 p.

Examines the careers of some two dozen immigrants who became active in a variety of American "radical" movements and tries to create a "radical profile" out of their collective biographies.

1221 O'Grady, Joseph P., ed. THE IMMIGRANTS' INFLUENCE ON WIL-SON'S PEACE POLICIES. Lexington: University of Kentucky Press, 1967. 329 p. Notes, index.

Collection of essays which focuses on ten immigrant groups which tried to influence Woodrow Wilson's plans for postwar Europe. Concludes that only the Jews and Poles actually influenced Wilson and that public opinion was not a major force in determining foreign policy during the period. Remaining immigrant groups studied were Germans, Irish, British, Italians, Magyars, South Slavs, Czechs, and Slovaks.

1222 Parenti, Michael. "Ethnic Politics and the Persistence of Ethnic Identification." AMERICAN POLITICAL SCIENCE REVIEW 61 (1967): 717-26.

Distinguishes between assimilation and acculturation as factors in political behavior and argues that ethnic identification is still a major determinant in voting.

1223 Scammon, Richard, and Wattenburg, Ben J. THE REAL MAJORITY. New York: Berkeley Publishing Corp., 1972. 347 p. Illustrations.

Argues that white lower and lower middle class ethnics, who form the backbone of the Democratic party, are in danger of being forced out of the party because of its emphasis on social issues. Urges a return to the center by emphasizing economic issues again.

1224 Swierenga, Robert P. "Ethnocultural Political Analysis: A New Approach to American Ethnic Studies." JOURNAL OF AMERICAN STUDIES 5 (1971): 59-79.

Discusses five major schools of interpretation of ethnic history --nationalist-nativist, filiopietistic, progressive, scientific, and

ethnocultural--and surveys the recent historiography supporting
the ethnocultural approach to political behavior.

1225 Tobias, Henry, and Woodhouse, Charles, eds. MINORITIES AND POLI-
TICS. Albuquerque: University of New Mexico Press, 1968. 131 p.
Notes.

Of the six essays, only Frances L. Swadesh's "The Alianza
Movement of New Mexico: The Interplay of Social Change
and Public Commentary" deals with an immigrant group in the
United States.

1226 Weed, Perry L. THE WHITE ETHNIC MOVEMENT AND ETHNIC POLI-
TICS. New York: Praeger, 1973. 220 p. Tables, bibliography.

Focuses on the motivations and organizations which produced
the emergence of white ethnic politics in the 1960s. Speculates on its impact on the strategies of the two major political
parties.

1227 Wolfinger, Raymond E. "The Development and Persistence of Ethnic Voting." AMERICAN POLITICAL SCIENCE REVIEW 59 (1965): 896-908.

Case study of ethnic politics focusing on the Italians of New
Haven, Connecticut, and their eventual adherence to the Republican party because of patronage and recognition disputes
with the Irish Democrats.

1228 Wyman, Roger E. VOTING BEHAVIOR IN THE PROGRESSIVE ERA: WIS-
CONSIN AS A CASE STUDY. Ph.D. dissertation, University of Wisconsin, Madison, 1976. 1109 p. Appendices, bibliography.

Uses small unit statistical analysis to delineate the voting behavior of the state's major ethnic groups. Concludes that
ethnic voting declined relative to ideological and class voting,
but still remained the most important determinant of political
behavior in the state prior to World War I.

Chapter 7

CENTERS, REPOSITORIES, SOCIETIES, DOCUMENTS,
AND JOURNALS

The following constitute depositories and organizations which distribute and publish primary materials for the study of immigration and ethnicity, but certain kinds of source materials have not been included for various reasons. Letters, diaries, and other manuscript material in private hands are obviously impossible to list. Foreign language newspapers are a valuable resource for those fluent in the language, but there have been literally thousands of them, many short-lived, and the relatively few that have survived in any number are usually included in the repositories and libraries mentioned below. Many states also had immigration bureaus, usually affiliated with agriculture or labor departments, but their publications were sporadic and usually of a purely promotional nature. Some of the few useful state publications are included below in "Miscellaneous Published Documents, Manuscripts, and Guides."

CENTERS, REPOSITORIES, AND SOCIETIES

1229 American Baptist Historical Society, 1106 South Goodman Street, Rochester, N.Y. 14620.

> Founded in 1853, it maintains a library and archives and publishes FOUNDATIONS.

1230 American Catholic Historical Association, Catholic University of America, 620 Michigan Avenue, N.E., Washington, D.C. 20017.

> Established in 1919, with a current membership of 1,100, it publishes the scholarly quarterly CATHOLIC HISTORICAL REVIEW.

1231 American Historical Society of Germans from Russia, 1004A 9th Avenue, Box 1424, Greeley, Colo. 80631.

> Formed in 1968, the organization has more than 2,500 members, publishes a magazine under the name of the society, and maintains a library and archives.

1232 American Hungarian Library and Historical Society, 215 East 82nd Street, New York, N.Y. 10028.

Organized in 1955 and with a membership of 450, the society "maintains collection of Hungariana; promotes research and study in the contribution of Hungarian culture to that of the United States. Presents scientific and cultural lectures, maintains a library of 3,000 volumes. Publishes studies on Hungarian culture."

1233 American Hungarian Studies Foundation, 177 Somerset Street, New Brunswick, N.J. 08903.

Established in 1954, the Foundation publishes the HUNGARIAN STUDIES NEWSLETTER three times a year. It aids "persons and organizations of Hungarian origin; supports and promotes publications, research, educational programs, and academic studies of Hungarian culture in American universities, colleges and high schools." Maintains a library and museum collection of 33,000 books and rare volumes and manuscripts.

1234 American Irish Historical Society, 991 Fifth Avenue, New York, N.Y. 10028.

Founded in 1897, this organization annually publishes THE RE-CORDER. It has a library of 25,000 volumes on genealogy, Irish history, and the Irish in America. It also has papers relating to Irish immigration, mainly during the nineteenth century.

1235 American Italian Historical Association, 209 Flagg Place, Staten Island, N.Y. 10304.

With a present membership of nearly 400, the association both publishes a quarterly newsletter, annual proceedings, and books; and maintains an archives and library on Italian-American history. It is an organization of academics and ethnics "interested in collecting, preserving, publishing and popularizing material about the settlement and history of the Italians in the United States and Canada." Organized in 1966.

1236 American Jewish Archives, 3101 Clifton Avenue, Cincinnati, Ohio 45220.

Established in 1892, it now has more than 3,000 members and publishes the AMERICAN JEWISH HISTORICAL QUARTERLY. Its statement of purpose: "Collects, catalogs, publishes, and displays material on history of Jews in America; serves as an information center for inquiries; maintains archives of original source material; sponsors lectures and exhibitions."

1237 American Scandinavian Foundation, 127 East 73 Street, New York, N.Y. 10027.

Dedicated to furthering understanding between the United States and the Scandinavian countries through education, cultural exchange, publications, and special projects. Established in 1910, it has twenty-seven local groups with 5,500 members and a library of 6,000 volumes of Scandinavian literature in the original language and in translation.

1238 American Society for Ethnohistory, Arizona State Museum, University of Arizona, Tucson, Ariz. 85721.

Has a membership of 600 and publishes a quarterly, ETHNO-HISTORY. Previous to 1966 the society was called the American Indian Ethnohistoric Conference. It was formed "to promote and encourage original research in the documentary history of the culture and movements of primitive peoples, and related problems of broader scope." Formed in 1953.

1239 American Society of Church History, Union Theological Seminary, 3401 Brook Road, Richmond, Va. 23227.

Established in 1888 with a current membership of 1,800. Publishes CHURCH HISTORY.

1240 American Swedish Historical Foundation and Museum, 1900 Pattison Avenue, Philadelphia, Pa. 19145.

Organized in 1926 and with a membership of 1,000, it publishes a newsletter, quarterly, and a yearbook. Its collections include microfilm and originals of material on early Swedish settlement in America, manuscripts of prominent Swedish Americans, and various church and town records.

1241 American Swedish Institute, 2600 Park Avenue, Minneapolis, Minn. 55407.

Founded in 1929; present membership of 5,300. Publishes a newsletter, HAPPENINGS, ten times a year and maintains a museum and library. Formed "to preserve the Swedish cultural heritage and develop close relations between the United States and Sweden."

1242 Archives and Museum of the Polish Roman Catholic Union, 984 North Milwaukee Avenue, Chicago, Ill. 60622.

Its collections relate chiefly to Polish culture and to the history of Poles in America. Included are papers of individuals and organizations, from the sixteenth century to the present.

1243 Augustana College Library, Rock Island, Ill. 61603.

Nineteenth- and twentieth-century items relating to the Augustana Synod of the Evangelical Lutheran church and to Swedish immigration to the United States, including letters, diaries, minutes, and journals.

1244 Balch Institute, 123 South Broad Street, 1627 Fidelity Building, Philadelphia, Pa. 19109.

Founded in 1971, the institute "houses 400,000 books, 20 million manuscripts, 20,000 reels of microfilm, and large numbers of ethnic and minority group newspapers, the nation's most comprehensive collection of materials concerning all national groups who came to North America."

1245 Burton Historical Collection, 5201 Woodward Street, Detroit Public Library, Detroit, Mich. 48202.

Manuscripts and materials on Armenians, Bulgarians, Croatians, Finns, Greeks, Hungarians, Latvians, Lithuanians, Poles, Rumanians, Russians, Syrians, Ukrainians, Yugoslavs; and material used by Lois Rankin in researching ethnic groups in Detroit.

1246 Center for Migration Studies, Brooklyn College, City University of New York, 210 Livingston, New York, N.Y. 11210.

Designed to aid scholars in the collection, preservation, and analysis of primary and secondary materials for the study of migration processes. The Archives of Migration houses manuscripts, photographs, and taped autobiographies and interviews with significant persons involved in various aspects of migration. Publishes the quarterly INTERNATIONAL MIGRATION REVIEW as well as books and pamphlets on migration. Important articles from the journal are annotated separately.

1247 Center for the Study of American Pluralism, National Opinion Research Center, 6030 Ellis Avenue, Chicago, Ill. 60637.

Uses random sample survey data on selected ethnic populations to determine the persistence and influence of ethnically based behavior in present-day America. Publishes ETHNICITY, a quarterly journal.

1248 Center for Urban Ethnography, University of Pennsylvania, Philadelphia, Pa. 19104.

1249 Chicago Historical Society Library, North Clark and West North Streets, Chicago, Ill. 60610.

Holdings include collections on immigration, especially in Chicago, as well as the records of the Polish American Democratic Organization, the Gads Hill Center (includes material on Polish people in Chicago), and the Chicago Commons. Also has in-

formation on Poles, Italians, and blacks. The Mary E. Mc-
Dowell Papers include information on Slavs in Chicago during
the 1930s.

1250 China Institute in America, 125 East 65th Street, New York, N.Y.
10021.

Organized in 1926 and with a current membership of 1,000,
the Institute is designed "to introduce Americans to Chinese
culture, and help Chinese to adjust to this country; to improve
community relations."

1251 Chinese Historical Society of America, 17 Adler Place, San Francisco,
Calif. 94133.

Established in 1963 and with a present membership of 350, it
maintains a library and archives and publishes the BULLETIN
OF THE CHINESE HISTORICAL SOCIETY OF AMERICA.

1252 College of the Holy Cross Library, Worcester, Mass. 01610.

Howe's collection of nineteen volumes of manuscripts concerning Irish immigrants and their descendants in Worcester, 1840-
1900.

1253 Commission on Archives and History of the United Methodist Church, Lake
Janaluska, N.C. 28745.

Gathers and preserves historical data, books, and archives relating to the origin and development of the United Methodist
church. Publishes monthly newsletter and METHODIST HIS-
TORY, a quarterly. Has regional and local chapters, a museum, and two libraries with 40,000 volumes.

1254 Czechoslovak Society of Arts and Sciences in America, 381 Park Avenue
South, New York, N.Y. 10016.

With 1,500 members, the society publishes ZPRAVY SVU ten
times a year, and PROMENY quarterly. Activities mainly
involve cultural, social, and scientific lectures, concerts and
exhibitions. Formed in 1958.

1255 Ethnic Studies Program, Pennsylvania Historical and Museum Commission,
Box 1026, Harrisburg, Pa. 17120.

Materials available for researchers include oral interviews,
newspapers, and church anniversary histories.

1256 Finnish-American Historical Archives, Suomi College, Hancock, Mich.
49930.

Collects documents on the history of the Finns in the United States and Canada. Also contains more than forty reels of microfilm of letters from Finnish immigrants to the United States sent to family and friends in Finland. Established in 1932.

1257 Finnish American Historical Society of the West, Box 3515, Portland, Oreg. 97208.

Founded in 1962 with a present membership of nearly 500, the organization publishes FINAM NEWSLETTER.

1258 Fisk, Margaret, ed. ENCYCLOPEDIA OF ASSOCIATIONS. Vol. 1: NATIONAL ORGANIZATIONS OF THE UNITED STATES. 11th ed. Detroit: Gale Research Co., 1977. 1,456 p. Index.

A detailed guide to organizations, listing title, date of founding, address, membership, purpose, and publications. The chapter on cultural organizations is particularly good for a listing of ethnic organizations.

1259 German Society of Pennsylvania, 611 Spring Garden Street, Philadelphia, Pa. 19123.

Founded in 1764 and with a present membership of more than 500, this society is the oldest German society in America. It maintains a library of over 50,000 volumes, 85 percent of which are in German.

1260 Hamer, Philip M., ed. A GUIDE TO ARCHIVES AND MANUSCRIPTS IN THE UNITED STATES. New Haven, Conn.: Yale University Press, 1965. 775 p. Index.

Although somewhat dated, this is a single volume summary of archival and manuscript repositories in the United States, arranged alphabetically by state and then by city and institution within each state, covering 1,300 depositories. Entries list briefly the major holdings, size of collections, and a descriptive notation. Compiled for the National Historical Publications Commission.

1261 Hispanic Society of America, Broadway between 155th and 156th Streets, New York, N.Y. 10032.

Founded in 1904, has 400 members and maintains a museum and reference library of over 100,000 manuscripts and 15,000 books printed before 1701. Publishes books and produces films and recordings related to these collections.

1262 Historical Foundation of the Presbyterian and Reformed Churches, Box 847, Montreat, N.C. 28757.

Currently includes 4,500 members and publishes a magazine, THE HISTORICAL FOUNDATION NEWS. Maintains an archives, library and museum. Established in 1927.

1263 Historical Society of Western Pennsylvania, 4338 Bigelow Boulevard, Pittsburgh, Pa. 15213.

Papers relating to activities of Polish Americans in the Pittsburgh region.

1264 Historical Society of York County, 250 East Market Street, York, Pa. 17403.

Materials on the social and cultural history of the Pennsylvania Germans, the Scotch-Irish, and the Quakers.

1265 Hoover Institution on War, Revolution, and Peace, Stanford University, Stanford, Calif. 94305.

Houses material relating both to the Japanese-American removal from the Pacific Coast and to studies of acculturation patterns of minority groups.

1266 Hungarian Cultural Foundation, P.O. Box 364, Stone Mountain, Ga. 30083.

Organized in 1966 and with a membership of fifty which organizes exhibits and lectures and seeks to preserve the Hungarian cultural heritage in the United States.

1267 Immigration History Research, Immigration History Research Center, University of Minnesota, 826 Berry Street, St. Paul, Minnesota, 55114.

Publishes a GUIDE TO MANUSCRIPT HOLDINGS and a periodical, SPECTRUM. The Archives contains an imprint collection of over 25,000 volumes, 1,700 periodical titles, files of 250 newspaper titles, 2,500 reels of microfilm, and nearly 2,000 linear feet of manuscripts. (The Center's holdings deal with those groups who emigrated from Eastern, Central, and Southern Europe and the Middle East to the United States and Canada.) The GUIDE lists holdings by ethnic groups, and includes collections of typical ethnic institutions and individual leaders. SPECTRUM contains reports on research at the IHRC, on grants connected with the institution, and on the Center's administration, conferences, projects, and recent acquisitions, as well as articles concerning methodology and research.

1268 Immigration History Society, Minnesota Historical Society, 690 Cedar Street, St. Paul, Minn. 55101.

The society publishes the IMMIGRATION HISTORY NEWSLETTER semiannually. It was founded "to promote the study of the history of immigration to the United States and Canada from all parts of the world...." It was established in 1965 and has a current membership of 550.

1269 Institute on Plurism and Group Identity, An American Jewish Committee Project on Group Life and Ethnic America, 4408 Eighth Street, N.E., Washington, D.C. 20017.

Renders technical assistance to neighborhood-based community organizations and develops models for improving the quality of life in ethnic, working-class areas. Publishes periodical reprints, case studies, and workbooks. Affiliated with the United States Catholic Conference.

1270 Italian Historical Society of America, 111 Columbia Heights, Brooklyn, N.Y. 11201.

Founded in 1949 and with a present membership of 700, the society publishes the quarterly ITALIAN-AMERICAN REVIEW and a newsletter. It was organized "to perpetuate Italian heritage in America and to gather historical data on Americans of Italian descent."

1271 Jewish Publication Society of America, 1528 Walnut Street, Phildelphia, Pa. 19102.

Organized in 1845, has 13,500 members, and publishes the AMERICAN JEWISH YEARBOOK and more than 800 books on Jewish history, religion, and literature.

1272 Kosciuszko Foundation, 15 East 65th Street, New York, N.Y. 10021.

Supports publication of a newsletter and scholarly books and articles. It maintains a reference library and acts as a clearinghouse for information on Polish and American cultural relations. Established in 1925 with present membership of 2,000.

1273 Leo Baeck Institute, 129 East 73rd Street, New York, N.Y. 10021.

Publishes a quarterly BULLETIN, a YEARBOOK, monographs, reprints, lectures, etc. It is "a research center for the political, cultural, social and economic history of Jews in German-speaking countries from the Enlightenment to the rise of National Socialism." Maintains an extensive archives and library.

1274 Luso-American Education Foundation, P.O. Box 1768, Oakland, Calif. 94604.

Publishes a quarterly, FOUNDATION NEWS. It attempts "to foster, sponsor and perpetuate the ethnic and national culture brought to America by emigrants from Portugal."

1275 Luther College Library, Decorah, Iowa. 52101.

Contains 27,000 manuscripts relating chiefly to Norwegian Americans and the Norwegian Lutheran church, 1844-1955.

1276 McDonald, Donna, ed. DIRECTORY: HISTORICAL SOCIETIES AND AGENCIES IN THE UNITED STATES AND CANADA, 1973-74. Nashville: American Association for State and Local History, 1972. 378 p. Index.

Regularly published alphabetical list of historical societies by state and by city. Provides information about date of founding, size of membership, and major program areas of each agency, including several dealing with immigration and ethnicity.

1277 Manuscripts Division, Library of Congress, 1st Street, between East Capitol Street and Independence Avenue, S.E., Washington, D.C. 20540.

Manuscript collections on all aspects of immigration, including the papers of Arnold L. Gesell relating to German immigration, 1870-1910; Thomas Capek on Czechs and Bohemians in Great Britain and the United States; and Edward O. Tabor on activities of Czechoslovak Americans.

1278 Maryland Historical Society, 201 West Monument, Baltimore, Md. 21201.

Large collection of papers of the Hibernian Society, an organization founded to provide relief for Irish emigrants to Baltimore, 1816-1945.

1279 Michigan Historical Collections, University of Michigan, Ann Arbor, Mich. 48104.

Materials relating to immigrant settlements in Michigan and Dutch migration to America, some of which were collected by Henry Stephen Lucas for his research on NETHERLANDERS IN AMERICA.

1280 Midwest Women's Historical Collection, University of Illinois at Chicago Circle, Chicago, Ill. 60637.

Includes records of the Immigrants' Protective League, 1904-67. The league was an organization concerned with legal, social, and economic problems of immigrants in Chicago.

1281 Mormon History Association, 1800 Hempstead Road, Salt Lake City, Utah 84112.

Founded in 1965 and has a membership of 630. Statement of purpose: "To foster scholarly research and publication in the field of Mormon history and to promote fellowship and communication among scholars interested in Mormon history."

1282 Museum of the Netherlands Pioneer and Historical Foundation, Holland, Mich. 49423.

Records concerned with the colonization and development of western Michigan by Dutch immigrants and their descendants.

1283 National Archives, 1100 L Street, N.W., Washington, D.C. 20005.

Holdings: Passenger lists of vessels entering U.S. ports from 1840, land entry papers from 1796, extensive census data, and records of the various federal agencies dealing with immigration and naturalization.

1284 National Project on Ethnic America, American Jewish Committee, Institute of Human Relations, 165 East 56th Street, New York, N.Y. 10022.

Concerned with the problems of lower middle class white ethnics, especially youth and women, and their relationships with nonwhite minorities. Publishes a Middle American Pamphlet Series, periodical reprints, and a bibliography on ethnicity.

1285 Norwegian-American Historical Association, St. Olaf College, Northfield, Minn. 55057.

Founded in 1925 with a present membership in excess of 1,000, its major programs include a library, archives, newsletter, and other publications. Manuscript holdings relate chiefly to Norwegian settlement in Minnesota, immigration to the United States, and information on the Norwegian Lutheran church in America.

1286 Polish American Historical Association, Polish Museum of America, 984 North Milwaukee Avenue, Chicago, Ill. 60622.

Publishes a quarterly bulletin and a semiannual journal, POLISH AMERICAN STUDIES. Its purpose is "to promote interest in and studies of Polish American history and its Polish roots, furthering scholarly research and publications in the field."

1287 Presbyterian Historical Society, 425 Lombard Street, Philadelphia, Pa. 19147.

Records of the Presbyterian church in the United States, including information on missionary work among the Chinese in California.

1288 Radcliffe College Library, Women's Archives, Cambridge, Mass. 02138.

Records of immigrant women, their protection, and life in America.

1289 Rochester Theological Institute Library, 177 Thurston Road, Rochester, N.Y. 14619.

Records relating chiefly to German Baptist clergymen in the United States and their seminary, 1835 to present.

1290 Slavic American Studies, City College of New York, New York, N.Y. 10031.

Offers courses in Slavic-American heritage and independent study opportunities in the history, cultural contributions, and current problems of Slavic Americans.

1291 Social Welfare History Archives, University of Minnesota Library, Minneapolis, Minn. 55455.

A two-volume guide to their holdings has been published. Collections include the records of welfare organizations, immigration and social uplift agencies, private papers of persons active in welfare reform, and the archives of various national organizations.

1292 Society for Italian Historical Studies, University of Connecticut, Storrs, Conn. 06268.

Statement of purpose: "To promote professional study, criticism, and research in Italian history and culture and to further the common interests of those interested in these purposes."

1293 Society for the History of the Germans in Maryland, 231 St. Paul Place, Baltimore, Md. 21202.

Established in 1886, now with 110 members, publishes THE REPORT: A JOURNAL OF GERMAN-AMERICAN HISTORY.

1294 State Historical Society of Wisconsin, 816 State Street, Madison, Wis. 53706.

Various collections of immigrant letters and diaries concerning immigration to Wisconsin and the upper Midwest, generally in the nineteenth century. Major immigrant groups included Germans and Scandinavians. Microfilm edition of the "Finnish-American Collection" consists of nearly 7,000 letters from the first half of the twentieth century, written by Finnish-American emigrants to their relatives in the Satakunta region of Finland.

1295 Swedish Colonial Society, 1300 Locust Street, Philadelphia, Pa. 19107.

Founded in 1909, has more than 500 members and supports a small publication program.

1296 Swedish Pioneer Historical Society, 5125 North Spaulding Avenue, Chicago, Ill. 60625.

Publishes the SWEDISH PIONEER HISTORICAL QUARTERLY as well as books and pamphlets. Its purpose is "to record the achievements of the Swedish pioneers in America through the publication of historical studies, immigrant history, biographical sketches, translations, etc." It maintains a library of more than 2,000 volumes on Swedes in America from 1850 to the present.

1297 Swiss American Historical Society, 216 East 39th Street, Norfolk, Va. 23504.

This society was founded in 1927 and now has 250 members. It publishes a newsletter and books.

1298 Truman, Harry S. Presidential Library, Independence, Mo. 64055.

Includes the correspondence, transcripts of hearings, and miscellaneous materials of the President's Commission on Immigration and Naturalization, 1952-53.

1299 University of Illinois, Chicago Circle Campus Library, 601 South Morgan Street, Chicago, Ill. 60680.

Includes manuscript collections on anti-Semitism, naturalization of immigrants, Jewish refugees, the German Aid Society of Chicago, and the Immigrants' Protective League.

1300 University of Texas Library, Austin, Tex. 78712.

Documents immigration to Texas, especially the records of the Berlin Association for Centralization of Emigration and Colonization operations in Texas and Germany, the John Shiller Papers on Czech settlement in America, and collections on English and French immigration to Texas.

1301 Wynar, Lubomyr R., ed. THE ENCYCLOPEDIA DIRECTORY OF ETHNIC ORGANIZATIONS IN THE UNITED STATES. Littleton, Colo.: Libraries Unlimited, 1975. 414 p.

Contains addresses, staff size, date of founding, number of branches, membership, dues, special requirements for affiliation, and functions of approximately 1,500 ethnic organizations, arranged by nationality.

1302 Yale University Library, New Haven, Conn. 06520.

Records of the American Immigration Conference Board, an anti-Communist organization concerned with limiting immigration in the 1920s and 1930s. Also has manuscripts relating to immigration.

1303 Yivo Institute for Jewish Research (YIVO), 1048 Fifth Avenue, New York, N.Y. 10028.

Publishes scholarly books and periodicals. "Engages in research in the social sciences and humanities as they relate to the Jewish field; collects and preserves documentary and archival material pertaining to Jewish life; trains younger scholars through the Max Weinreich Center for Advanced Jewish Studies; disseminates information to universities, organizations, and the public." Maintains 300,000 volume library, and archives with over two million items.

CENSUS REPORTS

Each decennial census since 1850 has contained valuable data on immigration. Because the information has varied over time, the census reports are arranged below in chronological order. Each annotation notes the subjects contained therein.

1304 U.S. Bureau of the Census. SEVENTH CENSUS OF THE UNITED STATES, 1850.

Contains minimal information on country of origin for immigrants to each state. THE COMPILATION volume (pp. 120-22) lists foreign born by country of origin for states and counties and the number of immigrants entering the United States annually. This is the first census to concern itself with the country of origin of immigrants.

1305 U.S. Bureau of the Census. EIGHTH CENSUS OF THE UNITED STATES, 1860.

Includes information for states and principal cities on the age, occupations, pecuniary means, birthplace, and destination of immigrants as well as their country of origin. Similar information is found in somewhat more detail in the section for each state.

1306 U.S. Bureau of the Census. NINTH CENSUS OF THE UNITED STATES, 1870.

Contains data on foreign born by country of origin for each state, its counties and the fifty largest cities in the United States. Also quantitative data on the number of foreign born and people of foreign parentage for each state. Has special information on immigrants from Great Britain, Ireland, Sweden, Norway, China, and the various German provinces.

1307 U.S. Bureau of the Census. TENTH CENSUS OF THE UNITED STATES, 1880.

Includes section on the distribution of the foreign born by topography, elevation above sea level, temperature, and rainfall levels. Details information on the distribution of the foreign born by country or origin for state and territory, county, and the fifty principal cities, and of those of foreign parentage for each state and territory. Also has section on the occupations of the foreign born in each of the fifty largest cities.

1308 U.S. Bureau of the Cenus. ELEVENTH CENSUS OF THE UNITED STATES, 1890.

Contains information on the country of origin of the foreign born by states, territories, counties, and cities over 25,000 people. Also includes information on people of foreign-born parents by the same jurisdictions and data on Chinese and Japanese immigrants by counties.

1309 U.S. Bureau of the Census. TWELFTH CENSUS OF THE UNITED STATES, 1900.

Includes data on foreign-born people by country of origin for states, territories, counties, and cities over 25,000; and on the children of foreign-born parents by states, territories, and cities over 25,000. Also contains special sections on Chinese and Japanese by counties and on citizenship and number of years in the United States.

1310 U.S. Bureau of the Census. THIRTEENTH CENSUS OF THE UNITED STATES, 1910.

Contains information on the foreign born, the children of foreign-born parents, and the children of mixed parentage by country of origin for states, counties, and principal cities by wards.

1311 U.S. Bureau of the Census. FOURTEENTH CENSUS OF THE UNITED STATES, 1920.

The second volume contains data on the country of origin for both immigrants and second generation Americans by country of origin, the year of immigration, the mother tongue of foreign white stock, and on illiteracy and school attendance in cities over 100,000. The third volume has information on foreign-born and second generation Americans by states, counties, and cities over 50,000.

1312 U.S. Bureau of the Census. FIFTEENTH CENSUS OF THE UNITED

STATES, 1930.

The second volume details country of origin, mother tongue, citizenship, year of immigration, age, distribution, marital condition, illiteracy, and inability to speak English for both foreign born and second generation by states and principal cities. The third volume provides the distribution of the foreign stock population by state, county, township, and wards of cities over 50,000 people.

1313 U.S. Bureau of the Census. SIXTEENTH CENSUS OF THE UNITED STATES, 1940.

Includes data on the foreign-born population of states, counties, and cities over 10,000 people. Has a special section on Japanese, Chinese, and Amerindians.

1314 U.S. Bureau of the Census. SEVENTEENTH CENSUS OF THE UNITED STATES, 1950.

Part 1 is a summary of data for the entire United States and the remaining parts are summaries for each state, territory, and the District of Columbia. Each part contains tables on the percentage of foreign born by country of origin, by state or territory.

1315 U.S. Bureau of the Census. EIGHTEENTH DECENNIAL CENSUS OF THE UNITED STATES, 1960.

Contains breakdown, by country of origins, for foreign born and children of foreign or mixed parentage for states and for Standard Metropolitan Statistical Areas of 250,000 population or more.

1316 U.S. Bureau of the Census. NINETEENTH DECENNIAL CENSUS OF THE UNITED STATES, 1970.

Contains information on foreign born and children of foreign or mixed parentage for each state and for Standard Metropolitan Statistical Areas over 100,000 population. Includes data on country of origin, mother tongue, citizenship states, and year of immigration.

1317 U.S. Bureau of the Census. A CENTURY OF POPULATION GROWTH FROM THE FIRST CENSUS OF THE UNITED STATES TO THE TWELFTH, 1890-1900. 1909. 303 p.

Partially deals with changing composition of the foreign-born population from colonial times to the onset of the twentieth century. Contains several tables.

1318 U.S. Bureau of the Census. HISTORICAL STATISTICS OF THE UNITED
STATES, COLONIAL TIMES TO 1957.

> Section C (pp. 48-66) has statistics on immigrants by country
> of origin, occupation, age, and sex; aliens admitted, deported,
> or excluded; naturalization and citizenship status; nativity
> of foreign parents of native white population; and foreign-born
> population by national origin from 1830 to 1957.

PUBLICATIONS OF THE IMMIGRATION AND NATURALIZATION SERVICE

The Immigration and Naturalization Service (INS) was created as the Bureau of
Immigration in the Department of the Treasury in 1892. From 1820 to 1870 annual reports on immigration were issued by the Department of State and from
1870 to 1892 by the Department of the Treasury as part of its annual REPORT
ON COMMERCE AND NAVIGATION. From 1903 to 1913 the INS was part
of the Department of Commerce and Labor and from 1913 to 1940 was an agency of the Department of Labor. Since 1940 the Service has been under the
Department of Justice.

1319 U.S. Immigration and Naturalization Service. ADMINISTRATIVE DECI-
SIONS UNDER THE IMMIGRATION AND NATURALIZATION LAWS OF
THE UNITED STATES. 13 vols. 1940-1971.

> Compilation of precedent-making decisions on immigration made
> by the attorney general, the commissioner of immigration and
> naturalization, the Board of Immigration Appeals, and other
> designated officials of the service.

1320 U.S. Immigration and Naturalization Service. ANNUAL INDICATOR OF
IMMIGRATION INTO THE UNITED STATES OF ALIENS IN PROFESSION-
AL AND RELATED OCCUPATIONS. 1967- .

> Largely statistical summary reflecting the preponderance of
> professional persons in recent immigration.

1321 U.S. Immigration and Naturalization Service. ANNUAL REPORT OF THE
COMMISSIONER GENERAL. 1892- .

> Submitted each year by the commissioner general to his cabi-
> net level superior. Primarily a statistical summary of immigra-
> tion and naturalization broken down by various indices, along
> with a description of the internal management of the service
> and recommendations for changes in the immigration and natu-
> ralization laws. From 1903 to 1913 separate reports were is-
> sued by the Naturalization and Information Divisions of INS.

1322 U.S. Immigration and Naturalization Service. CITIZENSHIP DAY AND
CONSTITUTION WEEK BULLETIN. 1940- .

Illustrates the service's efforts to celebrate the importance of naturalization by setting aside special citizenship days with appropriate ceremonies.

1323 U.S. Immigration and Naturalization Service. ESSENTIAL PROCEDURE AND REQUIREMENTS FOR NATURALIZATION UNDER GENERAL LAW. 1933- .

Issued annually. Contains information on special requirements for U.S. entry and/or naturalization pertaining to widows and orphans of citizens, veterans, Filipinos, expatriates, and others.

1324 U.S. Immigration and Naturalization Service. FEDERAL TEXTBOOKS ON CITIZENSHIP TRAINING. 1935- .

Series of texts issued since 1935 on American history, government, language, community, and citizenship for use in naturalization classes. Most also include an instructor's manual and a home study course. Valuable primarily as an illustration of the tremendous emphasis that the service places upon assimilation, acculturation, and naturalization.

1325 U.S. Immigration and Naturalization Service. GENERAL ORDERS AND PROCEDURES. 1913- .

Circulated irregularly to all INS personnel to inform them of procedures, administrative codes, deportation regulations, analysis of immigration figures, documents required of immigrants, new interpretations of laws, changes of entry ports, legal requirements for deportation, and similar matters.

1326 U.S. Immigration and Naturalization Service. IMMIGRATION BULLETIN. Washington, D.C.: Government Publishing Office, January 1906–August 1919.

Largely statistical monthly summaries of immigration and emigration figures and passenger movement in and out of the United States. Title varies.

1327 U.S. Immigration and Naturalization Service. LAWS APPLICABLE TO IMMIGRATION AND NATURALIZATION: EMBODYING STATISTICS OF A PERMANENT CHARACTER, AND TREATIES, PROCLAMATIONS, EXECUTIVE ORDERS, AND REORGANIZATION PLANS AFFECTING THE IMMIGRATION AND NATURALIZATION SERVICE. 8 vols. Washington, D.C.: Government Printing Office, 1952.

Supplements were issued in 1953, 1954, 1959, and 1962. Annual brief summaries of the practical applications of the laws are issued under the title UNITED STATES IMMIGRATION LAWS: GENERAL INFORMATION.

1328 U.S. Immigration and Naturalization Service. LECTURE COURSE OF STUDY FOR IMMIGRATION AND NATURALIZATION PERSONNEL, 1935.

Two series of thirty-six lectures issued between February 12, 1934, and February 18, 1935. Topics include morale boosting pleas, but are mostly administrative, legal, fiscal, procedural, and clerical.

1329 U.S. Immigration and Naturalization Service. MONTHLY REVIEW. Washington, D.C.: Government Printing Office, July 1940-July 1952.

Primarily a professional journal for members of the INS. Contains summaries of changes in legislation, important administrative and judicial decisions, a survey of the literature being published on immigration and naturalization, and articles on related subjects. Since August 1952 it has been published quarterly as the IMMIGRATION AND NATURALIZATION REPORTER.

1330 U.S. Immigration and Naturalization Service. REGULATIONS, RULES, AND INSTRUCTIONS. 1933- .

Instructions to personnel on procedures and information of value in their work.

CONGRESSIONAL HEARINGS

From 1892 to 1946 immigration laws were formulated by the House Committee on Immigration and Naturalization and from 1906 to 1946 by the Senate Immigration Committee. After 1946 the committees' functions were assumed by the Judiciary Committees of the respective houses. The following is a chronological list of the most significant hearings held on immigration policy from the 1890s to the present. No annotations are presented as the titles adequately convey the content.

U.S. Congress. House Committee on Immigration and Naturalization

1331 HEARINGS ON IMMIGRATION AND NATURALIZATION BILL, January 20-May 21, 1910. 61st Cong., 2d Sess. 522 p.

1332 HEARINGS RELATIVE TO DILLINGHAM BILL TO REGULATE THE IMMIGRATION OF ALIENS TO AND RESIDENCE OF ALIENS IN THE UNITED STATES, May 4-8, 1912. 62d Cong., 2d Sess. 224 p.

1333 HEARINGS ON PERCENTAGE PLAN FOR RESTRICTION OF IMMIGRATION, June 12-20, September 25, 1919. 66th Cong., 1st Sess. 296 p.

1334 BIOLOGICAL ASPECTS OF IMMIGRATION: TESTIMONY OF HARRY H. LAUGHLIN, April 16-17, 1920. 66th Cong., 2d Sess. 26 p.

1335 HEARINGS ON COMMUNIST AND ANARCHIST DEPORTATION CASES, April 21-24, 1920. 66th Cong., 2d Sess. 158 p.

1336 HEARINGS ON JAPANESE IMMIGRATION, at San Francisco and Sacramento, California (July 12-14, 1920); at Stockton, Angel Island, and San Francisco, California, (July 15-20, 1920); at Fresno, Livingston, Turlock, Auburn, and Los Angeles, California, (July 19-21, 1920); at Seattle and Tacoma, Washington, (July 26-29, August 2-3, 1920). 66th Cong., 2d Sess. 1,490 p.

1337 HEARINGS ON SPECIAL PROBLEMS RELATING TO THE EMERGENCY IMMIGRATION ACT OF 1921-1923. 67th Cong., 1st to 4th Sess. 480 p.

1338 HEARINGS ON OPERATION OF THE THREE PERCENTUM IMMIGRATION ACT, December 13, 1921-February 13, 1922. 67th Cong., 2d Sess. 504 p.

1339 HEARINGS ON IMMIGRATION AND LABOR, January 3-5, 22, 24, 1923. 67th Cong., 4th Sess. 111 p.

1340 HEARINGS ON THE RESTRICTION OF IMMIGRATION, December 26, 1923-February 12, 1924. 68th Cong., 1st Sess. 1,175 p.

1341 EUROPE AS AN IMMIGRANT-EXPORTING CONTINENT AND UNITED STATES AS AN IMMIGRANT RECEIVING NATION; TESTIMONY OF HARRY H. LAUGHLIN, March 8, 1924. 68th Cong., 1st Sess. Pp. 1231-1437.

1342 HEARINGS ON IMMIGRATION FROM LATIN AMERICA, THE WEST INDIES, AND CANADA, March 3, 1925. 68th Cong., 2d Sess. Pp. 303-345.

1343 HEARINGS ON IMMIGRATION FROM COUNTRIES OF WESTERN HEMISPHERE, February 21-April 5, 1928. 70th Cong., 1st Sess. 801 p.

1344 HEARINGS ON WESTERN HEMISPHERE IMMIGRATION, January 16-February 4, 1930. 71st Cong., 2d Sess. 457 p.

1345 HEARINGS ON EXCLUSION OF IMMIGRATION FROM THE PHILIPPINE ISLANDS, April 10-May 8, 1930. 71st Cong., 2d Sess. 300 p.

1346 HEARINGS TO RECONCILE NATURALIZATION PROCEDURE WITH THE BILL OF RIGHTS. January 26-27, 1932. 72d Cong., 1st Sess. 250 p.

1347 HEARINGS ON AMENDMENTS TO THE IMMIGRATION LAWS AS RECOMMENDED BY THE DEPARTMENT OF LABOR AND BY THE SECRETARY'S ELLIS ISLAND COMMITTEE, May 8-10, 1934. 73d Cong., 2d Sess. 219 p.

1348 HEARINGS ON DEPORTATION OF. ALIENS, April 9-11, 1935. 74th Cong., 1st Sess. 202 p.

1349 HEARINGS TO REVISE AND CODIFY THE NATIONALITY LAWS OF THE UNITED STATES INTO A COMPREHENSIVE NATIONALITY CODE, January 17-June 5, 1940. 76th Cong., 1st Sess. 710 p.

1350 HEARINGS TO PROVIDE A TEMPORARY HAVEN FROM THE DANGERS OF EFFECTS OF WAR FOR EUROPEAN CHILDREN UNDER THE AGE OF SIXTEEN, August 8-9, 1940. 76th Cong., 1st Sess. 303 p.

1351 HEARINGS ON REPEAL OF CHINESE EXCLUSION ACTS: BILLS TO REPEAL CHINESE EXCLUSION ACTS, TO PUT CHINESE ON A QUOTA BASIS AND TO PERMIT THEIR NATURALIZATION, May 19-June 3, 1943. 78th Cong., 1st Sess. 283 p.

1352 HEARINGS ON EXPATRIATION OF CERTAIN NATIONALS OF THE UNITED STATES, January 20-February 2, 1944. 78th Cong., 2d Sess. 64 p.

1353 HEARINGS TO GRANT A QUOTA TO EASTERN HEMISPHERE INDIANS AND TO MAKE THEM RACIALLY ELIGIBLE FOR NATURALIZATION, March 8-14, 1945. 79th Cong., 1st Sess. 154 p.

1354 HEARINGS ON STUDY OF IMMIGRATION AND NATURALIZATION LAWS AND PROBLEMS, April 24, May 2, 1945. 79th Cong., 1st Sess. 133 p.

1355 HEARINGS ON INVESTIGATION OF PROBLEMS PRESENTED BY REFUGEES AT FORT ONTARIO REFUGEE SHELTER, June 25-26, 1945. 79th Cong., 1st Sess. 183 p.

1356 HEARINGS ON STUDY OF PROBLEMS RELATING TO IMMIGRATION AND DEPORTATION AND OTHER MATTERS, August 6-December 21, 1945. 79th Cong., 1st Sess. 468 p.

U.S. Congress. House Committee on the Judiciary

1357 HEARINGS BEFORE SUBCOMMITTEE ON IMMIGRATION AND NATURAL-IZATION: PERMITTING ADMISSION OF 400,000 DISPLACED PERSONS INTO THE UNITED STATES, June 4–July 18, 1947. 80th Cong., 1st Sess. 693 p.

1358 HEARINGS BEFORE THE SUBCOMMITTEE ON IMMIGRATION AND NAT-URALIZATION: PROVIDING FOR EQUALITY UNDER IMMIGRATION AND NATURALIZATION LAWS, April 19–21, 1948. 80th Cong., 2d Sess. 210 p.

1359 HEARINGS ON THE DISPLACED PERSONS ACT OF 1948, March 3–9, 1949. 81st Cong., 1st Sess. 239 p.

1360 HEARINGS ON THE ADMISSION OF 300,000 IMMIGRANTS, May 22–June 3, 1952. 82d Cong., 2d Sess. 232 p.

1361 HEARINGS ON THE EMERGENCY IMMIGRATION PROGRAM, May 21–July 9, 1953. 83d Cong., 1st Sess. 246 p.

1362 IMMIGRATION AND NATURALIZATION ACT: WITH AMENDMENTS AND NOTES ON RELATED LAWS AND SUMMARIES OF PERTINENT JUDICIAL DECISIONS, 1958, 1960, 1961, 1964, 1965, 1969.

1363 HEARINGS ON IMMIGRATION, July 2–August 3, 1964, August 5–September 17, 1964, March 3–June 1, 1965. 88th Cong., 2d Sess. and 89th Cong., 1st Sess. 1,019 p.

1364 HEARINGS ON REVIEW OF THE OPERATION OF IMMIGRATION AND NATURALIZATION ACT AS AMENDED BY ACT OF OCTOBER 3, 1965, April 3–June 13, 1968. 90th Cong., 2d Sess. 153 p.

U.S. Congress. Senate Committee on Immigration

1365 HEARINGS TO CONTINUE IN FORCE LAWS PROHIBITING COMING OF CHINESE INTO THE UNITED STATES AND TO REGULATE, WITHIN THE UNITED STATES, ITS TERRITORIES, AND ALL POSSESSIONS AND ALL TERRITORY UNDER ITS JURISDICTION, AND DISTRICT OF CO-LUMBIA, ALL CHINESE PERSONS AND PERSONS OF CHINESE DE-SCENT, January 21–27, 1902. 57th Cong., 1st Sess. 491 p.

1366 HEARINGS ON THE GERMAN-AMERICAN ALLIANCE, February 23–April 13, 1918. 65th Cong., 2d Sess. 698 p.

1367 HEARINGS ON BILL FOR PROTECTION OF CITIZENS OF UNITED STATES BY TEMPORARY SUSPENSION OF IMMIGRATION, 1921. 67th Cong., 1st Sess. 731 p.

1368 HEARINGS ON JAPANESE IMMIGRATION LEGISLATION, March 11-15, 1924. 68th Cong., 1st Sess. 170 p.

1369 HEARINGS TO LIMIT IMMIGRATION OF ALIENS INTO THE UNITED STATES AND TO PROVIDE SYSTEM OF SELECTION IN CONNECTION THEREWITH, February 13-April 8, 1924. 68th Cong., 1st Sess. 314 p.

1370 HEARINGS ON RESTRICTION OF WESTERN HEMISPHERE IMMIGRATION, February 1-March 5, 1928. 70th Cong., 1st Sess. 192 p.

1371 HEARINGS ON THE NATIONAL ORIGINS PROVISION OF IMMIGRATION LAW, February 1-13, 1929. 70th Cong., 2d Sess. 177 p.

1372 HEARINGS ON SUSPENSION FOR TWO YEARS OF GENERAL IMMIGRATION INTO THE UNITED STATES, December 15-16, 18, 1930. 71st Cong., 3d Sess. 132 p.

1373 HEARINGS ON DEPORTATION OF CRIMINALS, PRESERVATION OF FAMILY UNITS, AND PERMITTING NONCRIMINAL ALIENS TO LEGALIZE THEIR STATUS, February 24-March 11, 1936. 74th Cong., 2d Sess. 231 p.

1374 HEARINGS TO PERMIT ALL PEOPLE FROM INDIA RESIDING IN THE UNITED STATES TO BE NATURALIZED, April 26, 1945. 79th Cong., 1st Sess. 41 p.

U.S. Congress. Senate Committee on the Judiciary

1375 HEARINGS BEFORE THE SUBCOMMITTEE ON AMENDMENTS TO THE DISPLACED PERSONS ACT, March 25, 1949-March 16, 1950. 81st Cong., 1st and 2d Sess. 1,248 p.

1376 HEARINGS BEFORE THE SUBCOMMITTEE ON IMMIGRATION AND NATURALIZATION: COMMUNIST ACTIVITIES AMONG ALIENS AND NATIONAL GROUPS, May 10-August 12, 1949. 81st Cong., 1st Sess. 895 p.

1377 HEARINGS ON REVISION OF IMMIGRATION, NATURALIZATION AND NATIONALITY LAWS, March 6-April 9, 1951. 82d Cong., 1st Sess. 787 p.

1378 HEARINGS ON INVESTIGATION OF ADMINISTRATION OF REFUGEE
RELIEF ACT, April 13-May 27, 1955. 84th Cong., 1st Sess. 376 p.

1379 HEARINGS ON AMENDMENTS TO REFUGEE RELIEF ACT OF 1953, June
8-21, 1955. 84th Cong., 1st Sess. 290 p.

1380 HEARINGS ON AMENDMENTS TO RELIEF ACT OF 1953, May 3, 1956.
84th Cong., 2d Sess. 105 p.

1381 HEARINGS BEFORE THE JOINT COMMITTEES ON THE JUDICIARY: RE-
VIEW OF IMMIGRATION, February 10-March 11, March 8-August 3,
1965. 89th Cong., 1st Sess. 961 p.

MISCELLANEOUS PUBLISHED DOCUMENTS, MANUSCRIPTS, AND GUIDES

1382 Abbott, Edith. HISTORICAL ASPECTS OF IMMIGRATION PROBLEMS:
SELECT DOCUMENTS. Chicago: University of Chicago Press, 1926.
881 p. Bibliography.

Massive collection of documents relating to the causes of emigration, the economic effects of immigration on the United
States, pauperism, crime, assimilation, and the debate over
the value of immigration.

1383 _____. IMMIGRATION: SELECT DOCUMENTS AND CASE RECORDS.
Chicago: University of Chicago Press, 1924. 802 p. Subject index.

Source book of published documents and case records dealing
with the immigrant journey, admission, exclusion and expul-
sion of immigrants, and the problems of adjustment faced by
a variety of national groups.

1384 Auerbach, Frank L. IMMIGRATION LAWS OF THE UNITED STATES.
2d ed. Indianapolis: Bobbs-Merrill Co., 1961. 584 p. Appendices,
footnotes, bibliography, index.

A reference book "integrating statutes, regulations, administrative practices, and leading court and administrative decisions." Includes a comprehensive index and a bibliography.

1385 _____. 1964 SUPPLEMENT TO THE SECOND EDITION OF IMMIGRA-
TION LAWS OF THE UNITED STATES. Indianapolis: Bobbs-Merrill Co.,
1964. 212 p. Appendices, footnotes, bibliography, index.

An update which "contains legislative, regulatory, and other
significant developments in the immigration field through February 18, 1964, Supreme Court decisions through 375 United

States 217, and administrative decisions through Interim Decision 1304." It also contains a cumulative index.

1386 California. Commission of Immigration and Housing. ANNUAL REPORT, 1913-1926. 7 vols. Sacramento. Illustrations, tables, appendix.

Contains information on immigrant education, housing, labor camps, complaints, geographic distribution, and unemployment, as well as a summary of legislation concerning immigrants.

1387 Chamber of Commerce of the United States of America, Immigration Committee. BULLETIN 1-26 (April 1, 1916-August 20, 1918). Washington, D.C.

Surveys conditions in 244 industrial cities in fourteen states. Focuses on language proficiency, citizenship status, employment, housing, sanitation, children, savings, investments, recreation facilities, and the general community life of immigrant workers.

1388 Ellis Island Committee. REPORT OF THE ELLIS ISLAND COMMITTEE. 1934. Reprint. New York: Jerome S. Ozer, 1971. 149 p. Maps.

Represents the findings and recommendations of a nonpartisan group of citizens under the chairmanship of Carleton H. Palmer and submitted to Secretary of Labor Frances Perkins.

1389 Immigrants' Protective League. ANNUAL REPORTS. Chicago: 1910-1918.

Briefly summarizes and evaluates the league's yearly work in the fields of information and social services, employment direction, and adult education.

1390 Massachusetts. Bureau of Statistics. THE IMMIGRANT POPULATION OF MASSACHUSETTS. Boston: Wright and Potter Printing Co., 1913. 90 p.

Statistical analyses of the foreign-born population in 1910, the distribution of immigrants in cities and industries, and of aliens deported from Massachusetts in 1912.

1391 New Jersey. Commission on Immigration. REPORT. Trenton: 1914. 201 p.

Examines conditions, welfare, distribution, and industrial opportunities of aliens in the United States. Commission appointed by Governor Woodrow Wilson.

1392 New York. Legislature. REPORT OF THE JOINT LEGISLATIVE COMMITTEE ON THE EXPLOITATION OF IMMIGRANTS. Legislative Document, no. 76. Albany, N.Y.: 1924. 166 p. Appendices.

Details the exploitation of immigrants by transmission agents, notaries public, transportation companies, employment agencies, workmen's compensation, insurance companies, and physicians.

1393 North American Civic League for Immigrants. ANNUAL REPORTS. Boston: 1908-1919.

Yearly reports of league activities, especially in the areas of education, protection of immigrants, and lobbying.

1394 Pennsylvania. Bureau of Statistics and Information. FIRST ANNUAL REPORT OF THE COMMISSIONER OF LABOR AND INDUSTRY, 1913. Harrisburg. Pp. 221-82.

Contains section on immigration, focusing on history, legislation, industry, education, living conditions, unemployment, the labor market, and the activities of private employment agencies.

1395 Rhode Island. Bureau of Industrial Statistics. "Some Nativity and Race Factors in Rhode Island." In TWENTY-THIRD ANNUAL REPORT OF THE BUREAU OF INDUSTRIAL STATISTICS, 1910, pp. 219-424. Appendices.

Contains data on the ethnic makeup of the state's foreign-born population, the causes of migration, comparative fecundity, illiteracy rate, criminality, occupation, and pace of assimilation.

1396 U.S. Congress. House Committee on Education and Labor. General Subcommittee on Education. HEARINGS ON H.R. 14910: THE ETHNIC HERITAGE STUDIES CENTERS BILL, February 16-May 6, 1970. 91st Cong., 2d Sess. 363 p.

Contains testimony by scores of educators and officials of ethnic organizations stressing the advantages of ethnic heritage study centers for preventing confrontations and divisiveness between ethnic groups and the need for cultural pluralism in the development of ethnic studies curriculum materials.

1397 U.S. Congress. House Committee on the Judiciary. ALIENS IN THE UNITED STATES. 89th Cong., 1st Sess. 1965. 1,014 p.

Recommends changes in the legal status of aliens and in the requirements for registration and reporting.

1398 _____. IMMIGRATION AND NATURALIZATION ACT: WITH AMENDMENTS AND NOTES ON RELATED LAWS AND SUMMARIES OF PERTINENT JUDICIAL DECISIONS. 85th Cong., 2d Sess. 1958.

1399 U.S. Congress. House Committee on the Judiciary. Subcommittee no. 1. STUDY OF POPULATION AND IMMIGRATION PROBLEMS. 88th Cong., 1st Sess. 1962. Nos. 1-17.

Includes reports on the population of western Europe; immigra-

tion to the United States, 1853-1926; numbers of visas issued
and denied; judicial decisions; impact on the labor market; and
deportation and repatriation of security risks. Each report issued separately; number of pages varies.

1400 U.S. Congress. Joint Special Committee to Investigate Chinese Immigration. REPORT. 44th Cong., 2d Sess. 1877. 1,281 p.

Proceedings of committee hearings held in San Francisco in
October and November 1876. Contains testimony on various
phases of the question of Chinese immigration by more than
100 witnesses.

1401 U.S. Congress. Senate Committee on Immigration. SENATE REPORT
1333. 52d Cong., 2d Sess. 1893. 279 p.

Contains transcript of the committee hearing and supporting
documents relating to the proposal of William E. Chandler to
suspend immigration for one year in order to revise laws re-
gulating it.

1402 U.S. Congress. Senate Committee on the Judiciary. THE IMMIGRATION
AND NATURALIZATION SYSTEMS OF THE UNITED STATES. 81st Cong.,
2d Sess. 1950. 925 p.

Studies the background of the immigration and naturalization
systems as they existed in 1950, the immigrant population,
excluded classes, and other pertinent data. Used as a justification for the McCarran-Walter Act of 1952.

1403 U.S. Department of Labor. IMMIGRANTS AND THE AMERICAN LABOR
MARKET. 1974. 58 p. Appendix.

Discusses the demographic and occupational characteristics of
present-day immigrants and their adjustment to the labor market and makes recommendations for changes in immigration
policy.

1404 U.S. Department of State. ADMISSION OF ALIENS INTO THE UNITED
STATES. 1936. 174 p.

Concerned with the provisions of the 1924 immigration restriction act and its administration. Also describes in detail the
operation of that and subsequent legislation.

1405 _____. ADMISSION OF CHINESE INTO THE UNITED STATES.
1941. 35 p.

Summarizes all the provisions of the immigration laws as they
applied to the Chinese just prior to the easing of restrictions
during World War II.

1406 _____. THE IMMIGRATION WORK OF THE DEPARTMENT OF STATE AND ITS CONSULAR OFFICES. 1939. 69 p.

Describes the work of consular officers in granting or withholding visas to potential immigrants at their port of embarkation. Also includes statistical summary of their activities.

1407 U.S. Department of State. Bureau of Foreign Commerce. EMIGRATION AND IMMIGRATION: REPORTS OF THE CONSULAR OFFICERS OF THE UNITED STATES. 1956- .

Reports by U.S. consuls on emigration from major cities in Europe, immigration into British North America, Mexico, Central and South America, and the West Indies. Deals with statistics and causes of emigration. From 1856 to 1903 these reports were issued monthly by the Bureau of Foreign Commerce; between 1903 and 1912 they were issued by the Bureau of Statistics of the Commerce Department. After 1912 they were issued by the department's Foreign and Domestic Commerce Bureau. Those from 1873 to 1886 were issued as a separate volume.

1408 U.S. Immigration Commission (Dillingham Commission). REPORTS OF THE IMMIGRATION COMMISSION, 1907-11. Washington, D.C.: Government Printing Office, 1911. Vols. 1-2, Abstract of Reports; vol. 3, Statistical Review, 1820-1910; Distribution of Immigrants, 1850-1900; vol. 4, Emigration Conditions in Europe; vol. 5, Dictionary of Races or Peoples; vols. 6-25, Immigrants in Industries; vols. 26-27, Immigrants in Cities: A Study of the Populations of Selected Districts in New York, Chicago, Philadelphia, Boston, Cleveland, Buffalo, and Milwaukee; vol. 28, Occupation of First and Second Generation Immigrants and Fecundity of Immigrant Women; vols. 29-33, Children of Immigrants in the Schools; vols. 34-35, Immigrants as Charity Seekers; vol. 36, Immigration and Crime; vol. 37, Steerage Conditions, Importation and Harboring of Women for Immoral Purposes, Immigrant Homes and Aid Societies, Immigrant Banks; vol. 38, Changes in Bodily Form of Descendants of Immigrants; vol. 39, Immigration Legislation, Federal Court Decisions, Steerage Regulation 1819-1908, State Laws; vol. 40, Immigration Situation in Canada, Australia, New Zealand, Argentina and Brazil; vol. 41, Statistics and Recommendations Submitted by Societies and Organizations Interested in Immigration.

Report of the Senate Commission whose findings led to the National Origins Quota System. Characterized mainly by efforts to demonstrate the alleged inferiority of southern and eastern European immigrants as compared to those from northern and western Europe in the categories above. Valuable for its data, much of which fails to support the Commission's conclusions, and for understanding the milieu which produced immigration restriction.

1409 U.S. Laws, Statutes, etc. UNITED STATES CODE, ANNOTATED, TITLE 8, ALIENS AND NATIONALITY: COMPRISING ALL LAWS OF A GENERAL AND PERMANENT NATURE UNDER ARRANGEMENT OF OFFICIAL CODE OF THE LAWS OF THE UNITED STATES WITH ANNOTATIONS FROM FEDERAL AND STATE COURTS. St. Paul, Minn.: West Publishing Co., 1970. 507 p.

> Contains annotated collection of laws, amendments, and enactments through April 7, 1970, as well as historical notes on each subcategory of immigration and naturalization so that the reader may trace their historical evolution.

1410 _____. UNITED STATES STATUTES AT LARGE. 1789- .

> Contains, by year, statutes and resolutions related to immigration and naturalization, with a subject index for each volume. The first seventeen volumes (1789-1873) were published by Little, Brown and Co. of Boston. Since then they have been issued by the United States.

1411 U.S. Library of Congress. THE NATIONAL UNION CATALOG OF MANUSCRIPT COLLECTIONS. Washington, D.C.: Library of Congress, 1959- .

> Attempts to bring under bibliographic control manuscript collections in the United States that are generally open to scholars. Initial volumes contained their own index, but three-year cumulative indexes were included later. Entries are arranged by number, requiring use of the index for retrieval. A repository index lists collections by name of organization. Published annually.

1412 U.S. President's Commission on Immigration and Naturalization. WHOM SHALL WE WELCOME? 1953. 319 p. Appendices, index.

> Surveys the operations of the National Origins Quota Act, concludes that it "embodies policies and principles that are injurious to the nation," and recommends its abolition. Proposes the annual admission of a number of immigrants equal to 1 percent of the current U.S. population without regard to national origin, race, creed or color. Popularly known as the Perlman report.

JOURNALS

The following is a representative list of journals which deal on a regular basis with U.S. immigration, ethnicity, and related subjects. For more comprehensive listings of such publications see ULRICH'S INTERNATIONAL PERIODICAL DIRECTORY, 1975-76. (New York: R.R. Bowker Co., 1975, pp. 560-77); THE STANDARD PERIODICAL DIRECTORY, 1970 (edited by Leon Garry. New

York: Oxbridge Publishing Co., 1970, pp. 483-507); and ENCYCLOPEDIC DIRECTORY OF ETHNIC NEWSPAPERS AND PERIODICALS IN THE UNITED STATES (edited by Lubomyr Wynar. Littleton, Conn.: Libraries Unlimited, 1975).

1413 AMERASIA JOURNAL. Asian American Studies Center, University of California, Los Angeles, Calif. 90024.

1414 AMERICAN GERMAN REVIEW. National Carl Schurz Association, 339 Walnut Street, Philadelphia, Pa. 19106.

1415 AMERICAN JEWISH ARCHIVES. American Jewish Archives, 3101 Clifton Avenue, Cincinnati, Ohio 45220.

1416 AMERICAN JEWISH HISTORICAL QUARTERLY. American Jewish Historical Society, 2 Thornton Road, Waltham, Mass. 02154.

1417 AMERICAN PORTUGUESE CULTURAL SOCIETY BULLETIN. American Portuguese Historical Society, 29 Broadway, New York, N.Y. 10006.

1418 AMERICAN-SCANDINAVIAN REVIEW. American-Scandinavian Foundation, 127 East 73rd Street, New York, N.Y. 10021.

1419 ARMENIAN REVIEW. Hairenik Association, 212 Stuart Street, Boston, Mass. 02116.

1420 AZTLAN. Chicano Studies Center, University of California, Campbell Hall, Room 3122, 405 Hilgard Avenue, Los Angeles, Calif. 90024.

1421 AMERICAN-SWEDISH INSTITUTE. Bulletin of American-Swedish Institute, 2600 Park, Minneapolis, Minn. 55407.

1422 CATHOLIC HISTORICAL REVIEW. Catholic University of America Press, Catholic University of America, Washington, D.C. 20017.

1423 ENTRELINEAS. Penn Valley Community College, 3201 Southwest Trafficway, Kansas City, Mo. 64111.

1424 ETHNICITY. Center for the Study of American Pluralism, National Opinion Research Center, 6030 Ellis Avenue, Chicago, Ill. 60637.

1425 ETHNOHISTORY. American Society for Ethnohistory, Arizona State Museum, University of Arizona, Tucson, Ariz. 85721.

1426 FINAM NEWSLETTER. Finnish American Historical Society of the West, P.O. Box 3515, Portland, Oreg. 97208.

1427 GRITO. Journal of Contemporary Mexican-American Thought. Quinto Sol Publications, Box 9275, Berkeley, Calif. 94709.

1428 HAPPENINGS. American Swedish Institute, 2600 Park Avenue, Minneapolis, Minn. 55407.

1429 IMMIGRATION HISTORY NEWSLETTER. Minnesota Historical Society, 690 Cedar Avenue, St. Paul, Minn. 55101.

1430 INTERNATIONAL MIGRATION REVIEW. Center for Migration Studies, Brooklyn College, City University of New York, New York, N.Y. 11210.

1431 ITALIAN-AMERICAN REVIEW. Italian Historical Society of America, 26 Court Street, Brooklyn, N.Y. 11242.

1432 ITALIAN AMERICANA. State University of New York-Buffalo, 1300 Elmwood, Buffalo, N.Y. 14222.

1433 JEWISH QUARTERLY. Jewish Literary Publications, 68 Worcester Crescent, London NW7 4NA, England.

1434 JEWISH QUARTERLY REVIEW. Dropsie University for Hebrew and Cognate Learning, Broad and York Streets, Philadelphia, Pa. 19132.

1435 JOURNAL OF ETHNIC STUDIES. College of Ethnic Studies, Western Washington State College, Bellingham, Wash. 98225.

1436 POLISH AMERICAN STUDIES. Polish American Historical Association, Polish Museum of America, 984 Milwaukee Avenue, Chicago, Ill. 60622.

1437 RECORDER. American Irish Historical Society, 991 Fifth Avenue, New York, N.Y. 14221.

1438 SCANDINAVIAN STUDIES. Society for the Advancement of Scandinavian Studies, George Banta Co., 450 Ahnaip Street, Menasha, Wis. 54952.

1439 SLOVAKIA. Slovak League of America, 313 Ridge Avenue, Middleton, Pa. 17057.

1440 SWEDISH PIONEER. Swedish Pioneer Historical Society, 3225 Forster Avenue, Chicago, Ill. 60625.

1441 SPECTRUM. Immigration History Research Center, 826 Berry Street, St. Paul, Minn. 53144.

1442 UKRAINIAN QUARTERLY. Ukrainian Congress Committee of America, 302 West 13th Street, New York, N.Y. 10014.

1443 WESTERN STATES JEWISH HISTORICAL QUARTERLY. Southern California Jewish Historical Society, 2429 23 Street, Santa Monica, Calif. 90405.

1444 ZPRAVY SVU. Czechoslovak Society of Arts and Sciences, 381 Park Avenue South, New York, N.Y. 10010.

ADDENDUM

1445 Abramson, Harold J. ETHNIC DIVERSITY IN CATHOLIC AMERICA.
New York: John Wiley and Sons, 1973. 207 p. Appendix, bibliography, index.

Uses survey research data to contend that, contrary to the
notion of a religious melting pot, ethnically-based marriage
patterns still exist among American Catholics. Tests thesis
against a number of variables and against prevailing theories
of assimilation and acculturation.

1446 American Ethnic Research Institute (AERI), 6931 South Yosemite, Englewood, Colorado 80110.

Promotes historical, sociological, bibliographical, and other
research dealing with ethnic groups. Founded in 1975, AERI
conducts surveys of matters relating to ethnicity, sponsors conferences, and maintains a library.

1447 Bodnar, John E. "Materialism and Morality: Slavic-American Immigrants
and Education, 1890-1940." THE JOURNAL OF ETHNIC STUDIES 3
(1976): 1-20.

Argues from the Slavic experience that not all southern and
eastern European immigrants displayed a passionate desire for
an American education. Feels that cultural continuity was
often considered more important and that Slavic workers were
often highly skeptical of the American success myth.

1448 Center for the Study of Ethnic Publications, Kent State University, Room
318, Library, Kent, Ohio 44242.

Cooperates with scholarly, professional, and ethnic organizations in promoting research and maintaining bibliographical
control over non-English language ethnic publications in the
United States. Also has a special curriculum for library science students on the provision of services to ethnic organizations.

1449 Chudacoff, Howard P. MOBILE AMERICANS: RESIDENTIAL AND SOCIAL MOBILITY IN OMAHA, 1880-1920. New York: Oxford University Press, 1972. 195 p. Appendix, notes, index.

Primarily a study of social and spatial mobility in a midwestern city. One chapter deals specifically with "the ethnic dimension" and immigrants are discussed in other chapters.

1450 Douglass, William A., and Bilboa, Jon. AMERIKANUAK: BASQUES IN THE NEW WORLD. Reno: University of Nevada Press, 1975. 519 p. Appendices, notes, bibliography, index.

Focuses upon Basque migration to South America, California, and the American West from Spanish times to the present. Discusses their efforts to maintain ethnic identity through religion, politics, language, and cultural activities.

1451 Galush, William John. "Forming Polonia: A Study of Four Polish-American Communities, 1890-1940." Ph.D. dissertation, University of Minnesota, 1975. 339 p.

This study of the Polish immigrant population of four Polish Catholic parishes in Cleveland, Minneapolis, Utica, and New York Mills, reveals that the immigrants chose to preserve their ethnic identity through fraternal insurance lodges and national parishes. They developed national federations of local societies and the ethnic press grew. The second generation, however, tended to eschew such organizations.

1452 Hoglund, A. William. IMMIGRANTS AND THEIR CHILDREN: A BIBLIOGRAPHY OF DOCTORAL DISSERTATIONS, 1899-1975. Philadelphia: Balch Institute. In preparation.

Contains information on over 1,600 dissertations which deal mostly with the assimilation of immigrants and their children into American life in the nineteenth and twentieth centuries. Includes works in history, education, sociology, political science, languages, psychology, religion, geography, linguistics, and communications. Uses mostly general ethnic classifications to group the material.

1453 Karni, Michael Gary. "YHTEISHYVA--or, For the Common Good: Finnish Radicalism in the Western Great Lakes Region, 1900-1940." Ph.D. dissertation, University of Minnesota, 1975. 416 p.

Nearly 30 percent of Finnish immigrants after 1900 were radicals, either before they emigrated or shortly afterward. Identified first with the IWW and then the Communist party, the radicals waged an internal battle over the cooperative movement in 1929-30. From that time forward, Communist influence declined and radicalism moderated.

1454 Karni, Michael G[ary].; Kaups, Matti I.; and Ollila, Douglas J. THE
FINNISH EXPERIENCE IN THE WESTERN GREAT LAKES REGION: NEW
PERSPECTIVES. Introduction by Clarke A. Chambers and John I.
Kolehmainen. Vammala, Finland: Institute for Migration, 1975. 232 p.

Compilation of a series of papers read at a conference held at
the University of Minnesota–Duluth, by American and Finnish
scholars, on the reasons for the exodus, patterns of settlement
and institutional growth, and value conflict.

1455 Lopez, Lillian. PUERTO RICANS: A GUIDE TO INFORMATION
SOURCES. Detroit: Gale Research Co. In preparation.

1456 Renkiewicz, Frank. THE POLES IN AMERICA 1608–1972: A CHRONOL-
OGY AND FACT BOOK. Dobbs Ferry, N.Y.: Oceana Publications,
1973. 128 p. Appendices, bibliography, Index.

Includes a chronology of Polish Americans since the founding
of Jamestown, twenty-five documents, and a compilation of
fraternal societies, publications, and cultural institutions.

1457 Runblom, Harold, and Norman, Hans. FROM SWEDEN TO AMERICA:
A HISTORY OF THE MIGRATION. Minneapolis: University of Minnesota Press, 1976. 391 p. Bibliography, index.

Essentially the results of the Uppsala University Migration Research Project dealing with the causes and nature of Swedish
migration to America and continued contacts with the Old
Country.

1458 Speranza, Ginol. RACE OR NATION: A CONFLICT OF DIVIDED
LOYALTIES. New York: Arno Press, 1975. 278 p. Index.

Pro-restrictionist account by a prominent Italian immigrant.
Views immigrants from southern and eastern Europe as the
victims of "mass-alienage."

1459 Swe, Thein. ASIANS: A GUIDE TO INFORMATION SOURCES.
Detroit: Gale Research Co. In preparation.

1460 _____ . CHINESE: A GUIDE TO INFORMATION SOURCES.
Detroit: Gale Research Co.. In preparation.

1461 Szeplaki, Joseph. THE HUNGARIANS IN AMERICA: A CHRONOLOGY
AND FACT BOOK. Dobbs Ferry, N.Y.: Oceana Publications, 1975.
152 p. Appendix, bibliography, index.

Contains a chronology of Hungarian immigration from the six-

teenth century to the present, a collection of relevant documents and a compilation of Hungarian institutions in the
United States.

1462 Thernstrom, Stephan. POVERTY AND PROGRESS: SOCIAL MOBILITY
IN A NINETEENTH CENTURY CITY. Cambridge, Mass.: Harvard
University Press, 1964. 285 p. Appendix, notes, index.

Deals with the problem of social mobility in Boston between
1860 and 1880. Finds little occupational mobility among
Irish laborers over two generations, but some increase in property ownership.

1463 _____. THE OTHER BOSTONIANS: POVERTY AND PROGRESS
IN THE AMERICAN METROPOLIS 1880-1970. Cambridge, Mass.:
Harvard University Press, 1973. 345 p. Appendix, notes, index.

Concerned primarily with discerning patterns of social and occupational mobility in Boston. Specific chapters deal with
differences in mobility between Yankees and immigrant stock
people, among Protestants, Catholics, and Jews, and among
blacks and whites.

1464 Thistlewaite, Frank. THE ANGLO-AMERICAN CONNECTION IN THE
EARLY NINETEENTH CENTURY. Philadelphia: University of Pennsylvania Press, 1959. 222 p. Notes, index.

Discusses the continuing ties, economic, political, and intellectual, that persisted between British immigrants and their
homeland in the 1880s.

1465 Thomas, Brinley. INTERNATIONAL MIGRATION AND ECONOMIC
DEVELOPMENT: A TRENT REPORT AND BIBLIOGRAPHY. Paris:
United Nations Economic Social and Cultural Organization, 1961. 85 p.

Discuss trends in the study of international migration from
statistical, economic, demographic, and sociological perspectives. Includes a selected bibliography of 397 items.

1466 _____. MIGRATION AND ECONOMIC GROWTH: A STUDY OF
GREAT BRITAIN AND THE ATLANTIC ECONOMY. Cambridge:
At the University Press, 1973. 498 p. Appendices, bibliography,
index.

Primarily an effort to build an econometric model of migration
from Great Britain based upon the demographic, financial,
and economic variables that affected the migration cycle.

1467 Vecoli, Rudolph J. "Prelates and Peasants: Italian Immigrants and the
Catholic Church." JOURNAL OF SOCIAL HISTORY 2 (1969): 217-68.

Challenges the accepted generalizations about the success of
the Catholic church as an assimilative agent. His analysis
of the Italian experience shows the Church did not serve as
a primary agency for integrating the immigrants nor did it
serve as an effective means of social control. In fact many
Italians saw the Church in the United States as more American
and Irish than Catholic.

1468 Weinberg, Daniel Erwin. "The Foreign Language Information Service
and the Foreign Born, 1918-1939: A Case Study of Cultural Assimilation
Viewed as a Problem in Social Technology." Ph.D. dissertation, University of Minnesota, 1973. 277 p.

The Foreign Language and Information Service and its related
educational program reflected the values of the urban, educated WASPs who were its leaders. They were the professional technocrats who wanted to redesign society in the direction
of a harmonious and dependent relationship with the emerging
corporate society.

AUTHOR INDEX

In addition to authors, this index includes all editors, compilers, translators, and contributors cited in this text. References are to entry numbers and alphabetization is letter by letter.

A

Abbott, Edith 1382-83
Abbott, Grace 912
Abel, Theodore 956
Abramson, Harold J. 1165, 1445
Acuna, Rodolfo 778-79
Adamic, Louis 001-2, 658, 759
Adams, Walter 890
Adams, William Forbes 283
Addams, Jane 108
Aho, Gustaf A. 321
Alba, Jose C. 765
Albini, Joseph L. 423
Alexander, Robert C. 1034
Alford, Harold J. 887
Allswang, John M. 1194
Almaguer, Thomas 780
Almaraz, Felix, Jr. 841
Almquist, Alan J. 1067
Alvarez, Jose Hernandez 781
Alvarez, Rodolfo 782
Alvirez, David 814
Ambacher, Bruce I. 1190
American Jewish Committee 913
Amfitheatrof, E. 424
Ander, Oscar Fritiof 003, 095, 109, 113, 119, 124, 144, 169, 322-23, 354
Andersen, Arlow William 324-25
Anderson, Charles H. 004

Anderson, Nels 425
Anderson, Rasmus B. 326
Andrews, Theodore 581
Antin, Mary 1140
Appel, John J. p. xi, 110, 418, 914
Appel, Livia 063
Ardan, Ivan 606
Aswad, Barbara C. 645
Auerbach, Frank L. 1384-85
Avery, Elizabeth Huntington 178

B

Babcock, Kendrick C. 327
Bailey, Harry A., Jr. 1195
Bailey, Thomas A. 716
Baily, Samuel L. 426, 457
Bailyn, Bernard 019, 114, 135, 153, 161, 248, 611, 665, 791, 894
Baird, Charles W. 179
Baker, Donald G. 1035
Balch, Emily Greene 607
Barbash, Jack 1166
Baron, Salo W. 502
Baroni, Gino 1028
Barron, Milton L. 915-16
Barry, Colman J. 209, 1036
Barth, Gunther 677-78
Barton, Josef J. 646, 917
Bass, Herbert J. 1024

Author Index

Author Index

Author Index

Author Index

SUBJECT INDEX

References are to entry numbers. Underlined numbers refer to main entries within the book. Alphabetization is letter by letter.

A

Abolition, Irish reaction to 315.
  See also Slavery
Acculturation 050, 228, 235, 299,
    410, 415, 421, 434, 462-
    63, 522, 573, 697, 719,
    724, 726, 733, 739, 741,
    834, 838, 909, 930, 932, 976,
    979, 1007, 1009, 1011,
    1024-25, 1222, 1265, 1445.
  See also Assimilation; Cul-
    ture, immigrant; Melting pot
    theory; Pluralism
Adamic, Louis 036
Adult education for immigrants 1171,
    1389
Africans in the U.S. See Blacks in
    the U.S.
Agnew, Spiro 1212
Agricultural laborers 1016
  Chinese as 682, 685
  Italians as 067, 479
  Mexican Americans as 790, 794
    801, 806, 812, 827-28,
    832, 848, 852
  See also Farmers
Alabama. See Birmingham, Alabama,
    Jews in
Alaska, Norwegian immigrants in 392,
    396
Alienation of immigrant groups 033

Aliens 1132-33
  legal status of 038, 716, 723,
    725, 1332, 1373, 1397
  registration of 038
Altgeld, John Peter 045
American Asiatic Association 1083
American Baptist Historical Society
    1229
American Catholic Historical Society
    1230
American Ethnic Research Institute
    1446
American Federation of Labor 777,
    823
American Historical Society of Ger-
    mans from Russia 1231
American Hungarian Library and His-
    torical Society 1232
American Hungarian Studies Founda-
    tion 1233
American Immigrants in Canada 028
American Immigration Conference
    Board 1302
American Irish Historical Society
    1234
American Italian Historical Association
    1235
American Jewish Archives 1236
American Jewish Committee 526-27,
    1079
  Institute of Human Relations. Na-
    tional Project on Ethnic
    America 1284

279

Subject Index

B

Badillo, Herman 045
Baeck (Leo) Institute 1273
Balch Institute 1244
Bankers, Jewish 501
Baptist church, attitudes toward immigrants 1054
Baptist immigrants 417
historical societies devoted to 1229, 1289
Barlien, Hans 382
Basques in the U.S. 1450
Benedict, Ruth Fulton 995
Berlin Association for Centralization of Emigration and Colonization 1300
Birmingham, Alabama, Jews in 514
Blacks in the U.S. 002, 014, 032, 041, 914, 916, 929, 952, 954-55, 959, 966, 985, 990, 1015, 1020, 1031, 1097, 1174, 1190, 1216-17
California 074
Catholic church and 1185
military service and 1192
New York 877, 936, 961
Pennsylvania 232, 924
relations with immigrant groups 315, 436, 568, 578, 596, 937, 1046, 1053, 1055, 1062, 1073, 1152
replacement of in labor force by immigrants 067, 073, 085, 305-6
Wisconsin 889
Blauner, Robert 955
Bohemian immigrants. See Czechoslovakians in the U.S.
Boston, ethnic groups in 069, 1022, 1032, 1200, 1463
Irish 299, 1462
Italians 451, 464
BOSTON PILOT (newspaper) 315
Bourne, Randolph 995
Boycott, as a response to U.S. immigration laws 1083
Braceros. See Agricultural laborers, Mexican Americans as
Brazil, immigration to 130

British colonies, immigration to 979, 1221
Dutch 197, 204, 206
English 138
French 179, 195
German 217, 246, 269
Irish 308
Jews 547, 549, 551
legal aspects of 165
Scotch-Irish 140, 148, 150, 155, 162
Scottish 168
Welsh 141
See also Revolutionary War and the immigrant; names of individual colonies
British in the U.S. 012, 105, 131-77, 1464, 1466
statistics 1306
Utah 404
See also names of British groups
British Temperance Immigration Society of Liverpool 173
Brooklyn College. See Center for Migration Studies, Brooklyn College
Bryan, William Jennings 725, 1214
Buffalo, New York, immigrants in 1007
Italian 497
Burton Historical Collection, Detroit Public Library 1245
Business, attitudes toward immigration 1065-66, 1083, 1103. See also Industry and the immigrant
Business cycles, levels of and immigration 096, 102-3
Business districts, immigrant housing patterns and 1164
BYDELAG (Norwegian-American society) 373

C

California
immigrants in 1067
Armenian 675
British 133
Chinese 679, 682-86

rian and Reformed Churches
1262
Historical societies, immigrant 110,
919, 1229-1303
directories of 1258, 1260, 1276
See also names of individual historical societies
Historical Society of Western Pennsylvania 1263
Historical Society of York County
1264
Hoover Institution on War, Revolution,
and Peace, Stanford Univer-
sity 1265
Housing and housing patterns, immigrant 042, 071, 101, 221,
256, 302, 351, 435, 464,
470, 495, 596, 618, 695, 885,
898, 914, 959-60, 987, 989,
1027, 1032, 1164, 1386-87
length of residence 010
See also Geographical distribution
of immigrant groups; mobility
patterns of immigrant groups
Hudson Bay Co. 175
Hughes, Langston 929
Huguenots in the U.S. See French in
the U.S.
Hungarian Cultural Foundation 1266
Hungarians in the U.S. 657-58, 670,
904, 909, 1061, 1221, 1461
bibliography 653
biography 671
historical societies devoted to
1232-33, 1266
New York 906
Hungarian Revolution (1957), refugees
from 904, 906, 908

I

Ibsen, Henrik 396
Icelanders in the U.S. 382
Illegitimacy among immigrant groups
010. See also Fecundity
among immigrant groups
Illinois, immigrants in 077
German 213
Norwegian 324, 346
Scandanavian 388

Swedish 328, 356, 369, 377
See also Chicago
Illinois Central Railroad 077
Illinois Immigrants' Protective League
1170
Illiteracy among immigrants 1311-12,
1395
Immigrants and immigration
bibliography 034, 036, 039, 1411
biography 036, 045, 059-60
biological aspects of 1334, 1408
and the "brain-drain" 890, 892,
894-95, 897, 903
centers, repositories and societies
devoted to 1229-1303
documents relative to 1382-83
economics of 096-107, 1466
as a field of research and study
027, 033, 108-19, 396,
422a, 846-47, 939, 1028,
1290, 1396
general accounts of 001-062
government publications on 1304-
81, 1386, 1388, 1390-92,
1394-1412
International 120-30, 890, 1465
journals on 1413-44
the new immigration 418-676
the old immigration 131-417
Orientals as immigrants 677-777
promotion and recruitment of 063-
65, 067-68, 070, 075, 077,
079-81, 083, 085, 087-88,
112, 145, 171, 246, 253,
279, 300, 371-72
as social history 005, 019, 025,
029
recent ethnic groups (post 1920s)
778-911
in a specific locality 063-95
statistics 009-10, 031, 059, 419,
1304-18, 1321, 1326, 1399,
1407, 1408
the voyage to America 012, 016,
058, 253, 320, 620, 1383,
1408
See also Asylum, right of; Children
of immigrants; Citizenship
among immigrant groups; Crime
and the immigrant; Culture,

immigrant; Discrimination and prejudice toward immigrants; Economic life and conditions, immigrant; Expatriation; Education and intellectual life, immigrant; Ethnic groups and ethnicity; Industry and the immigrant; Labor and employment, immigrant; Naturalization; Occupations of immigrant groups; Political life and conditions, immigrant; Religious life and conditions, immigrant; Social life and conditions, immigrant; names of immigrants; immigrants by nationality

Immigrants in literature and the arts 013, 436, 465-67, 569, 929, 992, 1082. See also Literature and the arts, immigrant

Immigrants' Protective League of Chicago 1182, 1280, 1299, 1389

Immigration Act (1965) 420, 766

Immigration agents and recruiters. See Immigrants and immigration, promotion and recruitment in

Immigration History Research Center. See University of Minnesota. Immigration History Research Center

Immigration History Society, Minnesota Historical Society 1268

Immigration law and policy 038, 042-44, 048, 053, 120, 420, 696, 774, 790-91, 794, 827, 891, 938, 1045, 1056, 1058, 1066, 1074, 1076, 1087, 1095-96, 1101, 1103, 1106-7, 1109, 1325, 1327-29, 1331-81, 1384-85, 1394, 1398, 1401, 1403, 1405, 1408-10

administrative decisions in 1319
bibliography 034, 059
in colonial America 165
exclusion and restriction 031, 051, 418, 465, 483, 499, 504, 527, 556, 639, 642, 676,

680, 692, 698, 704-5, 708-9, 711-12, 714, 722, 729-30, 736, 771-72, 777, 812, 823, 835, 896, 901, 904, 1038, 1064, 1068, 1071-72, 1079-80, 1083, 1088, 1103, 1183, 1202-3, 1333, 1340, 1345, 1351, 1365, 1369-70, 1372, 1383, 1404
anti restriction 1140-50
pro restriction 1110-39, 1458
quota system 037, 044, 368, 555-56, 639, 1034, 1039, 1051, 1057, 1094, 1351, 1353
See also Citizenship among immigrant groups; Legal system, American; Naturalization

Immigration Restriction League 1102
Indentured servants 091
Chinese as 677
Irish as 307
Indiana, immigrants in
German 231
Swiss 186
See also Gary, Indiana; New Harmony, Indiana; South Bend, Indiana
Indians (American) 929, 940, 952, 954, 994, 1046, 1097
in California 074, 1053
relationships with early settlers 183, 212, 233
statistics 1313
in the U.S. Army 1192
Indians (Eastern) in the U.S. 770, 774
Congressional hearings on 1353, 1374
Indian Immigration and Naturalization Act (1946) 774
India League of America 774
Industrial Workers of the World 1180, 1453
Industry and the immigrant 014, 023, 101, 107, 123, 135, 158, 443, 493, 925, 930, 945, 981, 1146, 1174, 1178, 1184. See also Business; Labor and employment, immigrant; names of specific industries

Subject Index